JAEPL, Vol. 24, 2019

JAEPL

The Assembly for Expanded Perspectives on Learning (AEPL), an official assembly of the National Council of Teachers of English, is open to all those interested in extending the frontiers of teaching and learning beyond the traditional disciplines and methodologies.

The purposes of AEPL are to provide a common ground for theorists, researchers, and practitioners to explore innovative ideas; to participate in relevant programs and projects; to integrate these efforts with others in related disciplines; to keep abreast of activities along these lines of inquiry; and to promote scholarship on and publication of these activities.

The *Journal of the Assembly for Expanded Perspectives on Learning, JAEPL*, also provides a forum to encourage research, theory, and classroom practices involving expanded concepts of language. It contributes to a sense of community in which scholars and educators from pre-school through the university exchange points of view and boundary-pushing approaches to teaching and learning. *JAEPL* is especially interested in helping those teachers who experiment with new strategies for learning to share their practices and confirm their validity through publication in professional journals.

Topics of interest include but are not limited to:

- Aesthetic, emotional & moral intelligences
- Learning archetypes
- Kinesthetic knowledge & body wisdom
- Ethic of care in education
- Creativity & innovation
- Pedagogies of healing
- Holistic learning
- Humanistic & transpersonal psychology
- Environmentalism
- (Meta)Cognition
- Imaging & visual thinking
- Intuition & felt sense theory
- Meditation & pedagogical uses of silence
- Narration as knowledge
- Reflective teaching
- Spirituality
- New applications of writing & rhetoric
- Memory & transference
- Multimodality
- Social justice

Membership in AEPL is $30. Contact Jon Stansell, AEPL, Membership Chair, email: jon.stansell@gmail.com. Membership includes current year's issue of *JAEPL*.

Send submissions, address changes, and single hardcopy requests to Wendy Ryden, Co-Editor, *JAEPL*, email: wendy.ryden@liu.edu. Address letters to the editors and all other editorial correspondence to co-editors Wendy Ryden (wendy.ryden@liu.edu) or Peter H. Khost (peter.khost@stonybrook.edu).

AEPL website: www.aepl.org
Back issues of *JAEPL*: http://trace.tennessee.edu/jaepl/
Blog: https://aeplblog.wordpress.com/
Visit Facebook at **Assembly for Expanded Perspectives on Learning**
Production of *JAEPL* is managed by Parlor Press, www.parlorpress.com.

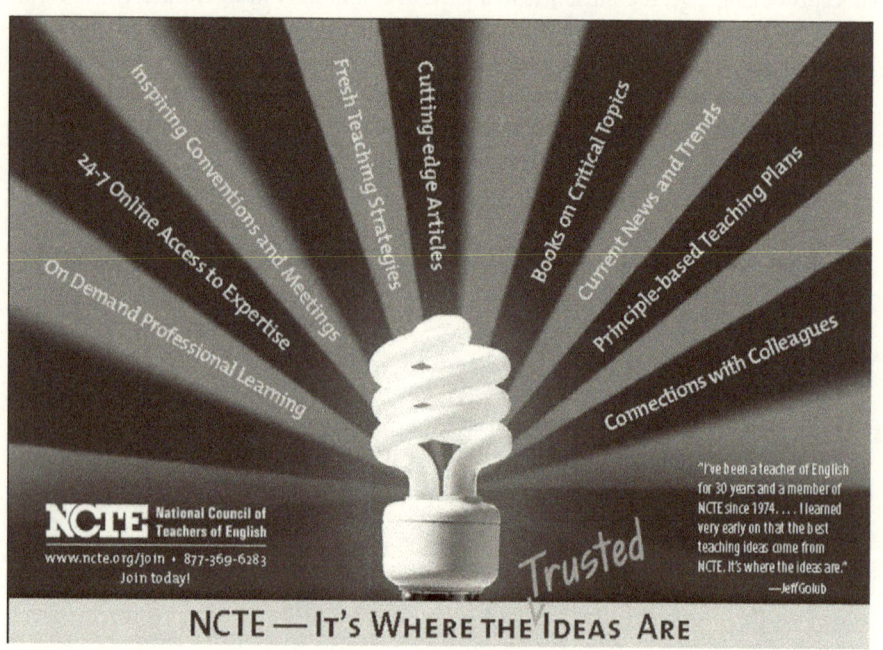

Executive Board, Assembly for Expanded Perspectives on Learning

Co-Chairs	Bruce Novak, Foundation for Ethics and Meaning
	Peter Huk, University of California, Santa Barbara
Conference Organizer	Nate Michelson, Stella and Charles Gutman Community College, CUNY
Secretary	Bob Lazaroff, Nassau Community College, SUNY
Treasurer	Keith Rhodes, University of Denver
Ex-officio	Marlowe Miller, University of Massachusetts, Lowell
	Vajra Watson, University of California, Davis
TRACE Website	Elizabeth DeGeorge, University of Tennessee, Knoxville
AEPL Website	Daniel J. Weinstein, Indiana University of Pennsylvania
Advisory Board	Chair: Peter Elbow, University of Massachusetts, Amherst
	Sheridan Blau, Teachers College, Columbia University
	Alice G. Brand, SUNY College at Brockport
	John Creger, American High School, Freemont, CA
	Richard L. Graves, Auburn University, Emeritus
	Doug Hesse, University of Denver
	Nel Noddings, Stanford University
	Sondra Perl, Lehman College, CUNY
	Kurt Spellmeyer, Rutgers University
	Charles Suhor, NCTE
	Peter Stillman, Charlottville, NY
	Jane Tompkins, University of Illinois at Chicago
	Robert Yagelski, SUNY Albany
Founding Members	Alice G. Brand, SUNY College at Brockport
	Richard L. Graves, Auburn University, Emeritus
	Charles Suhor, NCTE
Membership Contact	Sheila M. Kennedy, Lewis University
JAEPL Co-Editors	Wendy Ryden, Long Island University
	Peter H. Khost, Stony Brook University

JAEPL is a non-profit journal published yearly by the Assembly for Expanded Perspectives on Learning with support from Long Island University, Emory University, and TRACE at University of Tennessee, Knoxville. Back issues are archived at: http://trace.tennessee.edu/jaepl/.

JAEPL gratefully acknowledges this support as well as that of its manuscript readers, including, for this issue:

Tony Adams, Bradley University
Kati Ahern, SUNY Cortland,
Jennifer Clary-Lemon, University of Winnipeg
Sidney Dobrin, University of Florida
John Foran, UC Santa Barbara
Sandra Friedman, George Washington U
David Grant, University of Northern Iowa
Doug Hesse, University of Denver
Tom Hothem, U of California, Merced
Richard Kahn, Antioch U Los Angeles
Nate Mickelson, Stella & Charles Gutman Community College
Marlowe Miller, University of Massachusetts, Lowell
Kimberly Rose Moekle, Stanford University
Matthew Ortoleva, Worcester State University
Irene Papoulis, Trinity College
Catherine Prendergast, University of Illinois
David Schoem, University of Michigan
Kurt Spellmeyer, Rutgers University,
Daniel Weinstein, Indiana University of Pennsylvania
Robert Yagelski, University at Albany, SUNY

JAEPL

The Journal of the Assembly for Expanded Perspectives on Learning

Co-Editors

Wendy Ryden
Long Island University

Peter H. Khost
Stony Brook University

Book Review Editor
Irene Papoulis
Trinity College

"Connecting" Editor
Christy Wenger
Shepherd University

Copyright © 2019
by the Assembly for Expanded Perspectives on Learning
All rights reserved

(ISSN 1085-4630)

An affiliate of the National Council of Teachers of English
Member of the NCTE Information Exchange Agreement
Member of the Council of Editors of Learned Journals
Indexed with MLA Bibliography
Website: www.aepl.org
Blog: https://aeplblog.wordpress.com/
Visit Facebook at **Assembly for Expanded Perspectives on Learning**
Back issues available at: http://trace.tennessee.edu/jaepl/

Volume 24 • 2019

Contents

vii   Dear *JAEPL* Readers

Essays

Faith Kurtyka   1   "Be a Liberation Whatever": Social Justice Literacy in a Living-Learning Community
The author describes an assessment of a living-learning community—part residence life, part community service, and part academics—to understand how students learn "social justice literacy."

Mara Lee Grayson   17   Racial Literacy *Is* Literacy: Locating Racial Literacy in the College Composition Classroom
The author synthesizes the findings of a year-long teacher research project to explore the significance of racial literacy in the college composition classroom.

Special Section
Encountering the Natural World: Environmental Education in the Arts and Humanities

Wendy Ryden   47   Swamps, Flat Earthers, and Boughs of Holly: "Encountering" the Natural World and the Poetics of Environmental Literacy

Brian Glaser   52   Containing the Jeremiad: Understanding Paradigms of Anxiety in Global Climate Change Experience
This essay uses Bion's concept of "containing" to read the psychological dynamics of jeremiads about global climate change.

Amy Nolan   66   Seeking a Language that Heals: Teaching and Writing from a Ruined Landscape
I first heard Iowa referred to as a "ruined landscape" when I was riding a shuttle bus from an airport to a conference…. The statement led me to wonder … what does "ruined" mean?

Anastassiya Andrianova   81   Teaching Animals in the Post-Anthropocene: Zoopedagogy as a Challenge to Logocentrism
An essay on the theory and practice of zoopedagogy that invites students to explore alternative mode(l)s of communication while promoting environmentalism, critical thinking, and empathy.

Michael S. Geary   98   Writing about Wolves: Using Ecocomposition Pedagogy to Teach Social Justice in a Theme-Based Composition Course
Elements of ecocomposition are employed to construct a course that uses the relationship between wolves and humans as a social justice metaphor.

W. Kurt Stavenhagen   111   Relational Literacy
With relational literacy we counter an undue abstraction of the environment by mapping interspecies relationships and placing them within kinship narratives.

Book Reviews

Irene Papoulis	123	Present and Feeling
Dan Mrozowski	124	Newkirk, Thomas. *Embarrassment and the Emotional Underlife of Learning*
Jacquelyne Kibler	126	Young, Shinzen. *The Science of Enlightenment: How Meditation Works*
Christy I. Wenger	130	Peary, Alexandria. *Prolific Moment: Theory and Practice of Mindfulness for Writing*
Mary Leonard	135	De Luca, Geraldine. *Teaching toward Freedom: Supporting Voices and Silence in the English Classroom*
Sharon Marshall	137	Cooper, Brittney. *Eloquent Rage, A Black Feminist Discovers Her Superpower*

Connecting

Christy I. Wenger	139	Finding Meaning in our Work and Writing
Monica Mische	141	Response from Beyond
Kristina Fennelly	143	Reflecting on Arguing and Listening in Digital Spaces
Laurence Musgrove	147	Sunday Morning Before Midterms
Lindsey Allgood	148	Honoring Impulse, Attending to Gesture

155 **Contributors to *JAEPL*, Vol. 24**

Dear *JAEPL* Readers,

Volume 24 marks the beginning of a new co-editorship of the journal. It is with humble enthusiasm that we take up this mantle and hope to carry on the best of *JAEPL*'s work, even as we put our own brand on what it means to have expanded perspectives on learning.

As with many transitions, this one is bittersweet. The beginning of our period as coeditors marks the passing of a stellar era for *JAEPL* under the leadership of Joonna Trapp and Brad Peters. Without doubt, *JAEPL* flourished under their watch both in terms of quality and impact of the journal, and we are exceedingly grateful for the expertise and dedication that Joonna and Brad brought to their co-editorship. They have graciously offered to help us in assuming our new roles, and we will be taking advantage of their kind offer to ensure that we meet the high standards they have set. Many thanks, Joonna and Brad, and best of luck to you in your new endeavors. You have indeed left your mark.

We thank AEPL members and all our readers for your interest and commitment to the work carried out under the aegis of our organization. There has perhaps never been a more important time for pursuing our mission.

We especially would like to thank the following peer reviewers without whom this issue would not be possible: Tony Adams, Kati Ahern, Jennifer Clary-Lemon, Sid Dobrin, John Foran, Sandra Friedman, David Grant, Doug Hesse, Tom Hothem, Richard Kahn, Nate Mickelson, Marlowe Miller, Kimberly Moekle, Matthew Ortoleva, Irene Papoulis, Catherine Prendergast, David Schoem, Kurt Spellmeyer, Dan Weinstein, Bob Yagelski.

"Be a Liberation Whatever": Social Justice Literacy in a Living-Learning Community

Faith Kurtyka

Abstract: *This article describes an assessment of a living-learning community—part residence life, part community service, and part academics—to understand how students learn "social justice literacy."*

Living-learning communities, on-campus communities where students live together and take classes together, have been shown to lead to higher grades, higher retention rates, and more positive perceptions of college (Voss). Ideally, a living-learning community can become "a twenty-four-hour-a-day setting for intellectual engagement" (Schoem, "Sustaining" 132). In addition to these positive academic outcomes, living-learning communities are particularly interesting to scholars with expanded perspectives on learning because they blur the boundaries of the educational institution and students' daily lives to create a more holistic educational model. In effect, the classroom, residence hall, and the students' service sites all become what Vajra M. Watson calls "sites for soulful learning," because they are "both analytical and emotional; scientific and spiritual; theoretical and practical" (17).

In the Cortina Living-Learning Community (a.k.a "Cortina") at Creighton University, students live together, do three to five hours of service in the Omaha community together, and engage in a weekly formation time as well as semi-annual retreats. With an emphasis on faith, service, and justice, students take general education classes together every semester throughout their freshman and sophomore year, with an opportunity to continue involvement in the program via leadership opportunities in their junior and senior year. Rebecca Dora Christensen studied a similarly themed residential learning community—the Michigan Community Scholars Program—on the campus of the University of Michigan and found that students who participated in the community better understood their own positionality in society, cared more about social justice issues, and were more likely to find ways to carry out concrete actions that furthered the goals of social justice. David Schoem's study of the same community also found that "The agency and empowerment students feel about making a difference in the world is palpable" because individual students' excitement gets translated into a "contagious collective energy" ("Relational" 92).

While Cortina shares many of the same goals of the Michigan Community Scholars Program, Cortina emphasizes faith and spirituality as a necessary component of social justice work. The following goals for students in Cortina, developed by a coalition of faculty and residence life staff who administer the program, demonstrate how Cortina seeks to create a holistic, social-justice oriented, embodied, spiritual, and communal learning experience, and helps students develop mutually beneficial and compassionate relationships with people who suffer injustices:

- Demonstrate awareness of local, national, and global social realities.

- Engage with and think critically about questions concerning the meaning of justice and causes of injustice.
- Reflect and act in the context of a faith that does justice.
- Grow in their understanding of what it means to live in community. ("Cortina Vision Statement")

These goals are less reminiscent of the Bloom's taxonomy goals we might typically apply to an academic course (e.g., "Students will be able to analyze...") than reflective of an attempt to assimilate students into what James Paul Gee terms a "Discourse" of social justice. Gee defines "Discourses" as "ways of being in the world . . . forms of life which integrate words, acts, values, beliefs, attitudes, and social identities as well as gestures, glances, body positions, and clothes" (526). Gee situates his definition of "literacy" within this idea of a "Discourse": becoming literate is the mastering of a Discourse. Applying Gee's definition, Cortina is doing more than attempting to "teach social justice." Rather, Cortina aims to cultivate a social justice literacy or "way of being in the world" via being in relationship with people facing oppression, being aware of social structures that give rise to inequality, and taking concrete actions motivated by one's understanding of these injustices. Cortina does so through a living-learning structure that aims to integrate students' life experience, academic learning, spirituality, community, and connection to the world outside the university.

The Cortina Community draws its spiritual identity from its namesake, Fr. Jon Cortina, SJ, a Jesuit priest and engineering professor at the Universidad Centroamericana El Salvador during the civil war in El Salvador in the 1970s and 1980s. In 1989, six Jesuit priests in this community were killed because of their social justice teaching and activism during the war. While Fr. Cortina was traveling at the time, he continued the Jesuits' mission at the university and globally. Central to the Cortina Community's identity is the following quote from Fr. Cortina: "The main thing is to accompany people, and to be with them. And you [can] do liberation engineering, liberation theology, liberation ... whatever. Just be with them. Accompany their struggle for life. And that's it" (Doll). "Be a liberation whatever" appears on the group's promotional materials and social media and seeps into the way students talk about the program, as my data below will demonstrate. Fr. Cortina's emphasis on "being" aligns with Gee's definition of a literacy, expanding our perspectives on learning based on the transmission of knowledge to include ways of being present to others. For Fr. Cortina, as it was for Gee, learning is not simply a transmission of knowledge, but a *way of being* in the world.

This way of being also encompasses a mindful, aware presence, what Fr. Cortina calls "accompany[ing] people." Rather than trying to fix people or society's problems as a function of a white-savior complex, the goal is awareness, presence, or mindfulness of the suffering of others in an unjust society. Paula Mathieu argues that "awareness" is "a necessary addition to the intellectual training we give to student writers and teachers of writing" because awareness fosters reflection, introspection, and the ability to observe one's own thinking (15). Mindfulness is just as useful for writers and writing as it is for citizens engaged in social justice work.

If being a "liberation whatever" is the Discourse students must master, "social justice literacy" is the process of the mastery of this Discourse through a community, programs, and academics that work together. Having taught a composition class for Cortina for five years, I wanted to know the ways in which the program cultivated "social justice literacy" to help students become a "liberation whatever" and to what extent its hybrid nature—part academic, part service, and part residence life—enabled it to achieve its goals. I first describe how I used a grant from Creighton University's Center for Undergraduate Research and Scholarship to train four undergraduates in conducting one-on-one interviews and coding and analyzing interview data. Drilling down into four emergent codes from this data, I demonstrate what students learned from such an encompassing program. The Cortina Community is certainly an idealistic model; however, it still offers important insights into how we might be able to foster social justice literacy in just the time we have with students in our classrooms, regardless of the specific university setting.

I came into contact with Cortina because I teach composition, and in 2013 the director of Cortina asked me to develop a composition course specifically for first-year students in the program. The goal of my course was to introduce students to the main tenets of Cortina and work in conjunction with the living-learning aspects of the program. After discussing my method of assessing the program, I discuss the actual assignments I used in my composition class as a way of dovetailing with what students were learning elsewhere in the program. I want to note that the assignments I offer here are not merely teaching tips or techniques. Parker Palmer writes that "to teach is to create a space in which the community of truth is practiced" (90). By "the practice of the community of truth," Parker means the various practices that a community engages in to find its truth, such as certain methods of gathering or analyzing data. These assignments are intended as a way to "make space" for the practices of being an engaged citizen acting upon social justice issues in a community.

Method and Methodology

I have been teaching first-year students in the Cortina program for five years, and so I wanted to know how all the different parts of the program were contributing to students' learning social justice literacy, in particular what parts of the program were most meaningful to students. In the spring of 2017, I received a grant from my university's Center for Undergraduate Research and Scholarship to train four undergraduate students (not in the Cortina program) to conduct storytelling interviews one-on-one with students in the program (see the interview questions in Appendix A).[1] After we received the interview transcripts, I worked with the undergraduate student researchers to develop a coding scheme using grounded methodology (see the full set of codes in Appendix B). We coded one half of one interview together, discussed our results, refined the coding scheme, and then each student coded one interview on their own using the Dedoose qualitative analysis software. I met with each student individually after their coding session to answer questions they had or review segments that they found confusing. I met with the whole group one last time to discuss which codes they believed

---

1. This research was made possible through a grant from the Creighton Center for Undergraduate Research and Scholarship. I am grateful for the research assistance of Isabelle Senechal, Carly Rademacher, Mariam Abiyou, and Garret Fox.

were most significant for our findings, and these are the selected codes I will elaborate on below:

- Characterizing Cortina—Speaker makes a generalization about what Cortina is like or what it does, including values, beliefs, or functioning of the group.
- Elevating Cortina—Speaker describes something special about Cortina that sets the group apart from other people or groups, typically expressing positivity and excitement.
- Attributing Something Good Happening to Cortina—Speaker attributes growth, change, or learning to their participation in Cortina, including gratitude for an experience. Speaker makes a claim about something that happened in Cortina (negative or positive) having a positive larger meaning.
- Challenging Cortina—Speaker questions or challenges a common practice of Cortina.

We selected these codes because they explain the meaning of Cortina to students, what makes Cortina special, what makes Cortina great, and how students think critically about the program.

"You Can't Escape These People": Learning the Social Side of Civic Engagement

University instructors sometimes struggle with the idealistic notion of community formation, which can feel forced in the brief span of a quarter or semester and inauthentic when compared to a city or neighborhood community. In "Classrooms as Communities: At What Cost?," Roxanne Mountford writes, "In the classroom, students see themselves not as 'joining' a cause or group or community but rather as joining a coincidental grouping of individuals who are developing skills for future employment or self-interest" (306). In his review of the research on the concept of "community" in rhetoric and composition from 1980-2010, Paul Butler finds an imprecision in the use of the word "community," and that scholarship on community has "tended to blur the distinction between classroom communities, discourse communities, and other communities beyond the classroom (e.g., sites of service learning)" (24).

Cortina's learning community, however, seems to work precisely by uniting students around a passion for social justice issues and then blurring the lines between the usually distinct spaces of "classroom" and "service site" and "residence hall." While we might typically think of a community in terms of commonality, in the segments coded "Characterizing Cortina," students described Cortina as a space where they were challenged to encounter people different from themselves, both at their service sites and the students with whom they lived. One student noted the parallel between building relationships with people at the service sites and the challenge of living with people with different views: "[Cortina means] having had relationships with these service sites and with these people in Cortina that's going to facilitate [making] new relationships with new communities and with new people. And learning to understand someone who's—they have a completely different view on a subject than me."

I was surprised when students talked about "disagreements" among the community members because my sense of the students who signed up for the program was that they were all oriented toward social justice and service, and in my opinion, left-leaning in their politics. The student interviews, however, demonstrated that there existed enough variation in students' background experiences that students disagreed on the cause or root of many of the social justice issues they faced in their service sites: "I don't think there's a single person in Cortina who believes the same things about every issue. So, it's kind of interesting to see where everybody's coming from because a lot of the time people's opinions are the same. They're both like, 'This is bad, but why is this bad?' They are coming from two different places."

These nuances in the beliefs of different community members spurred students to think about different explanations for causes of social injustices and how groups across the political spectrum account for large-scale issues like poverty or racism. Students also learned how to get along with people *because* they were in proximity: "Literally, you're living next to these people. You can't escape them. You're forced to interact [with] them, which can be amazing, and can also be a big pain in the ass. I think the living part is you do life together. You go on those late-night Sonic runs. You cry about breakups together. You're there for one another when tragedy happens at home."

I characterize the learning here as more significant than just learning to get along with other people, which students could learn in many types of living environments. While students may learn from Cortina how to be an active citizen in traditional ways (by volunteering or voting), the community does a particularly good job with the *social* side of civic engagement via explicit and inexplicit community formation strategies. Cortina puts people in close enough proximity to each other with just enough disagreement that students learn to engage with each other civilly. As Nate Mickelson and Molly Makris write, civic engagement is often left out of outcomes for learning communities (LCs), but "structuring LCs around civic learning can enable students to develop academic skills while at the same time building new understanding of themselves as active citizens and potential change makers in larger communities." Students learn to talk and to listen, they grapple with difficult issues as a group rather than isolating themselves with like-minded individuals, and they approach each other with humility and respect. As Palmer writes, "The hallmark of the community of truth is in its claim that *reality is a web of communal relationships, and we can know reality only by being in community with it*" (95). Rather than seeing community as a space, structure, or organization, students in Cortina get in touch with "reality" via a web of interpersonal relationships because "community is the essential form of reality, the matrix of all being" (Palmer 97).

One student says that Cortina allowed her the space to admit when she didn't know something and the experience of learning about herself by learning about others:

> Asking people what they believed about stuff and not being 100% confident in what I believed, and I kind of came [to college] with a need to kind of explore things. I knew I didn't necessarily completely believe in the Christian faith, and being able to have discussions with people that are so firm in their faith, and have conversations with people who aren't at all, or have no faith, or are Muslim, or are Buddhist, or are this or that, you really can then develop your own spirituality. You can develop your own opinions, and whether your

opinion changes to that of another, it's strengthened either by the fact that you learned a new truth, or you were corrected....[And] you can stay til 4:00 a.m. because your room is right down the hall.

Cortina, then, might provide a different kind of model for a community for scholars of rhetoric and composition. By creating spaces *in between* and *outside of* the prescribed spaces of classroom or residence hall or service site, Cortina offers opportunities for students to engage in not just the motions and actions but also the social relationships that characterize effective and meaningful civic engagement. This outcome parallels Christensen's finding that "dialogic conversations" in co-curricular spaces like residence halls influenced their acquisition of social justice outcomes (253). These moments of civic engagement happen at the group's weekly "formation time," where the group comes together to discuss social justice issues, or during the van ride on the way home from a service site visit, or at 4:00 a.m. in a residence hall. To return to the concept of "social justice literacy," then, students in Cortina learn diverse ways of approaching social justice issues and learn to form their own opinions in dialogue and in listening to others.

Cortina's model fulfills several important tenets of community formation. In daily life in the residence hall, in classes, and in their service groups, students move through several small groups that contribute to the larger good of the community. Peter Block writes that to create a true "structure of belonging" that encapsulates individual's gifts and talents for the betterment of the whole, communities need "citizen-to-citizen engagement that constantly focuses on the well-being of the whole" (178). This one-on-one contact ideally happens in the context of small groups which are more effective than larger groups in valuing individuals' unique qualities. Block believes that small groups are "the unit of transformation" for a community because "small groups produce power when diversity of thinking and dissent are given space, commitments are made without barter, and the gifts of each person and our community are acknowledged and valued" (180). The smaller relationships that occur in Cortina, informally in the residence hall and formally in the service groups, become the units of transformation that allow individual students to be themselves while bearing in mind the social justice aims of the larger group, allowing for dissent and individuality within the larger community. Schoem notes the same phenomenon happening in the Michigan Community Scholars Program: "ongoing informal discussions of issues related to the program's mission and classes take place day and night" ("Relational" 92), creating a "unique 24/7 living dialogic community" (93).

To practice civic engagement in my composition class for Cortina students, we take a field trip to the Benson neighborhood, an up-and-coming diverse neighborhood to the north of downtown Omaha. Though a booming area in the 1950s and 1960s, Benson fell into disrepair in the 1970s and 1980s, with an increase in empty storefronts and run-down bars. In the last decade, and particularly the last five years, however, Benson has experienced a resurgence with a growth in restaurants, bars, shopping, and coffee shops. Over the course of one class period, we travel to Benson, and in groups of three to four, students complete the following assignment:

Benson Neighborhood Assignment

Complete one per group

Instructions:
1. Select one space in this neighborhood to map—it could be the inside of a business, an outdoor space, or a full block of houses or businesses. You're free to narrow or expand the map as much as you want, but the area should be something you can sketch a map of in about 30 minutes and should have at least one person you can talk to who is using the space.
2. You must talk with *at least one stranger* who uses this space and ask them 3-5 questions about how they and/or other people use the space.
3. Observe the space for 10 minutes or so. In the space below, sketch a map of what you believe to be the more important features of the area to the people who use it. Make notes on the map about notable features of the space.
4. Based on your limited time in this space . . .
   - How does this community use this space?
   - What does this map show about the community?
   - How accurately does this map represent/reflect the community?
   - How does this map represent the community's identity (or not)?

The goal of this assignment is to teach students a brief and non-intimidating form of civic engagement. They learn that you can't learn everything about a space just by googling or looking up Yelp reviews; you have to actually talk to people and visit places in person. Talking to members of the Benson community, like people walking their dogs or small business owners, helps students to practice the social side of civic engagement, as they listen to people talk about the way they define their space. Such conversations have led students to think about the forces of gentrification, the importance of local businesses, and the benefits of community organizing. They learn how to thin-slice a community to understand its values, the way one might have to make a quick judgment of a new neighborhood, workplace, or potential future in-laws. I emphasize that the goal is not to make snap judgements, but to work with the data available to make a tentative assessment of a community's situation.

"It's Kind of Like an Always Instead of Just a Sometimes": A Consistent Thread of Social Justice Through Students' Daily Lives

As a faculty member, I'm often struck by the disjointedness of students' daily lives: at 8 a.m. they are biologists in lab, at 10 a.m. they are swiping IDs at the rec center, at noon they are lunching with their sorority sisters, and at 3 p.m. they are rhetorically analyzing podcasts. This discontinuity is emphasized even more deeply when students work more jobs, live off-campus, or have families and other responsibilities. Such "institutional disconnects," as Julia Voss terms them, can be detrimental because many campus spaces may have similar goals and could benefit from "communication and coordination." As Palmer writes, "True community in any context requires a transcendent third thing that holds both me and thee accountable to something beyond ourselves" (117). In the segments coded "elevating Cortina," students discussed what they thought set Cortina apart or made it special; notably, these segments showed that Cortina created *continuity* or *fluidity* among the disparate aspects of everyday student life, what Palmer might identify as the "transcendent third thing." As one student says:

> In Cortina you go home and you are around people who think [about social justice issues] instead of just when you go to service. It's kind of like an always instead of just a sometimes. . .. It's more than just, service [once per week] or a service trip for one week. It's a year where you're doing service, reflecting on that. Learning new things about the world but you're also living with people who are going through the same thing.

While we can and should think about our classrooms as places where we can create continuities between students' everyday lives, living-learning communities provide spaces that we can use as a model for such integration. This coordination is a central mission of Jesuit Catholic higher education. Students "seek to resolve the feeling of disconnect in their lives. We need to develop appropriate processes that will facilitate the kind of intellectual, ethical, social, and religious integration that Jesuit and Catholic education has long espoused" (Society of Jesus 184). This integration is similar to Erin Penner Gallegos's concept of the "literacy landscape." Using the spatial metaphor of the "landscape," Gallegos offers the term "literacy landscape" as a means of considering how students' "lived literacy experiences—as well as their social, historical, economic, and cultural identities" can be incorporated with their academic identities, ideally so that "the classroom becomes contiguous with other places of comfort and becomes a place where students feel invited and authorized to speak." By creating a holistic space that continually links reflection on and practice of social justice, students become "authorized to speak" and act in the different social justice literacy landscapes of the university and their community.

I was surprised at how many students said that their most meaningful experiences in Cortina were not the classes, the group activities, or the service, but instead were individual conversations they had with others, often conducted in residence halls or during "late-night Sonic runs." In fact, I doubt that students would even identify these experiences as "learning." Cortina creates these meaningful learning experiences by pulling a thread of social justice through students' daily life experiences. One student described it articulately as a "blanket": "I feel like [Cortina is] just a blanket that comes around social justice and says, 'We're not just learning. We're having these discussions in community. We're having these discussions in class but we're reflecting on our own experience. And then we're putting that into action.'"

Cortina provides what Kris Gutiérrez and Joanne Larson call "expansive learning," a concept coined by Yrjö Engeström to refer to learning that takes place in informal, non-school settings. In these settings, "the knowledge and skills people acquire have *a highly positive social value because they are bound to practices and valued relationships with people in teaching roles.* And because learning is not the primary reason people participate in their everyday practices, *learning is continuous with experiences encountered in everyday life*" (Gutiérrez and Larson 70). This learning emerges from organic experiences, where people are trying to be a part of a community and have a genuine desire to learn the practices of that community. By offering students space to reflect both interpersonally and socially as well as communally and collectively, Cortina knits together the disparate threads that fray as students move through the spaces of their lives. Students' informal conversations are not to be dismissed but must be seen as examples of "expansive learning" that create continuities between students' learning experiences that thus lead to social justice literacy. These conversations form the connective tissue among the learning experiences of a living-learning community.

Gutiérrez and Larson stress that it's important to not just co-opt students' everyday literacy practices into the classroom, and it's important to me to not force students to have an "informal" conversation. I do, however, want to teach them that informal ways of communicating matter deeply and are worthy of analysis. In the assignment below, which comes at the beginning of the semester, we look at the specific practice of "code-switching" as a means of exploring the hidden values behind everyday conversation. Students read "How Code Switching Explains the World" (Demby), "Five Reasons Why People Code-Switch" (Thompson), and the NPR blog called "Code Switch" to understand some of the background of code switching.

Code-Switching Analysis

In this assignment, you'll examine the way you code-switch between two communities to understand how language connects to these communities' practices, beliefs, and norms. Below are the parts of this assignment, though you should choose an organization that makes sense for you:

1. Explain the most important characteristics of the two communities to which you belong.
2. Offer 2-3 different specific examples of how you code-switch between these two communities. When I say "specific," I mean that I want you to tell specific stories about how your language changes in these two different communities.
3. Analyze what the language use says about the *values* of these two different communities.
4. Analyze the effect of this code-switching on you. What does it say about your identity?

Reading and writing about code switching enables students to articulate the power dynamics of different social situations—an essential part of social justice literacy—and how their Discourses change in social situations. By drawing attention to this dynamic of everyday life, students learn to be attentive to their informal conversations and learn a new tool for understanding these conversations.

"I Don't Fix the Problems": Learning Humility in Service in Cortina

Many students come to Creighton and to Cortina with a background in doing service in high school; for some students, it's the *reason* they come to the university. Creighton conducts service trips on fall break and spring break throughout the US and has an entire center dedicated to service and justice. Residence halls, student organizations, and fraternities and sororities are also committed to service groups and projects. Cortina, however, seems successful at getting students to question the purpose and motive behind their service by encouraging them to see the big-picture social justice issues that play into their service sites. In the segments labeled "Attributing Something Good Happening to Cortina," students talked about the feelings of community and openness described above, but also attributed a newfound humility about service to their experiences in Cortina. Rather than checking off a box or padding a resume with service, students learn in Cortina that being present to people in their service sites is the most important "action" they can take. One student, "Angela," says: "One of the things that motivates me the most is I am a perfectionist and I like to fix things. I like to fix people's problems . . . but I also know I can't. . . . I know I'm not going to be the one to do anything. I'm just hopefully getting us on track towards that so somebody else can."

While we often talk about helping students "find their voice" and "taking action," social justice literacy also encompasses a humble acceptance of one's own positionality and limitations in the context of issues that cannot be solved with weekly service site visits. Angela, quoted above, is frank with her interviewer about these limitations. Once a week on Thursdays, Angela and another student meet students on campus and drive them down to the local homeless shelter where the students share a meal with the residents at the house, most of whom are experiencing homelessness as well as struggling with drug and alcohol issues.

> Interviewer: Do you find yourself, in your times on Thursdays, do you think that you are meeting a need?
>
> Angela: No.
>
> Interviewer: No?
>
> Angela: No. I'm doing nothing.
>
> Interviewer: What do you—
>
> Angela: You look shocked.
>
> Interviewer: Yeah, what do you mean by that?
>
> Angela: I'm not doing anything for anybody. I'm not meeting a need. The only need I think there is, and I don't know if I'm fulfilling it or not, I guess you can ask some of those guys. . . For me, those are my friends. Those are the guys I go and see every week. I think there is a need to be heard, but I don't know if I'm fulfilling that. I'm not going to say I am. I'll say no before anything because for me, I'm just there. I'm listening to the story and I'm not benefiting anybody else.

Significantly, many students noted that this view of service is a *departure* from their service experiences in high school, which were largely about racking up as many service hours as possible for their college applications. What is it about Cortina that allows for learning this type of humility and perspective? The regular service in Cortina combined with opportunities to reflect on their role in that service while learning about larger social inequalities seemed beneficial in understanding their position as "helper" or "server." Reflection, of course, is a best practice of service-learning pedagogy, allowing student "to make connections between their academic knowledge and skills and real-world situations," and as a best practice of service learning, reflection "should take place throughout the service-learning process" (Hanover Research 17). As James Dubinsky writes, "Creating reflection assignments that help students see the bridge they build as they participate in the social activity created through service learning enables them to ponder and evaluate their experience, consider its value, and transform it into knowledge they will use later as writers and citizens" (310).

Reflection, however, is well-tread territory, particularly at my Jesuit university. I believe Cortina demonstrates the outcomes of effective reflection, leading to social justice literacy, which encompasses an understanding of one's strengths and limitations in a service capacity and understanding the evolution of this identity as one's motivations for service change. For one student, "Harriet," becoming social-justice literate means realizing her expectations in a service setting and narrativizing a service experience in a way that makes sense of her new role in a service setting. As Harriet describes her service experience:

> I went to the Boys and Girls Club and each week, well I remember the first week I came in, I was like, "Okay, I gotta play with kids. I have to get in there and do this." Well, I noticed after like the first four weeks I started just watching TV with this kid every time. I remember looking around going, "I'm not serving. I'm watching TV. What am I doing?" And I can't remember who I had this conversation with. I told them, "I really don't feel like I'm doing service." And they said, "Harriet, have you ever just thought like the fact that you're sitting there with the kid and letting him tell you about the show and having a discussion with him about it, have you ever thought about just your presence there and listening to him? Ever thought of that being a service, of that meaning something to someone?" I was like, "I never thought of it like that. I thought service was really getting in there and doing something. But the smallest actions of service and love can just mean so much to someone. But yeah, every week. I'd walk over and he'd be like, "Let's watch it again!" "Okay!"

Harriet displays here a critical shift in her definition of service from "doing service" to "the smallest actions of service and love" and, more specifically, "presence" and "listening." Part of Harriet's social justice literacy is a stance of humility as well as what Kendall Leon et al. call an "embodied awareness" (48). In the context of service learning, this means that one is aware of one's relations to others in space. Likely, Harriet's previous service experience involved "doing" and "action" and her embodied awareness in the context of service and social justice literacy involves being at peace with the presence of her body in the physical space of another person.

Successful reflection in Cortina is also characterized by a healthy criticality. Suzanne Kesler Rumsey and Tanja Nihiser write of their frustrated attempts to find any publications about "failed" service learning projects because publications about service learning amount to a "plethora of overly-positive published experiences" (147). Rather than ignoring the missteps of service learning, they argue that mistakes and problems are an inherent part of the learning process: "[Service learning] expects things to go wrong. And it assumes that when things do go wrong, which will indeed happen, learning is

11

still possible. Moreover, the learning that all participants gain – students, community participants, and faculty alike – is the sort of learning that service learning continually purports: experiential, hands on, "real life" learning" (147). To theorize the process of failures in service learning, Rumsey and Nihiser articulate "a continuum of what we're calling *expectation, reality,* and *rectification*" (136). Both students and community partners have sets of expectations for how service learning will go, but encountering the reality of collaboration and communication across boundaries of school and community challenges them to "find equilibrium" between their expectations and reality to "rectify" the partnership (136).

To acknowledge the messiness of service learning, I want to read the segments labeled "Attributing Something Good Happening to Cortina" alongside the segments labeled "Challenging Cortina" to see how students move through this process in the context of Cortina. In addition to humility and embodied awareness, the "Challenging Cortina" segments show how part of social justice literacy is a critique of systems and structures of privilege, not just those that affect underserved populations in service sites, but also those that affect anyone in daily life.

One student, "Mark" became frustrated with "top-down" decision making in the Cortina community:

> I would say I have frustrations sometimes about the decisions that they make and the fact that the rest of the program necessarily doesn't get a voice. We kind of get told that things are happening. Especially, not all of the time, but sometimes some of the people are very disconnected because they don't have a service site that they lead. They are just in that position so some of the decisions they make are disconnected from where the freshman and sophomores are in the program. Whereas, I feel like, often times I'm more plugged in than they are.

Mark does not specifically connect the injustice of the Cortina leaders not listening to the voices of the rest of the students to the inequalities he sees at the service sites, but the critique remains. Mark's critique is also a part of social justice literacy: students learn to see injustices not just in prescribed locations but in their daily lives. Cortina enables this literacy by setting up circumstances where students can clearly see injustices at work and incorporating reflection that also allows them to see injustices existing in other spaces they move through, including the community itself.

For their final assignment in my class, students create a scripted, researched argument with a partner about a social justice issue to ultimately turn into a podcast.

Podcast Assignment

Now that you have become more aware of the way that words have power and the way that spaces make arguments, it's time to use your own words to make your own argument. In this unit, you'll work with a partner to create an argumentative podcast to be posted to Cortina's SoundCloud. Your podcast should bring attention to an issue that people don't know a lot about and should, in some way, be related to social justice. Consider Creighton students your audience. You may even select a topic related to Creighton and campus life

Your podcast will be a *scripted argument* between you and your partner. Your script should be written in a conversational style that is an "argument" between you and your partner. You and your partner arguing back and forth about this issue should make your audience more informed about the issue.

- Your podcast should be 8-10 minutes. This means your script will probably be around 5-7 pages, depending on how slow or fast you speak.
- Each person needs to find and use *at least two scholarly sources* to support their side of the argument. Any other sources are up to you.

This assignment combines the power of everyday conversation, civic engagement, research, and identifying and deconstructing a social justice issue. Rather than fearing argument, students are encouraged to dive in and engage in a researched argument with the goal of making their audience smarter. We use as examples the podcasts "Left Right Center" and "Intelligence Squared" as examples of researched arguments. They learn to identify and articulate a wide variety of social justice issues, including those that occur on our campus.

A Comprehensive Picture of Social Justice Literacy

Cortina offers opportunities for students to engage in not just the motions and actions but also the social relationships that characterize meaningful civic engagement, preparing them to be active and engaged citizens encountering people with whom they disagree. One fruit of these social relationships is informal, everyday conversations which help them see connections between the different aspects of their lives and social justice issues. Being social-justice literate means engaging in these informal conversations but also, through reflection and embodied awareness, being aware of one's own positionality when in a service situation. Social justice literacy also encompasses an awareness that injustices are not limited to what occurs at service sites but that power differentials exist everywhere in daily life.

From Cortina, we see the importance of encouraging students to relate social justice issues to events on campus or in the news, using "everyday conversation" as connective tissue between social justice issues. Students should be encouraged to reflect specifically on their physicality and implications of their body in the space of a service site, neighborhood, or other community space and how they relate to others in the space. Coming from a high school environment, especially one that emphasized attending college, students may see service more as resume-building than thinking about the complex relationships with those whom they serve. Reflecting on their past conceptions of and experience with service will help them form a more nuanced and authentic view of what it means to serve others as an adult and a community citizen. To become a "liberation whatever," students should be asked to look at the world through a social-justice lens to identify a variety of injustices in their everyday lives.

Appendix A—Interview Questions

5. How did you first get involved in Cortina?
6. What appealed to you most about the community?
7. Tell me about specific moments in your time in Cortina that were meaningful to you.
8. What does being in a living-learning community mean to you?
9. Tell me about moments of personal growth in Cortina for you.
10. Have you held a leadership position in Cortina? What was that like?
11. What have been some of your frustrations with Cortina?
12. How would you describe what it means to be a member of Cortina?
13. What is your vision for the future of Cortina?

Appendix B—Codes

Mark as a segment pieces of data where the speaker is responding to "What kind of a place/thing is Cortina?" Throughout the codes, "Cortina" refers to both the people and the program.

Reminiscing about Cortina

- Speaker expresses a positive opinion about a past time in Cortina, which could be nostalgic or romantic
- Speaker wishes something were true that is no longer true about Cortina

Elevating Cortina

- Speaker describes something special about Cortina that sets the group apart from other people or groups, typically expressing positivity and excitement

Attributing Something Good Happening to Cortina

- Speaker attributes growth, change, or learning to their participation in Cortina, including gratitude for an experience
- Speaker makes a claim about something that happened in Cortina (negative or positive) having a positive larger meaning

Characterizing Cortina
- Speaker makes a generalization about what Cortina is like or what it does, including values, beliefs, or functioning of the group

Explaining Cortina

- Speaker offers factual (non-debatable) information about what Cortina is or does or something that happened in Cortina

Challenging Cortina

- Speaker questions or challenges a practice of Cortina

Works Cited

Block, Peter. *Community: The Structure of Belonging* Berret-Koehler, 2009.

Butler, Paul. "Forget About Community: Narrative, Ethnographic Writing, and (Alternative) Discourse." *Open Words: Access and English Studies,* vol. 4, no. 2, 2010, pp. 23-47.

Christensen, Rebecca Dora. *Making a Difference: Residential Learning Community Students' Trajectories Toward Promoting Social Justice.* 2016. University of Michigan, doctoral dissertation.

"Cortina Vision Statement." *Creighton University Division of Student Life.* www.creighton.edu/studentlife/living/reslifeprograms/livinglearning/cortinacommunity/.

Demby, Gene. "How Code Switching Explains the World." *Code Switch: Race and Identity Remixed.* National Public Radio, 8 Apr. 2013.

Doll, Fr. Don, SJ. "Fr. Jon Cortina, SJ." *Magis Productions,* www.magisproductions.org/video-1/.

Dubinsky, James. "The Role of Reflection in Service-learning," *Business and Professional Communication Quarterly,* vol. 69, no. 3, 2006, 306-11.

Gallegos, Erin Penner. "Mapping Student Literacies: Reimagining College Writing Instruction within the Literacy Landscape." *Composition Forum,* vol. 27, 2013. www.compositionforum.com/issue/27/literacies.php.

Gee, James Paul. "Literacy, Discourse, and Linguistics: Introduction and What is Literacy?" *Literacy: A Critical Sourcebook,* edited by Ellen Cushman, Eugene R. Kintgen, Barry M. Kroll, and Mike Rose, Bedford, 2001, pp. 525-44.

Gutiérrez, Kris, and Joanne Larson. "Discussing Expanded Spaces for Learning." *Language Arts,* vol. 85, no. 1, 2007, pp. 69-77.

Hanover Research, Academy Administration Practice. "Best Practices for Scaling Service-Learning," Aug. 2014. www.hanoverresearch.com/media/Best-Practices-for-Scaling-Service-Learning.pdf.

Leon, Kendall, et al. "Developing Accounts of Instructor Learning: Recognizing the Impacts of Service-Learning Pedagogies on Writing Teachers." *Composition Studies,* vol. 45, no. 1, 2017, pp. 39-58.

Mathieu, Paula. "Being There: Mindfulness as Ethical Classroom Practice." *Journal of the Assembly for Expanded Perspectives on Learning,* vol. 21, 2015-2016, pp. 14-20.

Mickelson, Nate, and Molly Makris. "'Not only as Students, but as Citizens': Integrative Learning and Civic Research in a First-Year Learning Community Course." *Learning Communities Research and Practice,* vol. 5, no. 2, Article 2, 2017, washingtoncenter.evergreen.edu/lcrpjournal/vol5/iss2/2/.

Mountford, Roxanne. "Classrooms as Communities: At What Cost?" *JAC: A Journal of Rhetoric, Culture, and Politics,* vol. 15, no. 2, 1995, pp. 304-07.

Palmer, Parker. *The Courage to Teach: Exploring the Inner Landscape of a Teacher's Life.* Jossey-Bass, 1998.

Rumsey, Suzanne Kesler, and Tanja Nihiser. "Expectation, Reality, and Rectification: The Merits of Failed Service Learning." *Community Literacy Journal,* vol. 5, no. 2, 2010-2011, pp. 135-51.

Schoem, David. "Relational Teaching and Learning: The Classroom as Community and Community as Classroom." *Teaching the Whole Student: Engaged Learning With Heart, Mind, and Spirit*, edited by David Schoem, Christine Modey, and Edward St. John, Stylus Publishing, 2017, pp. 79-99.

—. "Sustaining Living-Learning Programs." *Sustaining and Improving Learning Communities*, edited by Jodi Levine Laufgraben and Nancy S. Shapiro, Jossey-Bass, 2004, pp. 130-56.

Society of Jesus of the United States. "Communal Reflection on the Mission of Jesuit Education in the United States: A Way of Proceeding." *A Jesuit Education Reader*, edited by George W. Traub, SJ, Loyola Press, 2008, 177-88.

Thompson, Matt. "Five Reasons Why People Code-Switch." *Code Switch: Race and Identity Remixed*. National Public Radio, 13 Apr. 2013.

Voss, Julia. "'Our Door is Always Open': Aligning Literacy Learning Practices." *Across the Disciplines: Special Issue on WAC and High-Impact Practices,* vol. 13, no. 4, 2016, wac.colostate.edu/atd/hip/voss2016.cfm.

Watson, Vajra M. "Life as Primary Text: English Classrooms as Sites for Soulful Learning." *Journal of the Assembly for Expanded Perspectives on Learning*, vol. 22, 2016-2017, pp. 6-18.

Racial Literacy *Is* Literacy: Locating Racial Literacy in the College Composition Classroom

Mara Lee Grayson

Abstract: *In order to develop pedagogies around racial literacy, we must first define the goals and bounds of racial literacy as praxis. In this paper, I synthesize the findings of a year-long teacher research project to explore the significance of racial literacy in the college composition classroom. Drawing from existing scholarship and my own research into racial literacy instruction, I offer four visions of racial literacy in the English classroom, the last of which is Racial Literacy as Literacy. I conclude by arguing that a racial literacy curriculum can teach students foundational concepts of textual analysis, audience awareness, authorial choice and positionality, and argumentation. In short, racial literacy is a culturally relevant, critical framework for literacy instruction.*

Race, class, ethnicity, gender, geography: these strands of subjectivity are woven into our educational infrastructure, simultaneously shaping our understanding of social, cultural, and intellectual concepts and being shaped by them. To attempt to extricate and explain the significance of one such factor in the sphere of American education and classroom interaction would be to simplify the complex dynamics at play within the network. However, because race is visible, both literally and as part of American discourse, it is both the easiest strand to locate, and also the one that, try as we might pull at it, never seems to come unraveled.

More than a decade ago, Allan Luke sought to reinvent the field of English education by drawing on linguistics, cultural studies, media studies, sociology, and other fields, to better respond to the "multilingual and multicultural, heteroglossic and multimediated world" of the twenty-first century (85). Literacy is not merely an academic skill, no matter how many standardized tests or other measurable assessments are applied to it; literacy is integral to understanding the ways in which language and texts (printed, media, or experiential) maintain or challenge social hierarchies and cultural hegemony. "English teaching and schooling," Luke argues, are "political interventions, struggles over the formation of ideologies and beliefs, identities and capital" (86). While some might believe – erroneously – that composition has nothing to do with race, it is hard to deny that the *teaching* of composition (like the broader field of English education) is concerned with questions of race, racism, antiracism, and social justice.

Racial literacy, a framework that in 2004 emerged simultaneously from the fields of sociology and legal studies and quickly made its way into English education, figuring into matters from policy to pedagogy, does not attempt simplicity. Racial literacy is a collection of skills that "probe the existence of racism and examine the effects of race and institutionalized systems on their experiences and representation in US society" (Sealey-Ruiz 386). Researchers have studied racial literacy pedagogy in English and composition classrooms at all levels from early childhood education (Husband; Rogers and Mosley, "Racial Literacy") and secondary English Language Arts (Vetter and Hungerford-Kressor) to undergraduate composition classrooms on racially diverse campuses (Grayson; Sealey-Ruiz) and racially homogeneous ones (Winans). Racial literacy in teacher education (Rogers and Mosley, "A Critical Discourse;" Sealey-Ruiz and Greene; Skerrett) prepares new teachers to work in diverse environments and to interrogate how their understandings of race are influenced by broader societal inequities and media stereotypes.

Racial literacy is not only about understanding race – it is a multilayered conceptual framework designed to help us do so. Racial literacy instruction is neither singular nor uniform; as such, scholarship on racial literacy pedagogy often leaves us with more questions than answers: What does racial literacy look like in the English classroom? How do we know when our students are practicing racial literacy? How can we develop pedagogies that speak to that process? In this article, I draw upon existing research and an original teacher research project to offer provisional answers to these questions and to explore a vision of racial literacy as a paradigm for literacy instruction.

Racial Literacy: Conceptual Origins

Though sociologist France Winddance Twine (2004) first employed the term *racial literacy* to categorize the practices White mothers of biracial children in the United Kingdom used to teach racial awareness and a positive Black identity to their children, the term has more widely been used to describe understanding of the role(s) race plays in all aspects of society, particularly in the United States of America. Twine's ethnographic study identified three practices that comprise racial literacy: the provision of conceptual and discursive practices with which to understand the function(s) of race, access to Black social networks, and exposure to Black-produced media and significant symbols of Black struggles. The first practice draws implicitly upon on the work of Paolo Freire and critical media literacy (Kellner and Share) while the second and third address, respectively, micro- and macro-identity.

Although Twine's initial conceptualization of racial literacy does not address the racialized experiences of non-Black people of color, legal scholar Lani Guinier contends that racial literacy must be contextual, responsive and interactive rather than static (114-15); must consider the "psychological, interpersonal, and structural dimensions" of race (115); and must interrogate "the dynamic relationship among race, class, geography, gender, and other explanatory variables" (115). Racial inequities are therefore representative of societal injustices that also affect other minoritized populations.

Twine's subsequent expanded framework (2010) is broader and more concrete. This iteration identifies the criteria of racial literacy as follows:

1. recognition of racism as a contemporary rather than historical problem,
2. consideration of the ways in which race and racism are influenced by other factors such as class, gender, and sexuality,
3. understanding of the cultural value of whiteness,
4. belief in the constructedness and socialization of racial identity,
5. development of language practices through which to discuss race, racism, and antiracism, and
6. ability to decode race and racialism. (Twine 92)

Some researchers have used only Guinier's framework (Rogers and Mosley, "Racial Literacy;" Skerrett), but most have incorporated elements from both scholars' work (Sealey-Ruiz; Vetter and Hungerford-Kressor; Winans). I have argued elsewhere that a holistic perspective must consider both frameworks and identify racial literacy as a "layered conceptual framework from which matters of race can be viewed on the systemic and situational levels" (Grayson, "Race Talk" 150).

Critical Race Theory (CRT) has influenced the framing of racial literacy (Rogers and Mosley, "Racial Literacy"), as has intersectionality (Nakagawa and Arzubiaga), "an analytic disposition" through which scholars can conceive of demographic categories "as always permeated by other categories, fluid and changing, always in the process of creating and being created by dynamics of power" (Cho et al. 795). Owing to its emphasis on analytical and discursive skills, racial literacy exemplifies one paradigm for engaging intersectionality in English education, English Language Arts, and composition studies (fields that are intrinsically intersectional, both due to their interdisciplinary roots and their marginalization within the contemporary neoliberal academy).

CRT scholars Delgado and Stefancic ask: "How can one talk back to the messages, scripts, and stereotypes that are embedded in the minds of one's fellow citizens and, indeed, the national psyche?" (33). My answer is through the discursive practices of racial literacy. I offer the following formulation as a means for understanding racial literacy: If CRT provides a theoretical framework for understanding race in American society and intersectionality provides the heuristic, then racial literacy is the praxis. In other words, *racial literacy* describes the activities necessary to understand race, racism, and antiracism.

To view this framework as an active practice, it is necessary to identify the particular skills and behaviors that enable individuals to practice racial literacy. While scholars have emphasized the "discursive" and "language" practices of, respectively, Twine's initial and expanded frameworks, few have delineated precisely what those practices are. Elsewhere I have identified four discursive practices students use to decode and respond to race and racism: personal sharing, labeling, interrogating stereotypes, and hedging (Grayson, "Race Talk" 150). These practices enable individuals to situate themselves in conversations about race and racism (through personal sharing), explore racialized discourse (through the assignment or interrogation of race labels), critique racialized representations in texts and media (through the recognition and counter-narrating of stereotypes), and acknowledge differences between their own positionality and that of their peers (through hedging and modifying statements). In student writing, these practices demonstrated increased awareness of rhetorical and compositional concepts such as authorial ethos, diction, textual representation, and audience (151).

The practices of racial literacy are not limited to one-time use; individuals continue to employ these strategies as they deepen their understanding. Racial literacy is not finite but ongoing: as Guinier explains, "it is about learning rather than knowing" (115).

What path(s) does this learning travel? What shape(s) does it assume?

Researching Racial Literacy

Though pedagogies for racial literacy development vary, there are consistencies among the methodologies employed by researchers of racial literacy pedagogy, particularly those who employ the broad framework of teacher research. These consistencies include insider modes of observation (Husband; Vetter and Hungerford-Kressor), the collection and analysis of student-produced writing (Sealey-Ruiz; Winans), and discourse analysis methods of analyzing student conversation (Rogers and Mosely, "Critical," "Racial" ; Vetter and Hungerford-Kressor).

For one academic year (fall 2015 through spring 2016), I worked within the methodology of teacher research to explore the following: 1) How do students incorporate the discursive practices of racial literacy into their writing? and 2) How might the analytical and rhetorical skills students develop during the practice of racial literacy transfer to student writing? In other words, is it possible for the racial literacy curriculum to improve not only students' understanding of race, racism, and racialism, but also their critical writing skills?

Research Site and Participants

This IRB-approved research was conducted at a private university in a major metropolitan area in the United States. Though situated in a bustling area close to the city's financial district, the university boasts many trappings of a residential campus: six residence halls, a dining hall, and a full-service health center for students enrolled in university insurance plans. Given the high cost of tuition, ninety-six percent of new students receive some form of financial aid. Nearly fifty percent of undergraduate students on this campus identify as White non-Hispanic; fourteen percent as Hispanic or Latino/a; ten percent as African-American; and nine percent as Asian or Pacific Islander. Approximately ten percent are international students.[1]

All students in the study were enrolled in one of two sections (of which I was the instructor) of English 120: Critical Writing, the second of two First Year Composition (FYC) courses required of undergraduates. Given that I had designed the "racial literacy curriculum" for use with my own students, I was both the teacher of this curriculum and the researcher of its efficacy, a practice that is common in teacher research. The term "teacher research" represents a diverse set of approaches to data collection and analysis that both draws upon established methods and develops new ones (Baumann et al. 39); because no two classrooms are the same, no singular methodology can sufficiently serve all classroom-based inquiry.

Unlike my previous research into the discursive practices of racial literacy (Grayson, "Race Talk"), I was less interested in *how many* students employed particular terminology and approaches to race talk than I was in *how, when,* and *where* students employed them. As such, I looked at classroom discourse and written work provided by seven individual students. As Yolanda Sealey-Ruiz did in her own classroom research, I used a

---

1. Demographic information is readily available through the university's official website. To protect the privacy of participants, I have chosen not to identify the institution by name.

multiple-case framework (Yin), viewing each student as a single case within the bounds of the classroom. Using this framing in conjunction with the methodologies of teacher research enabled me to explore each student's work over time within a particular setting.

Student participants provided informed consent during the first week of class. On these forms students provided their names, preferred pseudonyms (for confidentiality), their primary racial self-identification(s), and their ages (all of which were 18 or older). While it can be challenging for a teacher to conduct research in her own classroom due to the pressure students may feel to participate, students were informed that neither the course material nor grading procedures would be influenced by my research endeavors and that I would not analyze student-produced data until the conclusion of the semester, after final grades were submitted. As in Sealey-Ruiz's research, students could opt out by transferring to one of more than thirty other sections of Critical Writing offered that semester (though none did so). Approximately one-third of the students enrolled in these courses had taken a first-semester FYC course with me the previous semester.

I did not analyze data from every student in the class, focusing instead on the work of a representative sampling of the larger demographic makeup of the class. Figure 1 displays the relationship between the racial makeup of the classrooms and the racial makeup of study participants. The sample is closely but not exactly representative for two reasons: first, given the number of students, it would have been mathematically impossible to ensure exact representation among the sample group. Second, non-White students are (slightly) overrepresented: Because one's understanding of race and related linguistic practices are largely influenced by racial self-identification (Helms; Tatum; Sue), I thought it necessary to include work by at least one student who identified as each of the races represented in the broader participant pool.

Table 1: Racial Makeup of Students and Study Participants

Primary Racial Identification*	Percentage (%) of Students Enrolled in Course (n=40)	Percentage (%) of Study Participants (n=7)‡
White	67.5	58
Black/African-American	12.5	14
Asian/Asian-American	7.5	14
Native American		
Pacific Islander		
Latino/a / Hispanic†	12.5	14

*As provided by students on consent forms.

†While not classified as a race on the U.S. Census, the university used "Hispanic or Latino/a" in demographic tracking of students.

‡Percentages are rounded to the nearest digit.

On written identity statements that were part of the racial literacy curriculum, students more fully self-identified as follows:

Table 2: Study Participants' Specific Racial and Ethnic Self-Identification

Student*	Self-Identification
Cesar	Mexican
Colin	White, American
Dakota	Black, Hispanic, Puerto-Rican, Dominican
Kelly	Asian-American, Vietnamese
Lisa	White
Sam	White, Jewish, American
Zeke	White, American-Canadian

*All names are pseudonyms, some of which were chosen by the students themselves.

Methods of Data Collection and Analysis

Primary data were collected in the form of student-produced written work: ungraded homework assignments, including reading responses and informal writing exercises employing rhetorical strategies discussed during class; identity statements; unofficial course evaluations submitted as part of an in-class activity at mid-semester; and final research papers submitted during the last week of the semester. Given my additional interest in classroom dialogue, I worked within the ethnographic tradition of participation observation. Based upon the content of the class session and the materials at my disposal, I alternated between the following modes of documentation: quick, informal jottings taken during class meetings (while students were doing group work or in-class writing, so as not to interrupt classroom proceedings); informal entries in my researcher journal immediately after class; and formal field notes or reflective journal entries recorded in my home office at the end of the workday.

As I analyzed student documents, I used a predetermined set of four prefigured codes (Crabtree and Miller) based upon the first four criteria set forth by Twine to identify students' developing comprehension of race, racism, and anti-racism in American society: 1) recognizing race as a contemporary problem; 2) understanding race's interaction with other factors, including gender, geography, and socioeconomic class; 3) acknowledging the cultural value of Whiteness; and 4) developing a belief in the social construction of racial identity. To better identify the fifth and sixth criteria of racial literacy (language practices and the ability to decode race and racism), I used the language practices of racial literacy I determined ("Race Talk") as additional codes for analysis. Because prefigured codes can be limiting (Creswell 185), I allowed additional emergent codes (Crabtree and Miller 151) to arise in student speech and writing. I employed methods of discourse analysis to examine students' language around matters of race and racism, looking at what students said and wrote as well as how they expressed themselves, to whom, and in what contexts. As a writing teacher, I additionally examined the stylistic and rhetorical elements of students' writing, including but not limited to syntax, pronoun use, and verb choice.

As a second level of analysis (see Table 4), I looked for the following literacy and rhetorical practices in student writing: positionality; audience awareness; language choice; and representation (Grayson, "Race Talk"). As additional practices arose in student papers, I reread all student work with those new codes in mind. My goal was to understand if and how students' composition skills might develop alongside the practice of racial literacy over the course of the semester.

When looking at a document, I followed this pattern of analysis:

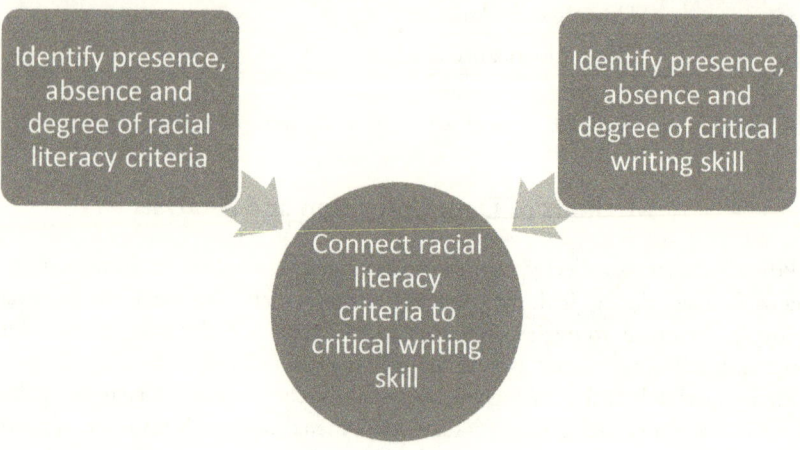

Figure 1: Analytical Considerations

To help explain how I identified racial literacy in student writing, the following table displays excerpts in which students demonstrated its characteristics.

Table 3: Racial Literacy in Student Writing

Student	Textual Evidence of Racial Literacy Characteristic*†‡			
	Recognizing Racism as a Contemporary Problem	*Acknowledging the Influence on Race of Other Demographic Factors*	*Understanding the Cultural Value of Whiteness*	*Belief in the Constructedness and Socialization of Racial Identity*
Cesar	"Every American should know that racism still exists in this country."	"People of the same race… Irish-Americans have a different heritage from Italian-Americans."		"I know that as soon as I say I am Mexican people think my family is either poor or part of a drug cartel."
Colin	"…modern day issues in society including… racism."	"Not everyone is affected by the same stereotypes…"	"White privilege is an upper hand in society that causes injustice on an unconscious level."	"I am extremely against labels, categories, and stereotypes."
Dakota	"The third component… is the belief that racism no longer exists."	"…influenced not only by what they see but also by the neighborhood they live in."	"…result of this country being founded by White men…"	"…we have had to label ourselves as black or white but never question why."
Kelly	"Asians have also been a target of racism and discrimination; however, their injustices are not covered nearly as much…"	"Society takes the silence of the Asian community as a green light to make these racist remarks… part of Asian culture is "keeping face"… to maintain a good reputation."	"White privilege… where some individuals get away with certain things because of their skin color."	
Lisa	"These statistics clearly reflect	"My dad's family live in south… they	"In order for racial oppression to	"…felt confused as a child growing up

	"the inequality and oppression that still exists in America."	would refer to people as 'rednecks'."	end, white privilege needs to be brought to attention."	thinking I was one thing, and then finding out I was something else."
Sam	"No progress leads to no eventual equality."	"Identity is cultivated through numerous channels."	"I cannot recall any instance where I was racially profiled or taken advantage of…"	
Zeke	"While I wish discrimination like this didn't take place, I am not naïve enough to believe that it does not exist."	"…one must contextualize…"	"…you never analyze the majority like that."	"I hope to continue delving deeper into who I am and exploring race as a social construct…"

* As identified by Twine (2010).
† I represent the fifth and sixth characteristics of racial literacy (language practices and the ability to decode, respectively) more fully in a separate table. (See Figure 3.)
‡ Students did not necessarily demonstrate every characteristic of racial literacy.

Despite my best attempts to be systematic enough about these coding procedures to ensure replicability for readers who may be interested in conducting similar research, as a teacher researcher one of my analytical tools was my knowledge of the students in my classrooms, which is not directly replicable. When a student used hedging language, for example, my knowledge of that student allowed me to identify whether or not hedging was unusual for that student. Some conclusions I have drawn, therefore, were informed not solely by raw data and replicable procedures of analysis but also by interpretation and intuition. To researchers who bristle at what they may see as a lax interpretation of data analysis, I argue that it is this familiarity with the classroom and its students that make teacher research a useful methodological framework for racial literacy inquiry. Regardless of the steps we set up, the final step of inductive thinking in the interpretation of empirical research is always the same: as anthropologist H. Russell Bernard has reminded us, "You think hard" (9).

Teacher research relies upon the teacher's insider perspective. Not only does the teacher researcher have access to data that may be unavailable to a researcher working from outside the classroom, her presence in and familiarity with the research setting often enable a more nuanced understanding of progression of the research over time than does a non-present, unfamiliar perspective. My position required that I regularly reflect upon the complexity of my dual role and its influences upon my inquiry and instruction; as such, I also had to be inordinately aware of my individual positionality. (I will discuss positionality – and how it might have influenced classroom activity or my interpretation thereof – in greater detail later in this essay.) Due to the contextual nature of race and racism, racial literacy research in particular demands a level of interpretation that an insider is in a strong position to identify. Therefore, I suggest that those interested in conducting similar research, rather than distancing themselves from the classrooms they study, embrace their emic positions and use their insider awareness to better explore the contextual practices of racial literacy.

To help readers understand my interpretive processes, I explain directly when my interpretation derives from my own knowledge of a student as well as from the data presented. I discuss additional coding and analytical procedures more thoroughly as I move through the rest of this essay.

Curricular Design

At the institution where I conducted my research, there are few departmental guidelines for the Critical Writing curricula, though printed materials and faculty development meetings make clear that instructors should focus on argumentation, document-based or other qualitative research, and the recognition of the discursive patterns and conventions of various forms of academic writing. Thematically, I built the curriculum upon Guinier's conception of racial literacy as a multilevel consideration of the interaction between race and Twine's revised racial literacy framework. In my previous racial literacy research, I allowed race talk to emerge organically during in-class discussion (Grayson, "Race Talk"); however, if we want to explore the possibility for the practices of racial literacy to transfer to student writing, it is necessary to explicitly acknowledge and implement a racial literacy curriculum.

It may be tempting for readers, particularly those who do not readily employ the framework of teacher research, to argue that *of course* students would practice racial literacy in a curriculum on racial literacy! However, because of the complexity of race and racism, sometimes even when students believe they are successfully navigating a critical curriculum, their struggles are evident to the teacher researcher. The additional perspective of researcher may enable teachers to more clearly see where their curricula are successful and where they are not. As Irene Lietz notes, while a White student in her classroom seems to "cope with" the "race-themed course better than many of her peers, her resistance, even as benign as it might appear in her essay and in class discussion, signals a struggle with the concepts of the course" (104). Lietz's reflection highlights that the researcher role may lead teachers to make observations they might have otherwise missed. As such, I argue that as educators we have both a right and an obligation to continually investigate the efficacy of our curricula.

The predominance of White students in my classrooms necessitated that I did not limit the curriculum to the provision of a framework through which to interpret information. Telling White students about racism is not enough; the racial literacy journey must be embodied and emotionally driven (Winans). As such, I began the semester by inviting students to assess their own relationships to race and racial identity. On an ungraded Identity Essay, students were asked to consider how they self-identified, how they learned about race and racism, and how they felt about being asked to identify themselves along racial, ethnic, national, and other demographic lines. The following are specific questions students were asked:

- How would you respond if someone asked "What are you?" How do you feel about that question?
- Have you ever been discriminated against? How so?
- Have you ever discriminated against someone else? How so? Why?
- When did you first learn about race?
- Was race talked about in your home?
- What does the word "culture" mean to you?
- Did you grow up near people who looked like you, spoke your language, or shared similar customs?
- Have you ever felt out of place because of your race, ethnicity, religion, socioeconomic class (or some part of your "culture," however you define that term)? (Grayson, "Teaching" 86)

I intentionally did *not* provide any background information on the theoretical framework of racial literacy prior to assigning this piece of writing. In my experience as an instructor, I have found that introducing students to theoretical material is most effective if they have already identified tangible applications or examples of that material in their own life experiences.

After students submitted the Identity Essay, we read excerpts from Twine's and Guinier's conceptualizations of racial literacy and discussed how those frameworks might help us to consider the functions of race in individual situations and more broadly in American society. Weekly readings thereafter considered the interaction of race with gender, socioeconomic class, and geography. As in other FYC racial literacy curricula, course texts were multimodal in nature (Sealey-Ruiz) to illuminate the numerous forms through which racial ideology is disseminated. We read scholarly essays and newspaper articles as well as short stories, song lyrics, and videos. Most materials addressed matters of race directly while others addressed race more obliquely.

Students wrote personal narratives and textual response essays; conducted research; engaged in small group and large class discussions; and shared their work with their classmates during informal presentations. Throughout the semester, students participated in Lead Discussant Groups, in which, once a week, two or three students led the rest of the class in a discussion or activity related to the readings that were due that day. Students did not choose their groups; instead they signed up for a group based upon the readings assigned for that week. Activities students led as lead discussants included small group discussions; surveys and questionnaires; and brief viewings of related film or viral clips. Students also participated in a Privilege Walk[2] and wrote "I Can / I Cannot" statements (McIntosh) to explore how their experiences, beliefs, and culture(s) contributed to their understanding of the world.

---

2. In a privilege walk, individuals line up in an open space. As a moderator reads a list of privileges, individuals take one step forward for each privilege they have experienced. In my classroom, students used pen and paper to ensure confidentiality.

Four Visions of Racial Literacy

Over the course of the semester, the practice of racial literacy seemed to manifest quite differently for individual students. Here I proffer four curricular visions of racial literacy for the English classroom: 1) Identity Development; 2) Critical Whiteness; 3) Antiracism and Social Justice; and 4) Literacy.

Racial Literacy as Identity Development

For many students, the path of racial literacy runs alongside the road to identity development. This makes sense given that individual racial identity is connected to the "larger cultural norms, social practices, and institutional systems related to race in the United States" (Wijeyesinghe and Jackson 6). In Twine's work with families, racial literacy was an identity-building process by which biracial children raised by White mothers could develop a positive, antiracist Black identity.

Skerrett, Pruitt, and Warrington call racial literacy a type of "specialized knowledge that derives from the lived realities of racial and other forms of oppression," adding that racial literacy acknowledges race as the "prevailing narrative in the lives of racially minoritized individuals and groups" (319). In this understanding, racial literacy is simultaneously developed through experience and intuitively held by those who are racially minoritized. CRT holds that people of color possess knowledge of race and racism unavailable to their White peers (Delgado and Stefancic). While some English educators have found that critical pedagogies may inadvertently marginalize White students (Hill), all individuals in the United States, including White people, are influenced by race and racism simply by virtue of living here (DiAngelo). On one hand, this makes racial literacy curricula even more beneficial for White students than for students of color: because many American Whites have little "regular, substantial contact with people of other races" (Trainor), they may emerge from segregated educational environments with a "sort of racial *il*literacy" (Winans 475, emphasis mine). On the other hand, because traditional classrooms tend to highlight White European ideologies and modes of discourse (Sue), critical pedagogies are necessary to address the experiences and needs of a diverse student population.

There is, however, a difference between the awareness an individual gains from lived experience and the critical consciousness that individual may develop to interpret and challenge racist acts and structures. In other words, by presuming that all students of color possess innate expertise on systemic racism, we risk conflating experiential knowledge with critical awareness; we also overlook the myriad ways in which systemic racism works on individuals, including and especially on people of color. Essentialism is the denial or flattening of distinctions between subgroups or individual members of racially defined groups in ways that, intentionally or inadvertently, create or maintain racial hierarchies (Omi and Winant 71-72). Individuals who experience racism do not necessarily experience or interpret racism in the same ways, regardless of a shared racial identification.

Dakota, who identified at different times as Black, Hispanic, Puerto Rican, Jamaican, and "human," resisted the Black and White binary of American racial discourse and challenged the label of Blackness that, in his experience, others had readily assigned him. Much of his writing explored the essentialism that influences social perspectives of Black men. Intriguingly, by the end of the semester, Dakota had begun to reaffirm his Black identity. Helms has found that there is a point in the lives of Black individuals when "it becomes impossible to deny the reality that they cannot become an accepted part of 'the White world;'" for some people, like Dakota, this "encounter" may initiate the move toward a more positive Black racial identity (25).

While psychological perspectives on identity development typically emphasize an individual's progression through a sequence of cognitive stages, the sociological approach of *symbolic interactionism* suggests that "individuals make meaning through microscale interactions with others" (Renn 17). Through this lens, we can explore how small social networks contribute to individuals' symbolic understanding of race and identity over time, such as when one moves from a "racially homogeneous setting to one that is diverse, or vice versa" (17).

Dakota wrote that in his high school White people were the minority but that entering the private university changed the way he saw himself: "here I feel like the minority." He attributed this feeling to more than skin color, however; having grown up with little money, he was frustrated by how "wasteful" his peers seemed to be. This observation represented a shift in micro-identity, while Dakota's inquiries into the larger sociological contexts of race contributed to his macro-identification with historically-situated Black struggles. Constantine, Richardson, Benjamin, and Wilson suggest that Black Identity Development theorists more fully address "the impact of *other* salient sociodemographic identities on racial identity development" (98). The racial literacy framework may provide the tools through which to expand one's understanding of a complex, intersectional process of identity development. As my class and I examined the interaction of race with socioeconomic class, geography, gender, and other variables, Dakota began to explore what it means to be a Black man in the United States. His final paper was an exploration entitled "Why Are White People Afraid of Black Men?" The more disconnected he felt from his classmates, the more he began to align himself with the Black part of his racial identity.

While Dakota struggled to clarify his racial identity, Sam, a White-identifying student, struggled with understanding that he even *had* a racialized identity. In a personal narrative he wrote:

> The unconscious and invisible fact of my race and ethnicity never really played a defined role within my life. I cannot recall any instance where I was racially profiled, or taken advantage of due to my race or religion. However, I know that such a problem is real, and such a problem needs to be changed… I have never really put much thought into the matter until I was asked to write this paper.

While Sam claims that race hadn't played a role in his life, his language points to his awareness, albeit cursory, that race *has* influenced his life; he does not, however, yet understand the nature of that influence. His description of his race as "unconscious" and "invisible" hint at an early understanding of the privilege he was afforded by virtue of his skin color. He admits that he has never before considered this, but instead of reflecting upon his own experiences, he uses distancing language ("such a problem") and emphasizes the cognitive ("I know") rather than emotive or experiential components of identity. Vetter and Hungerford-Kressor report a similar phenomenon: their students "argued that racial identities, in general, are learned... They did not recognize, however, that *their* racial identities are learned too" (92).

During Sam's lead discussant activity, he and another student shared how their identities had shifted during their transition from high school to college and invited their peers to discuss how they had (or had not) changed since entering college. This activity showed me that Sam recognized identity not as static but instead as directly influenced by demographic and contextual factors. Like the students in Vetter and Hungerford-Kressor's study who "appeared to be on the verge of viewing racism as an institutional and societal issue" but "did not take responsibility for it" (92), Sam was beginning to understand how racism worked, even if he could not yet articulate how it worked *on him*.

For students like Sam, it is important to emphasize the personal rather than conceptual components of the racial literacy curriculum. Because teacher research ultimately seeks "to promote the educational, social, and emotional well-being of the students we teach" (Baumann et al. 3), Sam's struggles necessitated that I be dynamic and adaptable in both pedagogy and methodology. As such, I assigned positionality cluster maps (Grayson, "Teaching") to help students plot the myriad social and cultural influences upon their self and social identities as well as the ways in which they view the world. Though individuals may enact multiple identities in the various discursive spaces they occupy, "people tend to think more holistically about identity"; the positionality map "can help students break down that holistic social identity into specific, identifiable components" such as race, ethnicity, language(s) spoken, and socioeconomic class, among other forms of social stratification. "Concrete examples also help students better understand concepts that might otherwise seem theoretical, such as intersectionality" (91).

On his final paper, Sam wrote about "governmental inefficiencies," focusing on the United States postal service.[3] I was not surprised by his chosen topic, nor was I surprised when I read his first paragraph, which proposed the privatization of mail service. I was surprised, however, that during his final presentation, Sam explained that because he was raised in a politically conservative family, his upbringing had likely influenced his perspective on society. Though a simple statement made on the last day of the semester might sound like a minimal marker of progress in racial literacy development, I believe this moment to be significant. While Sam had not yet begun to establish positionality in his writing, he had for the first time begun to situate his intellectual understanding among the cultures and communities of which he was a part.

Racial Literacy as Critical Whiteness

For many white students in my classroom, understanding white privilege was the lens through which they practiced racial literacy. As was the case with Sam, while all people are racialized, white people are often less aware than people of color of the role race plays in their lives (Helms). Not only do many American whites have little "regu-

---

3. I did not require that the formal research paper directly address race or racism; students were invited to pursue their own inquiries, provided they addressed the social and ideological implications of their findings. After all, race factors implicitly if not apparently into everyday life (Delgado and Stefancic; DiAngelo; Sue).

lar, substantial contact with people of other races" (Winans), the dominant discourses in segregated environments implicitly sustain and legitimize such segregation and contribute to the type of education conferred.

Colin initially struggled with assigning himself an identity label. On his identity essay, he wrote: "I simply want to identify as 'Me.' I am extremely against labels, categories, and stereotypes." Building upon Helms's model of white identity development, Beverly Tatum adds that whites who are aware of white racial privilege may resist the label in part because the models of whiteness in modern racial discourse are undesirable. Despite Colin's desire to move away from a distinct racial identification, he seemed to understand that he could not escape being racialized as a member of American society; moreover, Colin recognized that most of the time, he benefited from that racialization: "Physically I am a skinny, white, above-average looking (I like to believe) male. In society's case, I should be able to do anything I want. However, I am also gay."

While Colin understood that white skin and male gender afforded him considerable privilege, he also knew his sexuality diluted that privilege. Additionally, the directness with which he contrasts his culturally dominant race and gender with his non-dominant sexuality – "I *should* be able... *However*, I am also gay" (emphases mine) – displays his acknowledgment of the role his homosexuality has played in determining how he makes sense of racism. Implicit in this statement is Colin's acknowledgement that as a homosexual man in a heteronormative society, despite the privilege afforded him by the color of his skin, he has also been minoritized. It appears that this experience of being marginalized has led to his alignment with the oppressed rather than the oppressor. Identity development theorists have suggested that the steps toward a positive White identity begin when a person comes in "contact" (Helms) with non-Whites and begins to recognize the different lived experiences of Whites and people of color. Colin's sexuality seemed to function as a sort of gateway – by coming into contact with differential treatment in his predominantly White community, he was encouraged to further critique both the sexual and racial normativity of American society.

Colin articulated the struggle of understanding Whiteness in his research paper, a project for which he had interviewed a racially diverse group of his peers to better understand how young people made sense of White privilege. Colin suggested that White people "focus on the smaller effects of the privilege" that they receive on a daily basis – such as "a free bus ride" or "cup of coffee," two examples Colin identified from previous studies – in order to understand the White privilege and racism intrinsic to American society. The ability to see that individual incidences are indicative of systemic racism is an integral part of racial literacy.

Lisa also took on White privilege for her final research project. Understanding Whiteness was new for Lisa, and she began her written paper with a reflection on a recent experience that had made her aware of her own racialized identity as a White woman:

> For the past 18 years I've lived in a small suburban upper class town in New Jersey. My town was primarily White and, for the most part, conservative. Living in New York City for the past eight months has exposed me to new situations. One afternoon, I was on the subway, minding my own business with my headphones in... I found a woman staring at me. I immediately looked away, but she started talking to me. She said, "You're a privileged White girl."

This was the first time in my life that my race was commented on and I didn't know how to react, so I just turned up my music and looked away. This stuck in my head all day and made me consider why she said what she did. I've come to the conclusion that in order for racial oppression to end, White privilege needs to be brought to attention.

Lisa's reflection echoes Winans's observation that for White people, racial literacy must be understood emotionally and through lived experience (476). What Lisa has omitted, however, is the essentialism in the stranger's comment. While she provides little information enough here, in other writings she shared that she and her family had very little money. Just as the lived experiences of racism differ, so too do the experiences of privilege; reducing oneself or another to "a privileged White girl" overlooks the complexity of what privilege means in a capitalist economic system. Speaking only about White privilege without discussion of other societal factors both side steps consideration of how socioeconomic class and racism influence the lived experiences of poor Whites and masks how White privilege really works – consider, for example, the racial achievement gaps that exist "among students within the *same* socioeconomic levels" (Singleton and Linton 4, emphasis mine).

For students who have not been aware of the effects of systemic racism on their daily lives, racial literacy may be about moving outside their own perspectives. Once White students recognize the differences between their lived experiences and those of their peers of color, they are able to develop a more critical perspective of what it means to be White in American society. That perspective is often accompanied by disillusionment (Helms), frustration, and guilt.

In my work on designing racial literacy curricula, I recall the story of "Andrew," a White identifying student who visited my office to confess that he was frustrated with the course. When asked why, he replied: "White people kind of suck!" (Grayson, "Teaching" 71). This sentiment is common among white people as they begin to recognize how deeply situated racism is, and that they have, by virtue of their skin color, somehow been complicit in the maintenance of White privilege. Particularly notable was that Andrew did not address this dissonance in the classroom among his peers but privately in his instructor's office. Irene Lietz noted similar behavior in "Roberta," the white student she interviewed about her experience in a race-themed writing class: "As a white student with a white teacher in the privacy of my office, Roberta felt safe enough to admit that she questioned her own sincerity and ability to live with integrity as a racially aware person" (106).

Andrew's and Roberta's experiences highlight how important it is for instructors – particularly those who identify or are identified as White – to consider their own positionality as they design and teach critical pedagogies. While some race talk facilitators remain impersonal during discussion, I feel strongly that, as a white woman who works with students of color, I must openly acknowledge my positionality, especially in the racial literacy classroom. Despite how important I believe racial literacy curricula to be, I acknowledge that race talk and self-reflection are not always easy or comfortable. If we invite students to engage with difficult subjects in the classroom, we must be willing to let ourselves be vulnerable. During her study of antiracist literature instruction, Carlin Borsheim-Black found that when a White teacher shared her experiences with racialization, students felt more comfortable sharing as well; during these discussions, Whiteness was made "more visible, less neutral" (416).

Racial Literacy as Antiracism

Sealey-Ruiz laments that her students "did not move to action – the next preferred step in racial literacy development" (394). In fact, despite the body of literature on racial literacy pedagogies, I have found few studies conducted within the racial literacy framework that emphasize antiracist action beyond the classroom. Sealey-Ruiz suggests that the youth of traditionally-aged college students and the time limitations of a single semester may be contributing factors.

I posit two possible reasons for the lack of action: first, curricular limitations, and second, a vague definition of what antiracist action entails. To briefly address the former: instructors are limited by time, departmental requirements, and resources. One teacher who participated in Borsheim-Black's study confessed that departmental requirements "limited the extent to which she felt she could implement an antiracist approach" (415). Regardless of the frameworks we employ, we must recognize that we cannot do everything in one semester. Additionally, activism today does not always look like the activism of the 1960s (Barnhardt). Given its influence and visibility, social media – rather than physical protests and rallies – has become a primary site of social action (Gerbaudo; Tatarchevskiy). Discourse and the reframing of problematic discourses can effect change (Fairclough; Rogers and Mosley, "A Critical Discourse").

Racial literacy is an individualized practice and each student must progress at her own pace; as such, to force students into collective activist action can actually be seen as an act of imperialism. Given that critical pedagogues must "dance between challenging students to growth and learning and scaring them into retreat" (Lietz 100), pushing students too soon toward activism may cause them to retreat. Instead, instructors should focus initially on encouraging an antiracist stance through critical self-reflection.

Understanding and improving the self can be seen as a precursor to advocating for larger-scale social change. Until one can articulate the relationship between her own identity and the racial social hierarchy – and why that hierarchy is problematic – she may have neither the incentive nor the awareness to contemplate how that hierarchy might be dismantled. Ignoring one's Whiteness, for example, is tantamount to embracing the privilege it affords (Helms; Tatum; Painter). Instructors can introduce assignments that provoke student engagement with the world beyond the classroom, such as analytical essays or participant action research projects that investigate inequity in the media, on the school campus, or in the local community.

Racial Literacy as Literacy

Johnson argues that the fields of composition and rhetoric must embrace a framework of racial literacy to rethink the ways in which we theorize and teach about race; to do so "requires theorizing and teaching about race as a discursive system, not as individual words people use or as individual attitudes or behaviors" (160). However, it appears that in Johnson's classrooms, as in the classrooms Sealey-Ruiz studied, students used their writing to address race rather than using race or racial literacy as the paradigmatic discursive system she claims it is.

Table 4 demonstrates how students in the Critical Writing classroom I studied employed the literacy practices inspired by racial literacy in their writing:

Table 4: Discursive and Decoding Practices in Student Writing

Student	Positionality	Audience Awareness	Diction	Authorial Choice	Critical Analysis of Media/Textual Representation	Drawing Conclusions from Individual Situations
Cesar	"As a Mexican…"	"My answer changed when I realized less than 1 out of 20 non-Mexicans know where Merida is."	"I don't have a word for it… but in Spanish I have a word for it."	"I wish I could copy and paste one of these articles here so that you can read how ridiculous it is but I'll try to summarize the advice it gives readers."		"…is only one of many similar situations Black and other minority communities are undergoing today."
Colin	"I am a white individual so it could appear that I may not have a clear understanding…"	"She spoke differently depending upon what she was focused on."	"To understand… we must agree on a definition."	"This research is supposed to… guide people like myself…"		"Small issues like a free bus ride… are the beginning results of white privilege existing on an unconscious level."
Dakota	"In high school the minority there were white people… here I feel like the minority."	"Viewers… may not get the inside of issues in the black community and most likely cannot relate."	"The suggestion isn't bad but the way he phrases it is."	"I guess I'll speak as a black person, then."	"Since most of the media is white, the media can only give a view of the black community from outside looking in."	"They would think of me as an African-American before anything else. I believe that is something that is internalized in Americans."

Textual Evidence of Discursive and Decoding Practices*†

Kelly	"Coming from a diverse town… allowed me to have an open-minded mentality."			"I primarily reached out to those of East Asian descent rather than including those of South Asian descent to narrow down my research."	"…in movies, Asians are either praised or bullied for excelling in academics."	"It could also be inferred that the parents who faced discrimination would want their kids to take advantage of the opportunities that they did not have access to."
Lisa	"Growing up thinking that discrimination is ordinary was detrimental on my idea of society."		"Who really owns words?"	"While race plays a large role in determining privilege, so does gender; however, I am only addressing the component of race."	"The company has a celebrity representative… who is African-American, but previously did not sell cosmetics shades for darker skin tones."	
Sam	"I have never really put much thought into the matter and it was not until I was asked to write this paper that I sat and reevaluated."	"…the connection between him and his audience…"	"I've been working on… changing my word use."			
Zeke	"I believe it was this interest that led me to become an actor and actually emulate other characters' lives."			"…uses formal elements in unconventional ways in order to bring attention to these issues in urban communities."	"Hip-hop music, rap videos, and fashion labels take on these entities and reflect them onto their audiences, predominantly African-Americans."	"Conspicuous consumption… may change one's inner reality and raise one psychologically to a higher social status, it does not change the overall reality of the society."

* Discursive and decoding practices, the fifth and sixth criteria identified by Twine, include findings from previous research (Grayson, 2017) as well as from new data collected in the Critical Writing classroom.
† Students did not necessarily demonstrate every skill represented here.

In the next section, I examine how a vision of racial literacy as literacy speaks both to the conceptual framework and the particular goals of the composition classroom.

Racial Literacy as Literacy: A Potential Paradigm for Critical Writing

To explore racial literacy as a paradigm for literacy instruction in the college composition classroom, I discuss in the following subsections the literacy and rhetorical concepts students learn through racial literacy.

Establishing Authorial Positionality

Through sharing their interpretations of texts and "real world" situations in the classroom and self-reflection in informal writing assignments, students began to identify their own positionality in relation to issues of race, racism, and racialization. They were then better able to establish their authorial positionality in their own essays on topics including but not limited to matters of race. Reflection upon personal experience in extended dialogue or individual memoir-writing might be especially useful in helping students recognize their own positionality. Individuals must identify the "assumptions that [they] take as universal truths but which, instead, have been crafted by [their] own unique identity and experiences in the world" (Takacs 27).

In Colin's final paper on White privilege, he included a "Researcher Positionality" statement. While such a statement could come off as forced or even an afterthought, Colin used this section to also state his objective and build a bridge between himself and his audience. While the language is a bit clunky, the intentions are clear:

> I am a White individual, so it could appear that I may not have a clear understanding of how being neglected may feel because I will never be able to experience the injustice from the point of view of a non-White individual... This research is supposed to be able to guide people like myself who were or are unable to truly understand how it feels to be in a non-White individual's shoes on a day-to-day basis.

If I am to be critical, I might say that one cannot "truly understand how it feels" to be in another's shoes; that presumption is problematic and does not reflect an understanding of the "radically different experiences" of people of different races in the United States (Delgado and Stefancic 12). However, I am impressed with Colin's acknowledgement that his perspective is racially and experientially situated and his attempt to use that perspective as a tool for communication with the reader rather than sidestepping the issue. Interestingly, after this statement, Colin steers the paper away from his own voice and highlights the perspectives and language of the people he interviewed as part of his research. Knowing when to relinquish authority and allow your participants' voices to come through is a key component of writing qualitative research (Blakeslee et al.).

Considering Diction, Authorial Choice, and Audience

Discussing word choice and representation with regards to race encouraged students to attend to the deliberateness and authorial choice behind a writer's diction. There is a tendency to assume that good writing just happens, believing what some have called the "inspiration" myth (Smith) or the "notion of discovery" (Flower and Hayes). By making clear the intentionality behind word choice, students begin to recognize the constructedness of text, as well as the authorial intent and audience awareness that are necessarily part of crafting a written document.

During a lead discussant activity, Lisa and Kelly engaged the class in a word association game about the cultural value of words: "Who really owns words?" they asked. They asked students to qualify as positive or negative groups of words that may have similar dictionary denotations but in fact have different social usages and connotations. One such grouping was *Intelligent, Smart,* and *Clever*. After completing a handout, students discussed their reasoning; most, it seemed, had come up with the same labels. With more syllables, *intelligent* was voted to be the most complimentary of the three, though some students argued it was "cold" due to its academic association; *smart* was also seen as complimentary but more likely to be used in a non-academic setting; *clever*, students argued, could be used pejoratively and should not automatically be assumed to be a compliment.

Conversations about language, especially those that were racially charged, directly connected to conversations about audience. Zeke's lead discussant group showed a clip from *Straight Outta Compton*, the 2015 biopic of rappers NWA, in which a Black LAPD officer harasses the protagonists, using epithets like "nigger" and "boy" and referring to their White manager as their "master." While the lead discussants wanted to focus on how the Black officer's behavior made him complicit in Black oppression, classroom conversation quickly turned to what students referred to as "the N-word" and its re-appropriation by Black youth and hip-hop culture. They also speculated as to why people talk around the term rather than quoting directly, which students suggested depended upon who was saying it, to whom, as well as the context in which it was uttered. They learned that it isn't only words that matter, but who says them, with what intent, to whom, and how that audience might interpret them. Through discussion of racial slurs, students developed a critical awareness of how the components of a rhetorical situation work together to make meaning.

Critical Analysis of Media and Textual Representation

Many students reflected upon the media's role in disseminating essentialist portrayals of people of color, drawing connections between media representation and racist ideology. Students were especially critical of media coverage around police brutality and Black Lives Matter, suggesting that the networks' interest in ratings outweighed their interest in social justice. This identification of how media messages are influenced by monetary profit is a core concept of critical media literacy (Kellner and Share 376).

Kelly, who identified racially as Asian-American and ethnically as Vietnamese, worked throughout the semester to explore the ways in which people of Asian descent are minoritized in American society. This is especially significant given that Asians and Asian-Americans are often excluded from discussions of racism (Sue). In one assignment, Kelly wrote about a studious television character who exemplified the model minority myth of Asian-Americans. In another, she explored the impact of cultural values on the academic performance of Asian-American students. She examined what she called the "forgotten" history of U.S. discrimination against Asian-Americans in order to contextualize stereotypes in the media; the model minority myth; and the academic experiences of Asian-American students. Kelly conducted interviews and surveys among youth she knew yet acknowledged the limitations of the research:

> These are typically the characteristics in which society has cast upon many Asian Americans: smart, good at math and science, and being overachievers. For some… these may be true; however, just like all other stereotypes, it's wrong to assume the same characteristics for a whole population… Interestingly, although in many cases people of Indian descent are also stereotyped as being math experts, there were not a lot of studies or scholarly articles that included those of South Asian descent.

Here Kelly points to a problem of the racial classifications we use – in racial discourse, Asian tends to be understood as *East* Asian; little research exists on the discrimination experienced by South Asian Americans (Kaduvetoor-Davidson and Inman). This essentialist construction of race, even within antiracist communities, can disenfranchise individuals whose identities are intersectional or whose interests, experiences, and attitudes differ from others in the same racial group (Delgado and Stefancic).

Performative Literacy

Frustrations arose in the racial literacy classroom as students began to recognize the complex web of entangled strands of individual identity and social positionality that, woven together, factor into any story, be it a printed text, narrative song, observation, or lived experience. These lived tapestries are even more difficult to deconstruct when race, intrinsic to our social institutions and cultural ideologies, is involved. Because racial literacy considers race alongside socioeconomic class and geography, students in my classes were able to interrogate the situational factors that influence how race functions in society. The interrogation of those factors, however, did not necessarily guarantee students would come to a single interpretation or solution. Students learned to sit with the discomfort of unknowing and the recognition that learning is a continual process of participating without potential for perfect mastery (Lave and Wenger).

Sheridan Blau defines performative literacy as "knowledge that enables readers to activate and use all other forms of knowledge that are required for the exercise of anything like a critical or disciplined literacy" (19). Two of its components are the "willingness to suspend closure – to tolerate problems rather than avoid them" and a "tolerance for ambiguity, paradox, and uncertainty." Strong readers accept limitations in their understanding; further, "the most productive readers will even sacrifice whatever comfort they may find in a coherent and apparently complete reading to notice discontinuities or possible contradictions in their understanding of a text" (19).

These behaviors are very similar to those employed by individuals as they practice racial literacy: they tolerate the discomfort that arises as they recognize the paradox between the systemic racism and professed post-racialism of American society; they sit with the ambiguity of their roles in that society; and they sacrifice their comfort as they begin to identify as racialized individuals.

To point, when a group of lead discussants broke the students into groups to identify the ways in which seemingly positive stereotypes are not as benign as they may seem,

Colin and Zeke were among the small group of students who been directed to identify positive stereotypes of white people. The group was mostly silent.

"This is difficult," Colin said. "I can't think of anything and I'm not sure why. I guess I don't think white people should be talking about white people like this."

Zeke added: "It's like you never analyze the majority like that." When final papers were assigned the following week, Colin told me immediately after class that he wanted to do research on white privilege so he could better understand his own.

Drawing Conclusions

In writing and discussion, students in my study shared their experiences as racialized individuals. Some, like Dakota, criticized the nature of racial identification. Here is an excerpt from his Identity Essay:

> I have many different nationalities that make me who I am but I know that if a person saw me on the street they would think of me as an African-American before anything else. I believe that it is something that is internalized in Americans. Since we are born we have had to label ourselves as Black or White but never question why.

While Dakota resisted the Black/White binary of American racial discourse, he seemed to understand the distinctions between self-identity and social identity. Dakota's experiences have informed him of the societal tendency toward binary conceptualizations of race. He invokes having "had to label" himself – perhaps, one might speculate, on something akin to the demographic self-reporting forms new students (and faculty) at the university are given – to make a larger claim about American people. This instance of sharing and speculation points to Dakota's development of an academic writing skill: By drawing connections between one's personal experiences and others' experiences, one begins to "pluralize," thereby "generalizing" and moving away from purely personal narratives toward the content and style of academic writing (Moffett, "Bridges" 7).

Racial Literacy Is Literacy

At mid-semester, during a class session for which no readings had been assigned, two students acting as lead discussants – with no input from me – invited their classmates to anonymously answer the following question: "What have you learned this semester?"

As I read the responses, I used five *in vivo* codes (codes that arise directly from the language of the data; see Miles et al.) that described what students said they had learned. These codes were: Racial literacy; Analyze texts; Focus/Main Idea; Skills and Techniques for Writing; and Critical Lenses. I added an additional code – Other – to label responses that did not fall into any of those categories. I consolidated those codes into larger, parent codes to identify the broader practice or field of knowledge to which those sub-codes belonged: Reading Skills; Writing Skills; and Race in Society. Figure 2 represents students' responses.

Figure 2: What Students Learned from the Racial Literacy Curriculum

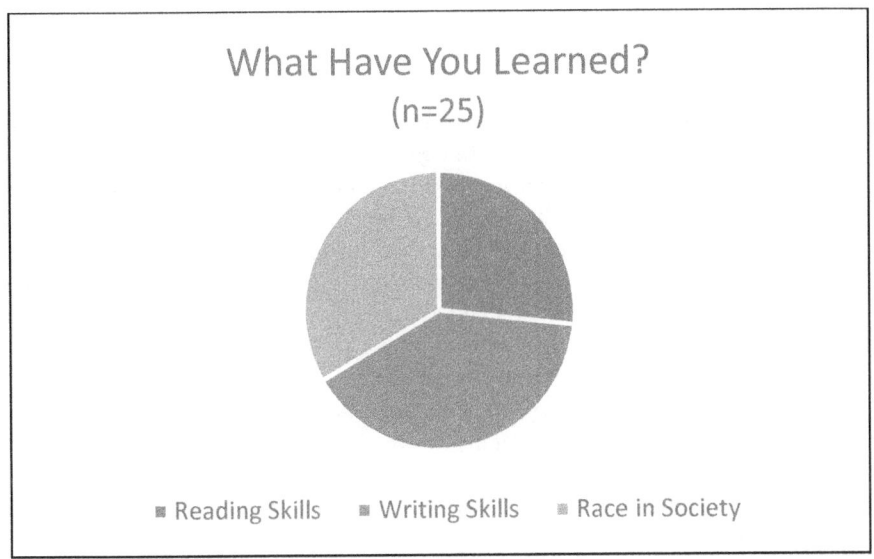

As a teacher researcher, I found these results heartening, in part because, more than once during the year in which I conducted this research, colleagues expressed concern that the explicit focus on race made my curriculum a better fit for a sociology class than a writing course. Halfway through the semester, however, students self-reported learning not only about the way race functions in society but also new reading and writing skills. Individual comments noted by students identified the following as some of the writing lessons they had learned:

- "how to analyze texts"
- "good ways to outline, format your piece"
- "stick to the main idea of your essay"
- "don't make assumptions in your writing"
- "process of organizing my thoughts"

Students told me throughout the semester during in-class discussions and on informal and formal course evaluations that they were surprised and pleased by how comfortable they were with the focus on racial literacy: on the last day of class, one student remarked that it was "super-interesting how open everyone is about this." On the mid-semester evaluation, a student wrote: "We can be completely open with our views. I like how even though they are very intense topics, I feel comfortable."

"Where else do we get to talk about these things?" is one comment I have heard in support of the racial literacy focus of my composition classes. While I am a strong proponent of engaging students through classroom discussion, the lack of free conversation elsewhere cannot be our sole justification for the implementation of racial literacy curricula in the English classroom. As such, while Sealey-Ruiz has suggested that students can use their writing to build racial literacy, I (Grayson, "Race Talk") have argued that racial literacy is particularly suited to FYC because students can use the racial literacy skills they practice to improve their writing.

Very broadly, being literate involves the abilities to decode, comprehend, interpret, critique, respond to, and communicate with various types of texts. The practice of racial literacy requires students to decode race and racism, comprehend the historical and contemporary structures of institutional racism, interpret individual examples of racism and racialism, critique inequity, respond to injustice, and communicate with classmates of similar and different experiences and understandings of the world. When students practice racial literacy, they demonstrate the literacy skills that have historically defined our field of instruction. By developing the discursive tools of racial literacy through critical reading, writing, and discussion, students learn to identify those practices and apply them to their work in academia.

In short, racial literacy *is* literacy.

As early as the second week of the semester, Zeke seemed to have a sense of how the practice of racial literacy gives language to concepts that are often understood more experientially than analytically. He wrote: "Twine's concept [of racial literacy], while technically foreign to me, I believe is something we all understand abstractly." I was impressed by this statement, not only because of the metacognition he refers to but also because of his recognition of the differences between the specialized language(s) of academia and the vernacular knowledge of the greater American public. Following Moffett's (*Teaching*) suggestion that rhetoric is innate, I contend that we teach rhetorical and literacy skills not because they are unfamiliar but so that students will be able to identify, refine, and expand upon what they already know and apply their skills in formal settings like academia. While some of the concepts and strategies learned and practiced in writing classes may be new to students, students enter the classroom with the experiential rhetorical knowledge that comes from a lifetime of interpersonal interaction and communication. This suggests that all students, regardless of their experiences or cultural identifications, raced as they are by virtue of living and attending school in the United States of America, have the potential to practice racial literacy.

Reflection: Limitations and Forward Steps

In her study of a critical race curriculum, Lietz found that, while in an interview years later, her student "insisted that she had changed since [their] first-year class" (107), her statements and behavior spoke to the contrary. In kind, it is possible (as frustrating as it may be to me or like-minded readers) that, for example, Sam, the student who struggled to understand his own white privilege, forgot about the concept after he submitted his final paper. It is possible that, despite having emailed me a few months later to thank me "for helping [him] adjust to college," he has never again considered how his racial or socioeconomic privilege played a role in that adjustment. It is possible that Sam's whiteness has become again an "invisible fact" he rarely notices, let alone considers critically. Given these possibilities, must I concede that the racial literacy curriculum is not as effective as I have made it out to be?

I will answer plainly: No.

In the racial literacy classroom, rather than instilling in students a particular set of beliefs informed by our own positionalities, we must engage them in questioning the beliefs they already hold; rather than telling students who they ought to be, we must encourage them to reflect upon who they already are and how they came to be that way. Those processes take time and a student who struggles with the racial literacy curriculum may not be able to apply its practices immediately, especially to situations that occur outside of the classroom. The racial literacy educator provides tools students can use to view more critically and dimensionally the worlds they inhabit and their roles therein; after pointing them in the right direction, however, there comes a time when the instructor must step back, confident that she has provided enough for her students to continue down the road on their own and with each other.

Racial literacy is not a destination. It is a way of traveling. We depart from different points, embark upon unique journeys, travel at our own paces, and arrive in different destinations. Just as we cannot expect every student who enters the English classroom to emerge the next Faulkner (or Faulknerian scholar), we cannot assume that one semester of a racial literacy curriculum will enable every student to be as engaged with questions of equity and antiracism as we are. It is our hope, of course, that students will return to these practices, but we must recognize that progress via racial literacy may take time. After all, how long has it taken some of us scholars to come to understand these concepts?

My study was conducted with a small population of students in a particular context, factors that may inspire debate about the generalizability of these findings. While larger or more longitudinal studies would be useful to examine the broader efficacy of the racial literacy framework, I do not believe that the time frame or limited participant pool are necessarily limitations. If anything, that this curriculum was successful in these particular FYC classrooms demonstrates two broader truths about classroom research: first, that when it comes to students' understanding of potentially sensitive or controversial issues educators must create learning environments that make students feel safe *and* invite them to tread into uncomfortable but necessary waters (Arao and Clemens; Grayson and Wolfsdorf); and second, that this type of research requires the sensitivity and familiarity of a framework like teacher research.

A considerable body of literature attests to the benefits of teacher research: in addition to potentially improving classroom instruction, teacher research may also help teachers discover a sense of agency in a system that often undervalues their efforts. Lankshear and Knobel describe teacher research as a means through which teachers may make "sound autonomous professional judgements and decisions appropriate to their status as professionals" (5). This is especially significant in an otherwise top-down educational system that emphasizes standardization and assessment.

A student-responsive, teacher-as-agent orientation to research is even more consequential where matters of equity are concerned. Educators and administrators "typically worry about racial inequality rather than the very idea of racial classification" (Pollock 13). Because avoiding racial markers simply hides the ways racial inequities manifest themselves, Mica Pollock suggests that conversations about race be framed with "honest, critically conscious discussion of *race talk itself and its dilemmas*" (218). Racial literacy will not, on its own, solve the inequities of our society or its educational institutions. But it may help us, and our students, name them.

Works Cited

Arao, Brian and Kristi Clemens, K. "From Safe Spaces to Brave Spaces: A New Way to Frame Dialogue around Diversity and Social Justice." *The Art of Effective Facilitation*, edited by Lisa M. Landreman, Stylus, 2013, pp. 135-150.

Barnhardt, Cassie L. "Campus Based Organizing: Tactical Repertoires of Contemporary Student Movements." *New Directions for Higher Education*, vol. 167, no. 1, 2014, pp. 43-48.

Baumann, James F., Betty Shockley, and JoBeth Allen. "Methodology in Teacher Research: Three Cases." *Perspectives in Reading Research*, no. 10, 1996, pp. 1-45.

Bernard, H. Russell. *Research methods in anthropology: Qualitative and quantitative approaches*. Altamira, 2006.

Blakeslee, Ann M, Caroline M. Cole, and Theresa Conefrey. "Constructing Voices in Writing Research: Developing Participatory Approaches to Situated Inquiry." *Ethics and Representation in Qualitative Studies of Literacy*, edited by Peter Mortensen and Gesa E. Kirsch, NCTE, 1996, pp. 134-154.

Blau, Sheridan. "Performative Literacy: The Habits of Mind of Highly Literate Readers." *Voices from the Middle*, vol. 10, no. 3, 2003, pp. 18-22.

Borsheim-Black, Carlin. " 'It's Pretty Much White': Challenges and Opportunities of an Antiracist Approach to Literature Instruction in a Multilayered White Context." *Research in the Teaching of English*, vol. 49, no. 4, 2015, pp. 407-429.

Cho, Sumi, Kimberle Williams Crenshaw, and Leslie McCall. "Toward a Field of Intersectionality Studies: Theory, Applications, and Praxis." *Signs: Journal of Women in Culture and Society*, vol. 38, no. 4, 2013, pp. 785-810.

Constantine, Madonna, Tina Q. Richardson, Eric M. Benjamin, and John W. Wilson. "An Overview of Black Racial Identity Theories: Limitations and Considerations for Future Theoretical Conceptualizations." *Applied and Preventive Psychology*, 1998, pp. 95-99.

Crabtree, Benjamin F. and William L. Miller. *Doing Qualitative Research*. Newbury Park: Sage, 1992.

Creswell, John W. *Qualitative Inquiry and Research Design: Choosing Among Five Approaches*. 3rd ed., Sage, 2013.

Delgado, Richard and Jean Stefancic. *Critical Race Theory: An Introduction*. 2nd ed., New York UP, 2012.

DiAngelo, Robin. *What Does It Mean to be White?: Developing White Racial Literacy*. Peter Lang, 2016.

Fairclough, Norman. *Discourse and Social Change*. Polity, 1992.

Flower, Linda and John R. Hayes. "The Cognition of Discovery: Defining a Rhetorical Problem." *College Composition and Communication*, vol. 31, no. 1, 1980, pp. 21-32.

Gerbaudo, Paolo. *Tweets and the Streets: Social Media and Contemporary Activism*. Pluto, 2012.

Grayson, Mara Lee. "Race Talk in the Composition Classroom: Narrative Song Lyrics as Texts for Racial Literacy." *Teaching English in the Two-Year College*, vol. 45, no. 2, 2017, pp. 143-167.

—. *Teaching Racial Literacy: Reflective Practices for Critical Writing*. Rowman and Littlefield, 2018.

Grayson, Mara Lee and Adam Wolfsdorf. "Courageous Conversations in the Age of the Trigger Warning." *From Disagreement to Discourse*, edited by Rhonda Bryant and Beth Durodoye, Information Age Publishing, 2019.

Guinier, Lani. "From Racial Liberalism to Racial Literacy: Brown v. Board of Education and the Interest-Divergence Dilemma." *The Journal of American History*, vol. 91, no. 1, 2004, pp. 92-118.

Helms, Janet E. "Toward a Model of White Racial Identity Development." *Black and White Racial Identity: Theory, Research, and Practice*, edited by Janet E. Helms, Praeger, 1990, pp. 49-66.

Hill, Marc Lamont. *Beats, Rhymes, and Classroom Life: Hip-Hop Pedagogy and the Politics of Identity*. Teachers College Press, 2009.

Husband, Terry. "Using Drama Pedagogy to Develop Critical Racial Literacy in an Early Childhood Classroom." *Perspectives and Provocations*, vol. 4, no. 1, 2014, pp. 16-51.

Johnson, Michelle T. *Race(ing) Around in Rhetoric and Composition Circles: Racial Literacy as the Way Out*. 2009. The University of North Carolina at Greensboro, PhD dissertation.

Kaduvetoor-Davidson, Anju and Arpana G. Inman. "South Asian Americans: Perceived Discrimination, Stress, and Well-Being." *Asian American Journal of Psychology*, vol. 43, no. 3, 2012, pp. 155-165.

Kellner, Douglas and Jeff Share. "Toward Critical Media Literacy: Core Concepts, Debates, Organizations, and Policy." *Discourse: Studies in the Cultural Politics of Education*, vol. 26, no. 4, 2005, pp. 369-86.

Lankshear, Colin and Michele Knobel. *A Handbook for Teacher Research: From Design to Implementation*. Open UP, 2004.

Lave, Jean and Etienne Wenger. *Situated Learning: Legitimate Peripheral Participation*. Cambridge UP, 1991.

Lietz, Irene A. " 'When Do I Cross the Street?' Roberta's Guilty Reflection." *The Journal of the Assembly for Expanded Perspectives on Learning*, vol. 21, 2015-2016, pp. 100-113.

Luke, Allan. "The Trouble with English." *Research in the Teaching of English*, vol. 39, no. 1, 2004, pp. 85-95.

McIntosh, Peggy. "White Privilege: Unpacking the Invisible Knapsack." *Peace and Freedom Magazine*, July/August 1989, pp. 10-12.

Miles, Matthew B., A. Michael Huberman, and Johnny Saldana. *Qualitative Data Analysis: A Methods Sourcebook*. 3rd ed, Sage, 2014.

Moffett, James. "Bridges: From Personal Writing to the Formal Essay." *National Writing Project*, March 1989. https://www.nwp.org/cs/public/print/resource/704.

—. *Teaching the Universe of Discourse*. Houghton Mifflin Company, 1968.

Nakagawa, Kathy and Angela E. Arzubiaga. "The Use of Social Media in Teaching Race." *Adult Learning*, vol. 25, no. 3, 2014, pp. 103-110.

Omi, Michael and Howard Winant. *Racial Formation in the United States: From the 1960s to the 1990s*. 2nd ed., Routledge, 1994.

Painter, Nell Irvin. "What is Whiteness?" *New York Times*, 21 Jun. 2015.

Pollock, Mica. *Colormute: Race Talk Dilemmas in an American School*. Princeton University Press, 2009.

Renn, Kristen A. "Creating and Re-Creating Race: The Emergence of Racial Identity as a Critical Element in Psychological, Sociological, and Ecological Perspectives on Human Development." *New Perspectives on Racial Identity Development: Integrating Emerging Frameworks*, edited by Charmaine L. Wijeyesinghe and Bailey W. Jackson III, 2nd ed., New York UP, 2012, pp. 11-32.

Rogers, Rebecca and Melissa Mosley. "A Critical Discourse Analysis of Racial Literacy in Teacher Education." *Linguistics and Education: An International Research Journal*, vol. 19, no. 2, 2008, pp. 107-131.

—. "Racial Literacy in a Second-Grade Classroom: Critical Race Theory, Whiteness Studies, and Literacy Research." *Reading Research Quarterly*, vol. 41, no. 4, 2006, pp. 462-495.

Sealey-Ruiz, Yolanda. "Building Racial Literacy in First-Year Composition." *Teaching English in the Two Year College*, vol. 40, no. 4, 2013, pp. 384-98.

Sealey-Ruiz, Yolanda and Perry Greene. "Popular Visual Images and the (Mis)Reading of Black Male Youth: A Case for Racial Literacy in Urban Preservice Teacher Education." *Teaching Education*, vol. 26, no. 1, 2015, 55-76.

Singleton, Glenn E. and Curtis Linton. *Courageous Conversations about Race: A Field Guide for Achieving Equity in Schools*. Corwin, 2006.

Skerrett, Allison. "English Teachers' Racial Literacy Knowledge and Practice." *Race Ethnicity and Education*, vol. 14, no. 3, 2011, pp. 313-330.

Skerrett, Allison, Alina Adonyi Pruitt, and Amber S. Warrington. "Racial and Related Forms of Specialist Knowledge on English Education Blogs." *English Education*, vol. 47, no. 4, 2015, pp. 314-346.

Smith, Michael. "Worshipping at the Altar: Creative Writing and the Myth of Inspiration." *Writing on the Edge*, vol. 22, no. 1, 2011, pp. 65-70.

Sue, Derald Wing. *Race Talk and the Conspiracy of Silence: Understanding and Facilitating Difficult Dialogues on Race*. Wiley, 2015.

Takacs, David. "How Does Your Positionality Bias Your Epistemology?" *Thought and Action*, Summer 2003, pp. 27-38.

Tatarchevskiy, Tatiana. "The 'Popular' Culture of Internet Activism." *New Media and Society*, vol. 13, no. 2, 2011, pp. 297-313.

Tatum, Beverly Daniel. "Talking about Race, Learning about Racism: The Application of Racial Identity Development Theory in the Classroom." *Harvard Educational Review*, vol. 62, no. 1, 1992, pp. 1-24.

Tatum, Beverly Daniel. "Teaching White Students about Racism: The Search for White Allies and the Restoration of Hope." *Teachers College Record*, vol. 95, no. 4, 1994, pp. 462-476.

Trainor, Jennifer Siebel. "The Emotioned Power of Racism: An Ethnographic Portrait of an All-White High School." *College Composition and Communication*, vol. 60, no. 1, 2008, pp. 82-112.

Twine, France Winddance. "A White Side of Black Britain: The Concept of Racial Literacy." *Ethnic and Racial Studies*, vol. 27, no. 6, 2004, pp. 878-907.

—. *A White Side of Black Britain: Interracial Intimacy and Racial Literacy*. Duke UP, 2010.

Vetter, Amy and Holly Hungerford-Kressor. "'We Gotta Change First': Racial Literacy in a High School English Classroom." *Journal of Language and Literacy Education*, vol. 10, no. 1, 2014, pp. 82-99.

Wijeyesinghe, Charmaine. L. and Bailey. W. Jackson, III. "Introduction." *New Perspectives on Racial Identity Development: Integrating Emerging Frameworks*, edited by Charmaine L. Wijeyesinghe, and Bailey W. Jackson, III, 2nd ed., New York UP, 2012, pp. 1-10.

Winans, Amy E. "Cultivating Racial Literacy in White, Segregated Settings: Emotions as Site of Ethnical Engagement and Inquiry." *Curriculum Inquiry*, vol. 40, no. 3, 2010, pp. 475-491.

Yin, Robert K. *Case Study Research: Design and Methods*. Sage, 2014.

Swamps, Flat Earthers, and Boughs of Holly: "Encountering" the Natural World and the Poetics of Environmental Literacy

Wendy Ryden

I will not start off with the litany: the ravages of climate and other anthropogenic *damage* (not *change*, see Freeman) to the environment that beset all living (indeed nonliving, too) things on this planet and beyond. Where would I begin, and where would I end? If you don't know the science about melting glaciers, species extinctions, and plastic chowder, you can readily find it. If you do know it, then chances are you understand what's it like to be me: waking up every day with a broken heart.

Our environmental crisis seems to be a perfect example of Oedipus's dilemma: knowing brings no profit to the wise. And yet many of us continue to do what we can: reduce our carbon footprint; try to educate where/when we can; agitate for the political change necessary to produce policies that are efficacious, just, "humane"; save an animal; plant a tree (or don't cut one down); have the courage to ask the neighbor not to use Round Up. Perhaps we do these things for no other reason than they are the right thing to do in the face of the inexorable. Still, many of us do nothing, or not enough, even if our sympathies lie with the planet and not the greedy oligarchs and klepto/plutocrats intent on destroying it. We are unable to de-normalize our routines, disrupt our ontological orientations, to properly account for what we intellectually understand to be a crisis of epic proportions. Sometimes it is just too hard; we cut corners; we forget; we put it out of our minds. Take selfies; photograph our dinners and bring the leftovers home in styrofoam and plastic bags.

I speak for myself: even as I, too, try to set aside my despair and live in accordance with the ways of other humans; even as I, too, give into exhaustion and denial, what makes the crisis real for me is what I believe to be my authentic connection to nonhuman beings and the natural world. This makes me a romantic, I think. That's OK. I do not see nature as the enemy of civilization, as the mythologies of some ancient (preindustrial) peoples seem to suggest. I do not fear being preyed on by lions (I don't live in a village close to where they roam) or being engulfed by forests or look at pristine lands and see opportunities for resource exploitation and development. Often, I see a wasteland, littered with plastic debris and strangling invasive vines, monoculture flora that supports little wildlife and is kept alive by polluting machines and chemicals. The crisis doesn't need to be made real for me. It is the neighborhood I live in. I am already swallowed whole by its abject ugliness and the human activity that supports the debacle. And yet within the tragedy are the sustaining moments of beauty: the bees buzzing on the asters in late autumn; the birds feeding on the flowers' seed in winter; the much maligned and needlessly feared opossum that comes to the compost pile; the sassafras that has found its way into my yard past the chopped-down, paved-over sub/urban disaster of my Long Island habitat; the rare moments when it is quiet enough to hear bird song and cicadas; looking a wren in the eye who waits a second before taking flight.

During one of the recent election cycles, I received a flier in the mail, one that epitomized the crude racism of dog whistle politics. One side depicted tattooed thugs from

MS 13; the other a suburban Long Island neighborhood complete with vulnerable white woman (no visible tattoos). I was meant to be horrified by the tattooed men and vote with the white woman talking to the strong white male leader, but liberal snowflake that I am, I found the scene of horror to be the suburban lawn depicted on the flier's "safe" side. Terrified by the sterile lawn, I wondered how anyone could find such a landscape sustaining, let alone safe. To me it is both a symptom and an embodiment of the psychosis, the necrophilia that has taken hold. A testament to the eye of the beholder. That we might see a staged image of tattooed men as the epitome of danger but be oblivious to the desolate ubiquity of the manicured suburban lawn—that is what I call a literacy crisis, and one that I ask teachers and scholars in the arts and humanities to address--for both themselves, their students, and their institutions.

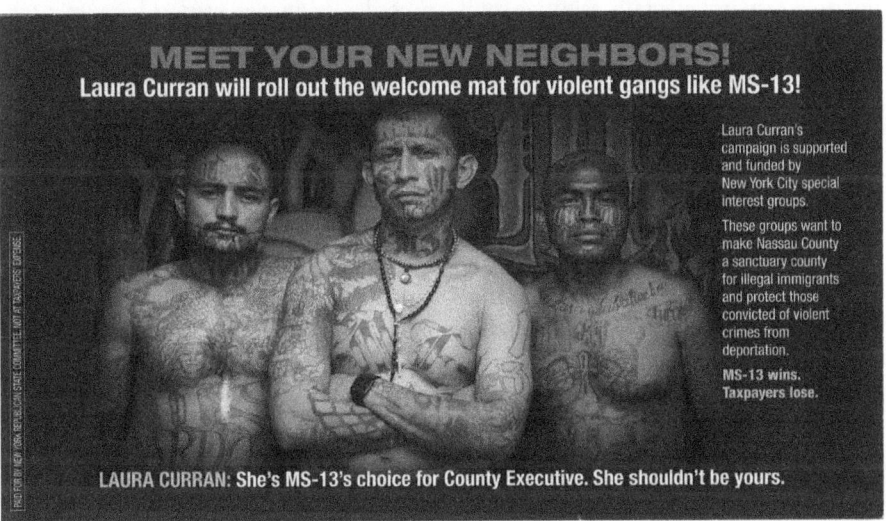

Of the many skin-crawling political slogans and tweets with which we have been inundated, "drain the swamp," the one some might see as the least egregious, brings home for me the antiprogressivism of the era with its outdated metaphor of environmental ineptitude that nonetheless contains our collective folk wisdom, or lack thereof. It is not incidental; language matters. (How many swamps were drained, I wonder, to make golf courses around the globe?) In the latter part of the twentieth century, we seemed to understand the importance of wetlands, a triumph of education and activism, as we passed legislation to protect them and enforced those laws. Now amid the zeitgeist of deregulation, of course it makes sense that the ill-advised metaphor resurfaces with a vengeance. As I write, "the wall" threatens to break out of its comic symbolic domain into an actual incarnation of lost wages, squandered tax dollars, and ecological devastation to an environmentally sensitive southern border. Language matters because it tells us something about how we think; who we are.

We live among climate deniers and flat earthers (many of whom take solace and pleasure in racism and xenophobia). Environmental *il*literacy is at the heart of our present crises and constitutes what Henry Giroux has called "weaponized" ignorance: "a malicious ignorance forged in the arrogance of refusing to think hard about an issue." Perhaps, as some suggest, we who are in the know need to craft more careful messages, more efficaciously manipulative arguments, that can circumvent protective reflexes of ignorance, by appealing to what's at stake for humans—and their children—in an apocalyptic future. Perhaps. But my educator's instincts incline me in a different direction, one that decenters that chauvinistic human subject towards a more liberating notion of the mindful, relational human.

In the beginning of the winter season, my native holly was covered with gorgeous red berries. I noticed the other day that not a single one is left. The quiet frisson of excitement I felt at the discovery is a nearly indescribable gift to me as I wonder about the critters (I strongly suspect the mockingbird as one) who feasted and left scat. My world opens up. The ecologist Stephen Harding speaks of the phenomenon of "encountering" nature and nonhumans:

> "Encountering" means really meeting something that goes beyond one's intellectual process.... "Encounter" is when that conceptual structure vanishes. And you actually meet the being as the being coming forth from itself as itself revealing itself to you in a way that is beyond your intellect in a way that is much more deeply intuitive and much harder to express. In fact, scientific language is inappropriate for this kind of encounter. It's poetry that does it. It's a poetic encounter.

Harding goes on to describe his experiences of empathetic encountering with muntjac deer that led him to profound connection with the earth itself. From a moment of encounter with one of the deer, he "could understand the wholeness of the muntjac and how they relate to the entire wood.... And it went further than that" where he "could also get a sense of the ecology of the whole forest," and then if he were "very lucky that wholeness would spread out," and he "would get a sense of the ecology of the entire earth." This "poetic" moment sounds similar to what Mary Oliver describes in the first two stanzas of "Moths":

> There's a kind of white moth, I don't know
> what kind, that glimmers
> by mid-May
> in the forest, just
> as the pink mocassin flowers
> are rising.
>
> If you notice anything,
> it leads you to notice
> more
> and more.

My encounter is not just with the unseen beings nourished with the fruit of the holly. It is with them, but also with the holly tree as it grows and changes. It is with the entirety of my modest backyard and the refuge it is able to provide, and beyond, and yet the encounter is contained/engendered in the particular moment/space/ drama of the disappearing drupes. My relation to all these things is indeed poetic and life-changing in its quietness, and its persuasive power far different from a fear-mongering, albeit accurate, diatribe about imminent destruction. My encounter places me in a relationship of sustaining care with other beings.

When I teach world literature during a fall semester, I save *Sir Gawain and the Green Knight* for the end, and I bring in a branch of holly, that indispensable prop carried by the Green Knight so relevant to the seasonal meaning of the poem: "... a bough of bright holly/That grows most greenly when bare are the groves" (72). Granted I am cheating a bit by showing students an American specimen, but I began the practice of taking the cutting to class a few years back, when I realized that some of my students did not know what holly was. I discovered that I should not take this environmental literacy for granted, but it becomes my privilege to share with them this pleasure of the holly.

Literacy, as we know, is not something we master but an ongoing project. Environmental il/literacy is very democratic: we all can and need to learn more. I learned recently, to my gratification, that great horned owls nest during the winter months. I wondered that I didn't know this beautiful thing but was nonetheless glad to find out. During a sustainability meeting on campus, I was surprised to discover that many of my colleagues present did not even know what a horse shoe crab is, let alone the marvel or crisis of it and its importance, especially given that we are located on Long Island. ("You mean those little things you buy at souvenir shops in South Carolina?" someone asked, referring, I guess, to the unlucky hermit crabs.) More ominously, another colleague, well-versed in social justice issues and a committed advocate for equality, announced to me his intention to treat his lawn with chemicals to achieve the aesthetic of wasteful monoculture. It was clear to me that facts would not "educate" him, by which I mean persuade him to choose a different lens through which he might consider his decision. So what would?

To assert that such individual choices might be inconsequential in scale compared to systemic commercial and corporate pollution and other global atrocities is, I believe, quite right and at the same time at least somewhat to miss the point. Encountering is as much a form of self-care as it is a form of caring for others, an ethical way of being in the world, another root/route of mindfulness and presence. The concept of encountering in Harding's sense might provide a foundation for environmental literacy as alternative (or at least addition) to the coopted rhetorics of ecologies and sustainability that have become yet another layer in our vast expanse of academese.

Perhaps the possibilities of encountering are more catholic than at first glance. A former student tells me that reading George Orwell's description of the dying elephant in our creative nonfiction class some years back (not a class steeped in environmental literacy) sparked in her a commitment to conservation of the species. Probably not what Orwell imagined, although who knows. She tells me she tries every day to improve her efforts to care for our world. A bit of balm for my broken heart—temporary, fleeting, but I take it.

Encountering is a basis for being, not a teleological solution for what ails us. It cannot make hard choices for us (deforest hardwood to make room for solar panels; cultivate nuclear power instead of fossil fuel; when/whether/how to harvest other living things). But in order to make such decisions (and compromises), we must bring our best, most aware, ethical, relational selves to bear on the questions. An environmental literacy that sees this as our objective might be worth creating, even as we contend with losses that can't be recovered; with futures that are inevitably dim.

Works Cited

Freeman, David. *Background Briefing with Ian Masters*. 23 August 2018. https://soundcloud.com/user-830442635/the-need-to-stop-talking-about-climate-change-and-start-talking-about-climate-damage-david-freeman.

Giroux, Henry. "Resisting the Weaponization of Ignorance in the Age of Trump." Truthout.org, 12 Feb. 2019.

Harding, David. "Encountering Another Being." *Empathy Media*, 5 Oct. 2017. http://ed.gr/fy18.

Oliver, Mary. "Moths." *Famous Poets and Poems*. http://famouspoetsandpoems.com/poets/mary_oliver/poems/15876.

Orwell, George. "Shooting an Elephant." Ebooks@Adelaide. https://ebooks.adelaide.edu.au/o/orwell/george/o79s/.

Sir Gawain and the Green Knight. Translated by Theodore Banks. *English Literature and Its Backgrounds*, Book I, edited by Bernard D. N. Grebanier and Stith Thompson, Dryden Press, 1939, pp. 69-100. https://ia601600.us.archive.org/31/items/in.ernet.dli.2015.215425/2015.215425.English-Literature.pdf.

Containing the Jeremiad: Understanding Paradigms of Anxiety in Global Climate Change Experience

Brian Glaser

Abstract: *This essay uses Bion's concept of "containing" to read the psychological dynamics of jeremiads about global climate change, arguing that their structure reveals a strategy of communication that may be useful for more broadly raising awareness about this challenging state of the planet. More specifically, I argue that contemporary global climate change jeremiads have a structure that first elicits alarm and then moves to discuss solutions, and that this structure may be beneficial to those who are awakening to the reality of global climate change by rendering anxiety bearable and therefore open to purposive and creative response.*

As the hubbub surrounding the hacked records of climatologists known as Climategate demonstrated, in talking about global climate change, we are dealing with a particularly unstable kind of common knowledge. But the community of experts has reached a consensus. Global climate change anxiety is realistic. One measure of the rising level of such anxiety in anglophone culture is not only a fictional treatment like Michael Crichton's *State of Fear* but also Hollywood's embrace of the issue as a source for the extravagant special-effects film, *The Day After Tomorrow*. But global warming anxiety has not only had a significant impact on some existing genres of science fiction writing and film. It has also, I would suggest, generated a new genre, one in which the relationship between realistic anxiety and imaginative response has a different character than in those texts where dire scenarios are elaborated on fictive grounds. For in global warming novels, imagining the unreal is a kind of path of escape from realistic anxiety. Even a relatively realistic fictional treatment of the effects of global warming like the one found in Kim Stanley Robinson's *Science in the Capital* trilogy moves the reader to some extent out of the world that is known by science and into a virtual environment that he or she can dispel. More readerly experience of those fictive future worlds is not more experience of the world that is actually warming.

I see a new genre in the growing number of nonfiction books which direct their imaginative energies towards anxiety about the world that is known scientifically and empirically. These books, I mean in this essay to claim, offer a diverse range of variations on a core theme, or perhaps, an experience—one that we might call the climate change experience. These are books that bring considerable imaginative resources to bear on one of the central challenges facing thinking people today—how to adapt to troublesome knowledge about the physical world. These works do this in a sustained, intensive way that writing is particularly good at facilitating. By reading these books as something more than what they might be taken to be in a casual reading—that is, as books for a general audience about a scientific subject—and paying some attention to where their considerable imaginative energies are located, I think we learn a good deal about the patterns with which anglophone culture is living out and living with the anxiety that has been brought to it by new knowledge of the warming globe: which frightening realities that culture is willing to look at, how its anxiety encourages it to think about itself differently, and what it is inclined to do when that anxiety becomes too much to bear.

Methodologically, my approach brings together thinking in the psychoanalytic tradition with those from a rhetorical branch of the study of texts. Bion's concept of containing, in which a therapeutic relationship allows for the transformation of intense anxiety into a more bearable state, can help us to explain the sudden ubiquity and popularity of texts that have been described as jeremiads—morally urgent discussions of a threatening fate and then highly specific arguments about what can be done to avoid that fate. To the arguments of those who see this centuries-old genre to have new life in an age of anthropogenic climate change, I offer the insights of a psychoanalytic thinker about how these texts might work most optimally, for teachers and critics as well as for general readers.

Global Anxiety

Bill McKibben was the first to sound the alarm in popular culture about global warming with his 1989 *The End of Nature*, a book that appeared in the wake of the groundbreaking and startling testimony of James Hansen about anthropogenic climate change before a congressional panel during a summer heat wave in 1988. In the two decades since, McKibben has broadened his efforts to take on imaginative projects that can probably be brought fairly well under the umbrella of the term sustainable living. As a complement to his work with 350.org, an organization mobilizing and coordinating demonstrations in support of national and international policies to lower the amount of carbon in the atmosphere to 350 parts per million, McKibben published in 2010 the manifesto *Eaarth: Making a Life on a Tough New Planet*. It is an anxious book. In it, McKibben, as Paul Greenberg noted in a *New York Times* review, "brings the reader uncomfortably close to climate change."

The book has a preface and four chapters. The preface establishes the anxious tone. Noting the melancholic mood of *The End of Nature*, McKibben draws a contrast between his point of view in writing that book and his current perspective: "that sadness has turned into a sharper-edged fear" (xii). The first chapter seeks to establish that fear as distinctive in a certain way to climate change. McKibben gives evidence from around the globe to demonstrate not merely that the average temperature is rising—that is not disputed—but that there is virtually no part of the world that is unaffected by this change. On one particularly dense page, he mentions the melting of the Arctic ice cap and the Greenland glacier, acidification of the oceans, drying of the Amazon rainforest, effects of rising sea levels on island nations like those in the Maldives as well as on the accessibility of drinking water in Bangladesh, and danger to the forests of North America from the pine beetle as well as threats to the cedars of Lebanon (45). So one of the early purposes of *Eaarth* is to globalize global warming anxiety, not only to raise the issues of environmental justice that appear in the text from time to time—the disappearance of island nations is one instance, the rise in dengue fever in Bangladesh is another—but also to make clear the power and inescapability of the changes that are underway (71-3). Though, as I will discuss briefly below, McKibben makes use of a subnational paradigm at certain crucial points in the book, his approach to anxiety about climate change is to accumulate enough instances that the reader senses in a concrete way that there is really no local counterforce adequate to this particular form of globalization.

If the book's anxiety is globalized in that way, it is also presented as the source of a smaller kind of community, one constituted by McKibben and his readers. "I know that I'm repeating myself," he says at the end of one catalogue of threatening changes. "I'm repeating myself on purpose. This is the biggest thing that's ever happened" (46). The purpose of the repetition is unstated but seems obvious—emphasis. But the emphasis has a rather textured communicative function. For his repetition conveys an emotional charge that is absent in scientific or even journalistic texts where statement of fact is the writer's job and repetition of information is more or less inappropriate. Here, rather, as at other points, McKibben both expresses and invites anxiety, offering his own ability to absorb distressing information about the consequences of climate change as a sort of path by which readers may themselves come to be able to do something inwardly with the data they've been given, to integrate it into their understanding of the world. The reader is allowed to participate in McKibben's anxious process of knowing with the implicit assurance that McKibben himself has found the anxiety it produces bearable, and that he can offer himself as a model of agency that is not paralyzed or undone by fear. In this way, a community is imagined, if not created.

And a good deal of the final two chapters of the book is a performance of purposive response to global warming anxiety. The second chapter "High Tide" continues the work of the first chapter, mostly by looking towards the future, discussing consequences of global warming that have not yet been pervasively felt—political destabilization and epidemiological issues, among others. After this continuing performance and evocation of anxiety, McKibben shifts remarkably in the last two chapters: "We've turned our sweet planet into Eaarth, which is not as nice. We're moving quickly from a world where we push nature around to a world where nature pushes back—and with far more power. But we've still got to live on that world, so we better start figuring out how" (101). In the text that follows there is both a shift in subject and a shift in mood—the threat is ominous but somewhat vague, whereas the response to that threat will be pragmatic and rather specific.

His suggestions about how to "live on that world" are in a way written around his investment in 350.org, which he mentions only at the very end of the book. Instead, he recommends in the third chapter "Backing Off," which involves thinking of the nation differently, "*The project we're now undertaking—maintenance, graceful decline, hunkering down, holding on against the storm—requires a different scale. Instead of continents and vast nations, we need to think about states, about towns, about neighborhoods, about blocks*" (124). In what is perhaps an unsurprising irony, McKibben makes this point about the importance of subnational thinking first through an extended history lesson about the conflicting views of national government held by Alexander Hamilton and Thomas Jefferson. His point is that what he calls the "National Project" is no longer relevant to the challenges facing Americans on "Eaarth," but also that there is an American tradition of thinking the subnational or the local (114). In the fourth chapter "Lightly, Carefully, Gracefully," McKibben argues for small-scale farming, non-carbon-based sources of energy, and sustainable communities linked and held together by the internet, again discussing both what needs to be done in his view and the evidence that such a program of action is practical. In the final pages of the book he tells the story of how 350.org came to be, ending with a prophecy that knits together much of what he has said in the course of the book: "We will keep fighting, in the hope that we can limit that damage. And in the process, with many others fighting similar battles, we'll help build the architecture for the world that comes next, the dispersed and localized societies that can survive the damage we can no longer prevent" (212). The announcement of Eaarth turns out to be an announcement of the end of civilization as we know it, but it is also the catalyst for a new idea of community that can be rationally understood, realistically created, and pleasurably sustained. The book does not aim to displace global warming anxiety, but rather to evoke it and then contain it—first to make it intensely felt, and then to make it bearable through a specific and carefully thought-out plan for a whole community.

McKibben's book moves away from an acute form of global warming anxiety. McKibben does not escape from problematic knowledge to the problem of knowledge—he does not use what we might call the epistemological defense—and indeed a part of the performance of his text is to use knowledge to arouse anxiety. But his book does do the work of coping with that anxiety by its end. Dreaming of alternative futures is meant to allay a state of fear. In this respect it might be said to be avoidant of difficult knowledge in its own way, since it supplants a focus on troublesome realities with what it seems fair to call utopian visions of the future. It is possible that in its fiercely optimistic schemes *Eaarth* is in its own flight from the anxiety that is emotionally concomitant with knowledge of global warming. But there is another way to understand what the second half of the book is doing, one that tells us something different about how the culture is coming to terms with global warming, and one that helps to make perhaps better sense of the prevalence of the basic structure of *Eaarth* among recent popular global warming books.

Containing and the Genre

In "Tracking the Elusive Jeremiad: The Rhetorical Character of American Environmental Discourse," John Opie and Norbert Elliot make the persuasive case that the form of the jeremiad in American literary history as analyzed by Perry Miller and Sacvan Berkovitch exerts a powerful influence on a tradition of environmental writing that extends from a seventeenth century sermon by Samuel Danforth through Al Gore's 1992 *Earth in the Balance*. In a diachronic analysis, they notice four markers of the genre: the jeremiad chides its audience for failures; it uses this chiding as a persuasive force; it aims to revitalize its community; and it provides a message of hope (10). Among the jeremiads they survey, they identify two classes—one which relies on emotional or pathetic appeals, and the other which makes use of logical, or what they call implementational, rhetoric. "If we generalize," the authors say about their conclusions at the start of the essay, "we might say that writers employing evocative strategies tend to perceive the world as wonderful in its immediacy and in need of our intuitive perception for its maintenance; writers employing implementational rhetoric tend to view the world as chaotic and in need of control" (10). Jeremiads on environmental issues are divided into those that use pathetic appeals and those that make logical ones, and this bifurcation also splits the texts along the lines of more positive and more negative or anxious attitudes, respectively.

There is reason to read McKibben's book as fitting quite neatly into the genre of the "elusive" environmental jeremiad as Opie and Elliott define it, since it does fault industrial civilization with causing climate change, and it seeks to offer something like hope in a way that will "revitalize" the community the book addresses. If it is somewhat problematic to call *Eaarth* an American jeremiad because of the global scope of its concern and the even anti-national color of its proposals, it still can be described as a jeremiad with strong links to the literary tradition that McKibben's national identity, place of residence, and historical frame of reference connect him to. Like many in its genre, it is a text that belongs to an American tradition, but that does not limit its impact on global and local levels of significance.

The greater difficulty in reading McKibben's book according to Opie and Elliot's otherwise largely appropriate schema is that their distinction between evocative and implementational subgenres would encourage one to make a limiting choice about the book at precisely the point where it very likely becomes distinctive in the development of the genre. For *Eaarth* is, as my brief analysis was intended to show, first evocative in its approach, and then implementational. McKibben invites anxiety, expresses anxiety, and then copes with anxiety. The pattern is deliberate, and it offers a specific and somewhat controlled path to take readers through the process of coming to terms emotionally with the experience of knowing the earth. It is, as I try to demonstrate below with a look at a number of other works in the genre, the pattern of the climate change experience.

Before I get to those works, and then to some reflections on the genre's role in the larger cultural project of knowing the environment, I want to introduce an idea that will be useful in understanding the therapeutic purpose of a jeremiad like McKibben's. The psychotherapist and theorist W. R. Bion employed the term "containing" to describe a dynamic process between two minds, a process by which what is initially an unbearable state of emotion for one of them gradually becomes tolerable because of the way that it is experienced and reflected on by the other. In a recent book that attempts to sort through how well Bion's term can be integrated into the field of psychology some fifty years after its coinage, Duncan Cartwright defines a contemporary understanding of therapeutic containing this way:

> It is a state of mind that attempts to apprehend experience that is felt at the edges of consciousness but cannot yet be understood, fully experienced, or held in mind. In this way Bion's view of analytical containment concerns a process of transformation whereby previously unbearable states of mind that prevent thinking and development are made more bearable and thinkable. As Bion put it, the containing process works on parts of the individual (or the analytic couple) that "feel the pain but will not suffer it and so cannot be said to discover it." (25-26)

Experiencing the way another can bear a state of mind that one finds intolerable oneself can empower one to "discover" the reality of that affect or emotional state, and so to integrate it into one's mental world and bring rational and conceptual faculties to bear on it.

That is what containing is. How does it work? As Cartwright notes, Bion explains the process through an analogy with what an infant experiences while nursing. In the course of that form of connectedness, Bion argues, the infant's own internal life is significantly impacted by what he calls the reverie of the mothering figure. The impression of balance and evenness created by this dreamlike state helps that figure to render manageable anxieties experienced by the infant. "Maternal reverie" returns initially intolerable anxieties that are projected by the infant in a form that is not debilitating: "Normal development follows if the relationship between the infant and breast permits the infant to project a feeling, say, that it is dying, into the mother and to reintroject it after its sojourn in the breast has made it tolerable to the infant psyche" (Bion, "A Theory" 309). In a word that one finds in a number of discussions of Bion's term, containing "detoxifies" anxiety by giving one the vicarious experience of being undisturbed by it. In another passage Cartwright draws attention to, Bion discusses his conclusions about a particular relationship this way: "An understanding mother"—the analogy with the therapist is implicit—"is able to experience the feeling of dread that this baby was striving to deal with by projective identification, and yet retain a balanced outlook" (Bion, "Attacks" 313). So the process of containing anxiety works through a projective identification, in which one mind locates its own unbearable anxiety in another with whom it identifies, and then is able to experience and cope with its own anxiety more fully by watching how that figure manages to function under the burden of its fear.

I think that approaching a work like *Eaarth* with the concept of containing as a resource for understanding can give us a sense of what the genre aims to do that is significantly more specific than Opie and Elliott's description. The climate change experience is not created by an address that first chastises and then inspires, evoking fear and then evoking hope, as the jeremiad is said to do. It is an attempt to make anxiety-producing knowledge fully affectively assimilated and, consequently, fully known. Fear is not, as Berkovitch would have it, the means to an end of producing a spirit of consensus. Coping with fear is, rather, a significant part of the work of knowing. The hope offered at the end of the text is in the service of enabling the reader to grapple and come to terms with a distressing but not overwhelming reality.[1]

If such a focus on how the text orchestrates an experience of anxiety is strongly interpretive, it is also less suspicious than the alternative way of reading the jeremiad criti-

---

1. At this point it is important to note that the infant's fear of death and the reader's fear of climate change catastrophe are different in at least one important way—the infant's fear is unrealistic while the threat of climate change is wholly realistic. This raises the question of whether containing is an appropriate strategy for addressing climate change, and whether it is not better to panic altogether than to have one's anxiety rendered bearable by the containing function of a text. On this point I would say only that I side with the tropism of psychoanalytic thought to insist that it is in general maladaptive to be overwhelmed. And yet it is also important to note that while I am prepared to defend my method against this challenge, and to decide in favor of containing as a paradigm for responding to anxiety, for the culture at large no such decision for or against has to be made—those who can turn panic into adaptive responses can do so without the influence of the containing jeremiad, which is all to the good.

cally. *Eaarth* does not marginalize or exclude dissent to invite and create a community, as Berkovitch claims about the genre. Rather, by first eliciting anxiety, and then inviting a kind of identification with the author's own expression of anxiety, and ultimately performing a balanced, poised response to that anxiety, *Eaarth*—and other books in its genre—allow readers to feel fear about global warming in a way that allows them to "discover," in Bion's words, the measure of its reality. The paradox is plain but remarkable: it is not the data or the drama but the reverie—the purposive dreaming about alternative futures—that functions to make global climate change an emotional reality for many readers.

Other Stars of the Genre

A number of books published within a few years of McKibben's have a similar structure. "Some may quibble about the timing," writes the environmental activist and educator David W. Orr in his 2009 treatise, *Down to the Wire*, "but it is clear we are headed toward a global disaster that has the potential to destroy civilization" (21). Orr, who rose to prominence among environmental writers in the early 1990s with a text championing the ideal of environmental literacy, makes quite clear nearly twenty years later in *Down to the Wire* that that form of knowledge is becoming increasingly frightful: "Climate change, like the threat of nuclear annihilation, puts all that humanity has struggled to achieve—our cultures, art, music, literatures, cities, institutions, customs, religions, and histories, as well as our posterity—at risk" (4).

Like McKibben, Orr seeks to both arouse and express anxiety. When he aims to create anxiety, as in the passage above, his focus is broad and often global. The expressions of anxiety, by contrast, work on an individual scale, as when he discusses in a postscript the source of his commitment to the cause of disseminating environmental knowledge. In the summer of 1980, Orr narrates, he was working on a farm in Arkansas with his brother. Temperatures hit record highs, climbing to well over 100 degrees. Nearly a decade before there was a widespread popular concern about global warming, he was left with a sense of apprehension about climate grounded in his body and its memories:

> After the summer of 1980, climate change was important to me, not because I'd thought a great deal about it in an air-conditioned office but because I had first felt it viscerally and somatically. My interest did not begin with any abstract intellectual process or deep thinking but rather with the felt experience of the thing, or what the thing will be like. That summer is recorded both mentally and bodily in memories of extreme heat with no respite. (218)

Orr's global warming anxiety is rooted in embodied experience, and his knowledge of "what the thing will be like" is a part of him at a level that is situated perhaps even more deeply than his capacity for reflection, thought, and judgment.

Something remarkable about this book, then, is that despite the intensity of its anxiety and the spirit of realism in its assessment of the threat, Orr insists on offering, what he calls in one chapter, "Hope at the End of Our Tether" (189). The particular emphasis of Orr's reverie is governance and leadership. He offers a model, based in heroic American leadership of the past—including a lengthy appreciation of Abraham Lincoln—for how forward-thinking legislators, politicians, and judges can stand at the head of a crusade to slow emissions of carbon dioxide and other greenhouse gasses. This is the basis for what Orr calls "hope of the millennial kind" (9). His plan has at its center both an immediate reduction in carbon emissions—he says less than many other authors about how this should be accomplished—and, just as crucially, a series of proposals for engaging communities of experts in the political and legislative processes. Power to make policy will devolve to those who understand the issue best. Orr appreciates, and even celebrates, the radical dimension of this vision: "Our situation calls for the transformation of governance and politics in ways that are somewhat comparable to that in U.S. history between the years of 1776 and 1800" (205). McKibben and Orr both draw on American history to demonstrate the plausibility of their grand plans. But where McKibben had proposed downscaling what he called the "National Project," Orr proposes reinventing it in a way that strengthens it and heightens its importance. Both follow their evocations of anxiety with sustained dreaming.

Another recent global warming book that is structured in a similar way is James Lovelock's *The Revenge of Gaia*. Lovelock calls the earth Gaia with the purpose of making a controversial—even eccentric— argument that there is a symbiotic relationship between the physical environment of the planet and the forms of life it sustains. The one modifies the other in support of the conservation of existing forms of life. Usually, in Lovelock's analysis, this mutual adaptation is brought about through modification of the chemical makeup of the atmosphere. This, he argues, has been the state of the planet since long before homo sapiens, and the Gaia principle will, he implies, outlast the species. But anthropogenic climate change complicates this picture—hence the title of Lovelock's book. The revenge of Gaia will be its refusal, as it were, to sustain many of the forms of life currently found on the planet:

> We suspect the existence of a threshold, set by the temperature or the level of carbon dioxide in the air; once this is passed nothing the nations of the world do will alter the outcome and the Earth will move irreversibly to a new hot state. We are now approaching one of these tipping points, and our future is like that of the passengers on a small pleasure boat sailing quietly above the Niagara Falls, not knowing that the engines are about to fail. (6)

Lovelock predicts a temperature rise that experts locate on the higher end of the spectrum of possibilities. He is less inclined than either Orr or McKibben to perform his own anxiety about this threat, but the ominous tone of the Niagara metaphor is present in a muted in way in a number of clear statements of his apprehension about what might be in store for a clearly warming planet: "Nothing in science is certain, but Gaia theory is now robustly supported by evidence from the Earth and it suggests that we have little time left if we are to avoid the unpleasant changes it forecasts" (65). Oscillating between doom and apprehension, Lovelock generates the impression that his spells of uncertainty are more defensive than genuine, that the revenge of Gaia will be realized either sooner or later, as his sailing metaphor suggests.

Like Orr and McKibben, however, Lovelock has a plan. Indeed he has two plans.[2] The main one is a hard sell for the importance of developing nuclear sources of energy. In "Sources of Energy," he discusses wind, solar, wave and tidal energy, hydro-electricity and bio fuels only long enough to argue that renewable sources are not viable responses to the need and demand for power. This leaves him with the alternatives of fossil fuels and nuclear energy, and he enthusiastically embraces the nuclear option, spending the rest of the chapter dismissing concerns about safety, even arguing against claims that the Chernobyl disaster should be taken as a caution against nuclear power. He makes no grand claims about how quickly the nuclear revolution might be realized, and he acknowledges the significant cost of that form of generation. But the longish interlude of dreaming about solutions in the book does counter the anxious projections that make up most of the rest of it.

The same pattern can be found in Thomas Friedman's extended screed, *Hot, Flat, and Crowded: Why We Need a Green Revolution—and How It Can Renew America*. (My discussion is of the edition extensively revised to incorporate reflections on the credit crisis and recession.) Much of the work of the first half of Friedman's book is to draw connections between population growth, the global rise of a middle class with attendant consumption patterns, and global climate change. Where any one of them is framed as a threat to the stability of the planet, the other two are often presented as exacerbating factors. So passages like this one, in which Friedman's alarm is clearly evident, in a sense have their anxiety-quotient amplified by the context of his larger argument:

> How bad could things get? . . . Since we can't stop CO_2 emissions cold, if they continue to grow at just the mid-range projections, "the cumulative warming by 2100 will be between 3 and 5 degrees Celsius over preindustrial conditions," says the Sigma Xi report [a report commissioned by the U.N.], which could trigger sea level rises, droughts, and floods of a biblical scale that will affect the livability of a range of human settlements. And these are just the mid-range projections. Many climatologists think things will get much hotter. (81)

Quoting Sigma Xi, Friedman claims that the goal of the global community in combating climate change should be to "avoid the unmanageable and manage the unavoidable" (81).

These are the basic data which Friedman connects to the phenomena of increasing global prosperity and population growth to give his meditations a sense of greater urgency. Unlike McKibben, who intensifies the anxiety of his book by listing and even imagining catastrophes in detail, Friedman's anxiety is sustained and deepened by an exploration of the logistics by which the planet becomes warmer:

> if we, as Americans, do not redefine what an American middle-class lifestyle is—and invent the tools and spread the know-how that enable another two or

---

2. Lovelock's more desperate plan, laid out in the final chapter of the book, is to compile a text that will serve as a kind of guidebook to Gaia for future human beings, once Gaia's revenge is complete: "What we need is a book of knowledge written so well as to constitute literature in its own right. Something for anyone interested in the state of the Earth and of us—a manual for living well and for survival" (157).

three billion people to enjoy it in a more sustainable fashion—we will need to colonize three more planets. . . . Cities all over the world have caught America's affluenza—surely one of the most infectious diseases ever known to man. (87-88)

The focus on America in this passage, and the book's subtitle, can be misleading—Friedman's net of apprehension is cast widely, and it brings in diverse phenomena like energy poverty in non-industrialized countries and what he calls "petrodictatorship." His recurrent preoccupation is about the globe, and his overriding fear is named in the lead word of his title: it is getting dangerously hot.

Like Orr and McKibben in their different ways, however, Friedman initially turns in his reverie to a fantasy of the nation. "Green Is the New Red, White, and Blue" reads one chapter heading. Friedman makes many recommendations, including, repeatedly, that the U.S. government send what he calls a price signal to make the cost of carbon-based fuels register some of the damage and risk that they entail, and that Americans shift to the use of appliances that are able to regulate when and how much they draw from the power grid. In one uninhibited rhapsody, Friedman imagines cars as energy storage units to be used for non-peak power, free home energy audits which result in rebates from energy companies, computers that draw nearly no power and net-zero school buildings. These are, he reports, not only realistic ideas but experimentally tested ones (283).

As this passage suggests, the second half of the book won't and can't really be contained by a national frame. In his discussion of the REDD proposal—Reduced Emissions from Deforestation and Forest Degradation, a program by which "developed countries would pay poor developing countries to keep their forests intact"—Friedman identifies a plan with international applicability (369). Similarly, in his provocative final chapter "China For a Day (But Not For Two)," Friedman's suggestion that America emulate the ability of China to implement centralized controls on the economy clearly has relevance to other developed nations. Specific and wide-ranging, Friedman's plan for a "green revolution" carries as much energy into hopeful visions of the global future as was present in the dire warnings of the first half of the book.

Another example of work arguably in the vein of the jeremiad is Philippe Squarzoni's *Climate Changed*. It is a graphic novel that narrates the author's search for a deeper understanding of the problem of global climate change and his interviews with many experts to think through both the source of the crisis and possible solutions. Like the other books described here, Squarzoni's account moves from problem to a kind of hopeful reverie. But because it is a graphic novel, it has recourse to two communicative strategies not found in the other books. One is that the concern of the experts interviewed comes across not only through their words but through their facial expressions and bodily posture. This helps to both intensify the sense of crisis and to magnify the urgency with which solutions are proposed. A second resource is humor—because of the contextualizing visual information, Squarzoni can create sometimes humorous tensions between what is said and what is seen. This is another kind of containing, I would argue—a sense of distance and poise in humor that detoxifies some of the anxiety that many of the figures in his book clearly feel.

Not all recent books about global warming for a popular audience are written according to this structure. Fred Pearce's *With Speed and Violence,* a 2007 book about mechanisms by which climate change could lead to drastic, irreversible shifts in environmental conditions for much of the globe, and the 2007 *Field Notes From a Catastrophe,* by Elizabeth Kolbert, a series of essays about how global warming is having an impact on a wide variety of scientific fields, both lay out their ominous warnings without any effort to offer hope or a plan for escape.[3] But books like these in a way make the two-part structure of books like *Eaarth, Down to the Wire, The Revenge of Gaia* and *Hot, Flat, and Crowded* more remarkable. For why, given the urgency of the problem these books address, should a plea for recognizing it be coupled with a far-fetched plan for redressing it? To emphasize that these books are written in the tradition of the jeremiad would beg the question: what makes that genre so appealing for the popularizers of climate change?

The Value of Containing

In a skeptical review in *Reason* charging that McKibben's *Eaarth* gleefully imagines "we'll have to return to living in villages and farms, becoming 21st-century peasants," Ronald Bailey reads the book as conforming to "the time-honored structure of environmentalist tracts, opening with a quick rehearsal of the science that allegedly seals our terrible fate, followed by a much longer disquisition outlining the author's elaborate plan for salvation" (58). In Bailey's view of the relevance of the form of the jeremiad to McKibben's text, the commonality signals the author's reliance on a formula to appeal to the expectations of an environmentalist base. This may be so. According to "Climate Change in the American Mind," a report released in June 2010 by the Yale Project on Climate Change Communication and the Center for Climate Change Communication at George Mason University, 12% of Americans are "very worried" about global warming (3). Clearly this is a rather large niche as markets go. The jeremiad form may indeed make a convenient match with the reading appetites of this anxious audience.

But if we think of a book like *Eaarth* as designed to have a therapeutic benefit for those who are engaged in the emotionally demanding process of assimilating knowledge of global climate change, its "time-honored structure" seems to be not so much tailored to the expectations of a sympathetic readership as it is designed to help a much larger audience move out of a state of denial. According to "Climate Change in the American Mind," 45% of Americans agree with the statement "There is a lot of disagreement

---

3. This may be a good place to address the omission in my review of climate change jeremiads of one of the most well-known books on the subject of climate change, Naomi Klein's *This Changes Everything.* One could certainly make the argument that her text carries out the process of containing that I have described. But my impression of the book is that it doesn't really shift from problem to solution so much as it broadens from a discussion of climate change into a much more far-reaching discussion of the problems of capitalism. It replaces, I would say, one problem with another, a problem even more intractable than climate change. So I could not in good faith argue that this book has the containing function of the others I have discussed. This choice clearly reveals at least some of my values and priorities, and—if it is not grandiose to say so—I hope it might invite a critical discussion on the question of anti-capitalist climate change rhetorics.

among scientists about whether or not global warming is happening" (3). This is a significantly larger number than those who know that most scientists are in agreement. Faced with anxiety-inducing knowledge about climate change, Americans are using some version of denial and unrealistic thinking en masse.

A few ecocritical thinkers have sought to redress this by turning their attention to the psychological challenges that accompany the experience of knowing that the world is warming. Frederick Buell's chapter on environmental degradation in *From Apocalypse to Way of Life* draws a distinction between what he calls a "many-stranded nature tradition" that "keeps people valuing, defending, experiencing, and scientifically investigating ecosystems and biota that, however degraded, still are the necessary and only planetary kin and companions human beings have," on the one hand, and, on the other a "focus on second nature" that "instructs people not just about ecological decline, but also the social deformation, human conflict, and injustice that are integral parts of environmental crisis" (110). Buell claims that it is the first of these that "leans toward . . . psychological solutions" in its contributions to the project of coping with or minimizing anthropogenic environmental degradation, of which global warming is a part (110). Buell is not specific about what the "psychological" dimensions of these solutions are—one thinks of the celebrated work of E. O. Wilson to raise awareness about human impacts on global biodiversity as an example. Wilson's "biophilia hypothesis," the claim that humans have an inborn affinity for living beings, offers theoretical grounds for both the pleasure and the ethical value of nature writing.

But as McKibben's *The End of Nature* suggested twenty years ago, the issue of climate change makes any turn to nature less simple than an opposition between first and second nature would have one believe. Buell's schema of a restorative world of nature set against a conflicted world of "social deformation" and "injustice" locates the psychological resources for coping with environmental degradation in a genre of cultural production that is characterized by defensive exclusions, if not nostalgia. This claim has limits—recent literature of global warming has in places been written from an elegiac perspective within the nature writing tradition, as for instance Robert Hass's "State of the Planet" and Jorie Graham's *Sea Change*. But to locate the psychological resources available to the culture for coming to terms with global warming mainly in nature writing significantly underestimates the range of genres in which this work can be carried out.

A report recently published by the British arm of the World Wildlife Foundation takes a broader and deeper view of how cultural forces can act as therapeutic facilitators of the process of coming to terms with global warming anxiety. In *Meeting Environmental Challenges: The Role of Human Identity*, Tom Crompton and Tim Kasser argue that there are "three therapeutic steps" to reducing "environmentally problematic defence and coping mechanisms," among which problematic mechanisms they include "strategies for reinterpreting the threat"—a fair description of the epistemological defense (48). The three steps are: to identify the maladaptive defense; to allow for the anxiety that has been sealed off to emerge into consciousness; and to develop more adaptive coping mechanisms (46-7). The alternative ways of coping that they recommend are "*problem-solving*" and "*mindfulness*" (50-1).

The work of Crompton and Kasser is important, particularly if we view it in an ecocritical context where arguments like Buell's are more the norm. Their short book is pretty obviously marred by uncritical parallels between the threat of death and the threat of environmental crisis, but it treats a question that has been neglected for a long time, perhaps too long. Likewise, I think that the argument I have been making here complements their ideas about how cultural texts can be therapeutic in the process of assimilating threatening knowledge about the planet. For where Crompton and Kasser present problem-solving as a part of developing more adaptive coping mechanisms for environmental challenges, I have tried to show that understanding how the process of containing is at work in efforts to face these challenges helps us to see that problem-solving can play a crucial role in allowing anxiety to be felt and so, eventually, more ably managed. Problem-solving, or environmental reverie, is *preliminary* to the work of knowing the earth, and of adapting optimally to climate change. It might be the path of strategic action by which human civilization can, in Friedman's words, avoid the unmanageable and manage the unavoidable. But what it is still likely doing more often is helping a culture be equal to what it knows.

And so it is not to the discredit of these books that they propose plans for action that are unlikely to be realized without an improbable and sweeping change in the way millions, and perhaps hundreds of millions, of people think about the problem they address. And their indisputable anthropocentrism, their almost exclusive focus on the human consequences of climate change, should be understood in the context of their rhetorical and affective strategies. For the work of their proposals is not to point in a practical way towards immediate solutions, as necessary as these appear to be. It is to help people apprehend the reality of the problem. I think it is quite likely that the project of coming to terms with knowledge of global climate change is demanding enough to require this sort of enduring engagement. These books are doing important therapeutic work that is not being carried out elsewhere in the space of environmental literature.

Works Cited

Bailey, Ronald. "On being a 21st-century peasant." Rev. of *Eaarth,* by Bill McKibben. *Reason,* vol. 42, no.3, 2010, pp. 58-60. *General OneFile.*

Bion, W. R. "Attacks on linking." *International Journal of Psychoanalysis*, vol. 40, 1959, pp. 308–15.

—. "A theory of thinking." *International Journal of Psychoanalysis,* vol. 43, 1962, pp. 306–10.

Buell, Frederick. *From Apocalypse to Way of Life.* Routledge, 2003.

Crichton, Michael. *State of Fear.* Harper, 2004.

Cartwright, Duncan. *Containing States of Mind.* Routledge, 2010.

"Climate Change in the American Mind." *Climate Change Communication.* Yale Project on Climate Change Communication and the Center for Climate Change Communication at George Mason University, June 2010. climatecommunication.yale.edu/wp-content/uploads/2016/02/2010_02_Americans-Global-Warming-Beliefs.pdf.

Crompton, Tom, and Tim Kasser. *Meeting Environmental Challenges: The Role of Human Identity*. WWF-UK, 2009.

The Day After Tomorrow. Directed by Roland Emmerich, Twentieth Century Fox, 2004.

Friedman, Thomas. *Hot, Flat, and Crowded*. Farrar, Straus and Giroux, 2009.

Greenberg, Paul. "Hot Planet, Cold Facts." Rev. of *Eaarth*, by Bill McKibben. *New York Times*, 7 May 2010. nytimes.com/2010/05/09/books/review/Greenberg-t.html.

Kolbert, Elizabeth. *Field Notes from a Catastrophe*. Bloomsbury, 2007.

Lovelock, James. *The Revenge of Gaia*. Basic Books, 2006.

McKibben, Bill. *Eaarth*. Times Books, 2010.

Opie, John, and Norbert Elliot. "Tracking the Elusive Jeremiad: The Rhetorical Character of American Environmental Discourse." *The Symbolic Earth*, edited by James G. Cantrill and Christine L. Oravec, UP of Kentucky, 1996, pp. 9–37.

Orr, David W. *Down to the Wire*. Oxford UP, 2009.

Pearce, Fred. *With Speed and Violence*. Beacon Press, 2007.

Squarzoni, Philippe. *Climate Changed*. Translated by Ivanka Hahnenberger, Abrams ComicArts, 2014.

Seeking a Language that Heals: Teaching and Writing from a Ruined Landscape

Amy Nolan

> *There seems to be no escape from our difficulties until the industrial system breaks down...and nature reasserts herself with grass and trees among the ruins.*
>
> —Robert Graves, *The White Goddess*

> *... to call the Midwest the heart of the country is not to get it right. It is more the gut. It is the gut of the nation.*
>
> —Michael Martone

A few years ago when I was riding a shuttle bus from an airport to a large writing conference, I sat next to a man who, like me, teaches at a small, liberal arts college in Iowa. This man, also like me, and like so many academics I have met here, was not from Iowa originally. As we introduced ourselves, I told him that I had moved here from Michigan, and that I'd never been to Iowa before my move. He grew quiet, his gaze grew distant and he looked out the window. In a tone not unlike a doctor telling a terminally ill patient that there is nothing more he can do, he said, "Iowa is a ruined landscape."

A year later, I heard another man, also an academic, utter the same phrase, which he followed by bitterly stating that he does not want to die here. The casual certainty with which both of these men had uttered the phrase troubled me. I wondered what "ruined" means to them. What constitutes a "ruined landscape" outside of what we readily recognize in a devastated war zone or place destroyed by a natural disaster? We write of how our actions and policies have shaped and ruined the land—but what of the reverse? What does it mean if our home is "ruined" and how does that shape our vision of ourselves? Further, what can ruined places teach us about holding contradictions in balance?

In the two men's comments was also a sense of wanting to have it both ways: to be able to reject Iowa as a place and idea, and to claim a privileged, academic status, as one who can endure calling such a place home—as one who understands himself as someone who does not need to care about a place where the job market had thrust him. I realized that a thinly veiled grief and fear live beneath this marked sense of superiority, which manifests itself in a sometimes-cynical over-investment in the illusion of distance: but the illusion covers up a sense of homelessness and disconnection that we cannot admit that we long for.

One could argue that our whole culture is based on notions of flight, fantasies of flight. So-called flyover zones could be defined as anything that we don't want to deal with—like the proliferation of cancer and other diseases as being connected to how much we are polluting the earth (and by extension, our own bodies). Too often, we enter fatalist thinking, which is already expected of the "armchair academic," or scholar who observes and critiques the world from a "safe" distance from the complicated places in our hearts. I wonder what we can learn from those places, what not only confronting them--and our own complicity in creating them and perpetuating them, while at the same time accepting our tendency to try to abdicate responsibility by ignoring them--can teach us about how we are shaped by these places, and what a study of ruin in this way can show us about where we go from here, especially if we feel paralyzed or overwhelmed by grief about the disappearing and polluted landscapes we call home. It's easy to dismiss a place as ruin while refusing to touch down on the ground; it's harder to allow the place and its complex history to talk to us, to shape us.

***

In the summer of 2017, I attended the Biannual Prairie Conference in Council Bluffs. While there, I listened to stories about the prairie, and learned of Iowans' long-lasting passion for trying to preserve what is left, and even restore what is possible. I talked with scholars, activists, students, writers and scientists, who told me that climate change is forcing *all* species to move north. The Midwest, especially Iowa, is actually a "bullseye" for mass extinctions that are occurring today. The thesis of every lover of the prairie, every piece of literature on the prairie, and every nature writer who discovers the prairie, is that Iowa is the most altered state in the country. Many bird, butterfly, reptile, and small mammal species rely on high quality grasslands to raise their young and thrive.

At the conference I learned that researchers are still collecting data on how crop erosion is affecting the soil, and they are still monitoring bird populations as they migrate. They placed tree swallow boxes in the prairie strips, and are hoping to help the honeybee population. Remnant prairies have been found in these unfarmable places, but average less than 15 acres, because they are isolated and cannot support species reproduction. The researchers say that we can protect what is left by creating roadside prairies, as well as in yards—as opposed to lawns. We can incorporate prairies into agriculture more deliberately, especially in places that cannot be farmed.

At the conference we took a field trip into the Loess Hills Prairie trail system. I ventured off alone, and walked beneath a canopy of massive oaks, river birches, and walnut trees. My head buzzed with the sound of the deep-summer cicadas' rhythmic rattle. It drowned out everything: other voices, cars, my own breathing. I was enveloped in a cathedral of sound—the sound of being under water—the rush of a river current. I closed my eyes and surrendered to it. I had never listened to cicadas so closely as I did that summer, four months before my mother died. In Michigan we don't have cicadas like we do in Iowa, where they grow to the size of fat moths. The cicada's song guides us through the dark night of the soul. Its vibration "has the ability to cleave us to our very core, open us, and remind us of what we need to hear" (Star Wolf and Cariad-Barrett 150). Cicadas pulse time. They *ride* time. Surrounded by the relentless, powerful rhythm that I felt in my chest, my belly, my throat, I felt like my body was disappearing into the sound—reminding me of something much bigger—something we are not in charge of, something that holds and protects us. I'd just been to Michigan to visit my mother who was dying of ovarian cancer. Her voice, along with fragments of stories that she has told me forever, were then coming at me from nowhere—pieces that I hadn't heard in years, like how she once told me that when she was a little girl another kid had said to be careful or the cicadas will sew your lips together.

I found in the cicadas what essayist Lynn Casteel Harper calls "the golden hour," where we feel the dance between darkness and light, "the ripening of what is before and within and beyond. The thin edge between life and death stirs my soul to inscrutable awareness. My heart aches…as the really real hovers near, waking me from drowsy numbness. For this brief time—which can only be witnessed, never willed—the inimitable heart of the universe swells across gulfs impassable in ordinary time" (9). When we are called to dwell in this place—this "thin edge"—we are being presented with a precious gift. Any time we are called upon to witness the truth of the present, no matter how painful or difficult, we are never more awake than this.

***

I call two places home: Iowa and Michigan. I was born in Mt. Clemens, a town situated just north of downtown Detroit. I was raised in Grayling, a small northern Michigan town, named after a now-extinct river trout. I moved to Iowa when I was thirty-six years old. I had never even driven through the state. I moved here because I had secured a rare tenure-track teaching position in creative writing. As a graduate of a doctoral program in a competitive field—contemporary American literature and film—I counted myself as deeply lucky. My husband and I have literally planted roots here: since we moved to Iowa we were married in our backyard, we have buried two beloved pets, we have planted ten different species of trees, vegetables and fruit.

Academics and economics uprooted me from my home state, but the sacred work of teaching in this particular place, my friendships, my colleagues, and the landscape, keep me staying in Iowa. Twelve years later, I still live, write, and teach here. At the midpoint of my career (on my twenty-sixth year in the classroom), I am re-learning how important it is, not only to encourage and create space for students to write about and reflect on their inner lives, but also their own responses to the changing landscape, especially that of where they are from. No matter if a student is from rural Iowa or Chicago or Swaziland—students long for stories—their own, and those of others—especially in this "flyover space" that we live and learn within. They long to dive in, to recognize themselves in the greater whole. I tell them, while the opposite may seem true, the way to that sense of the universal is through the specific, the small: that is why *your* stories are important.

The collapse of bee colonies, the disappearance of earthworms, both vital to our survival, speak to present and future ruin. Their message is that there is nowhere to run. So. Perhaps somehow, some way, we need to keep finding ways to connect, or re-connect, with what is here, with what shapes us—not despite, but perhaps because, it is wounded, and reflects something ruined and thus vulnerable in ourselves. In *Dwellings,* her collection of essays on how landscapes shape us, Linda Hogan writes, "What we are searching for is a language that heals this relationship [between us and the natural world], one that takes the side of the amazing and fragile life on our life-giving earth. Without it, we have no home, have no place of our own within the creation" (59-60).

As I continue to explore the many-layered notions of what ruins means, I am also learning how I might teach more effectively—that is, teach as if the local environment is not separate from the world of the text, of the importance of critical thinking, human interaction, and cultural literacy. I notice that I am becoming more comfortable with silence and the space it can provide: to open to the stories that find their way into the gaps. The increased anxiety, depression, a sense of overwhelm that many students are currently experiencing are, I argue, indicative of the sense of loss that they feel every day—that something is missing, and they do not have the language to express it. And that something, perhaps, is the story—however designed or shared—that connects lived experience, a sense of shifting identity, a sense of place or places, inner and outer, and how they come together in a way that lets us see, underneath all the noise and chatter, that nothing is *truly* lost.

In a recent poetry class, my students read a poem about a young boy who comes across a deer carcass at a winter camp, and in a moment of reverence, takes a bit of hair from the deer's body. After some discussion, including the possibility that the boy is a sociopath, silence pooled comfortably. I hadn't planned to, but in the moment it felt appropriate to share a story with them. That very morning I had stopped my car when I saw a dead raccoon in the road. I told them about how I had waited for traffic to clear, got out of my car, and walked over to the raccoon, carrying a flat piece of cardboard. The raccoon's fur was striking, with layers of silver, gray, brown, and black, and soft in appearance. I was also struck by how beautiful its hands were. I slid the cardboard under its body, which was surprisingly light, considering how big the raccoon had looked from the road—a dark lump on the pavement. I told the students that I felt the animal deserved respect—that I couldn't bear the thought of its body being squashed over and over, by car after car, as if it were a piece of trash. I carried the raccoon over to the grass, and then covered it with the cardboard, a makeshift lean-to. I told them that because we live here among the raccoons and deer and skunks and porcupines, we owe it to the world to pay attention as best as we can. To bear witness, to notice, to really *see* the world around us, in all its beauty, horror, and perhaps hardest of all, its woundedness.

I noticed that my students were completely quiet—and while their gazes were fixed on me, I could also see that their focus was inside, too. I realized that I had taken a risk—to share something of myself, something of my soul. And I could tell that they knew it. I knew that it was up to me, in the classroom, to hold the integrity of balance—to model vulnerability, and not force students to share in kind, but to let them know that they can depend on me as a teacher to hold ground, and hold the silence that allows stories to form.

The challenge is for those of us who teach to not view "the life of the mind" as more relevant than the ground on which we stand. To be fair, it is extremely difficult, since we are groomed right from the beginning toward the opposite approach. In the essay collection, *Black Earth Ivory Tower,* Brooks Blevins reflects on this widespread quality of what it means to be on the academic job market. Blevins writes: "[M]ost academics simply try to find that good, tenure-track job, wherever it may be, and adapt to the surroundings as best they can. After all, don't we make a living with our minds? What difference does it make *where* you teach World Civilization or Composition I? Isn't the physical world ultimately superfluous to the life and career of the intellectual?" (305)

In academia very often there does not seem to be a choice in where one "lands" when she applies for a job. According to Eric Zencey, "[Professors], citizens of the…mystical 'world city'…are expected to owe no allegiance to geographical territory; [they're] supposed to belong to the boundless world of books and ideas and eternal truths, not the infinitely particular world of watersheds, growing seasons, and ecological niches…[As a result, they] tend to mistake 'disconnected from locale' for 'educated.' They tend to think of education as little more than an organized assault on the parochial point of view, the view of the rooted 'I'" (15). Zencey's viewpoint is perhaps cynical, but I agree that not being rooted inhibits us from building history, memory, and connection. The plight of the academic is a microcosm of the plight of the average American citizen, whose ancestors, willingly or not, were uprooted from every corner of the globe.

Of this displacement, Laura Sayre writes, "One of the failings of graduate education…is the structural dislocation it forces upon you, the way in which it asks you to spend your late twenties—a period in which you might well be setting down roots for life—digging into a place only in order to be uprooted" (191). Perhaps our challenge as teachers is to have the courage not only to dig into where we are, but to address the conditions that require us to perpetuate detachment and disconnection from the landscape around us and under our feet. In what ways might we begin or continue to engage students in this way, whether in conversation, in reflection, in going outside and to see and feel the world around them right now? How might we find ways to help them, and ourselves, incorporate their stories into their chosen disciplines, and thus, into their very lives?

The cost of the sense of disconnection that we often feel, teachers and students alike, whether it is conscious or not, is rooted in the stories we tell ourselves: whether an overinvestment in the story of an "idealized past," or Edenic place that has been sullied; or its flipside, which is an overinvestment in the idea of inevitable extinction. These trap doors—the "lost Eden" story and the extinction ending story—can be barriers against speaking about place and galvanizing action to address the questions and problems that unfold, especially for addressing what constitutes "ruined landscapes." Both stories are dead ends: whether writers fixate on a "better time," or romanticize science and technology, especially the notion that they can "save" us, they miss the point, which in my view, is to simply stand still and behold what is here, all around us, and within us.

The importance of stories to help us understand and hold onto the feeling that might serve as a catalyst for action—stories unmediated by the pressure to analyze experience away, to theorize and quantify—cannot be underestimated. Stories not only hold cultures together by creating a common language; they offer multiple ways of seeing experience. They support the need—a desperate one—for empathy and understanding. My story touches, overlaps with yours, but your experience and story (even with its silences, laughter and tears) have value in and of themselves. While writing, by its very form, is an act that takes us away from the present, it also allows us to linger in it. To write is to have a broken heart—and the source of a broken heart is often the witnessing of that which seems irrevocable, beyond the reach of time. From that source, I might come to glimpse the possibilities and even hope—that hummingbird of a word—in the notion that staying with what is ruined could help us find and hear a language that gives us the strength to heal what has been broken.

***

At the beginning of my story there is a river—*a singing river*: a flowing, fast river full of stories: the source of my existence, and the source of my love for the world. We all come from stories, written and oral, told by both men and women, through films and music, too. Mine come from all of these things, and through listening to and watching the northern Michigan AuSable River, the tall pine trees, my grandmother, my mother, and the earth itself. The river helped me survive, and it is why I write. The river reminds us that the world is not fixed; it is an alive, ever-changing, place.

***

When I was one year old, I tumbled into the icy AuSable River on a winter afternoon. I had fallen off my grandparents' dock into the dark, clear current of the AuSable in northern Michigan, where fly-fishermen and women came to fish from all over the world. In winter, there was no sound but the river singing its exciting, tumbling song, and I was floating due east, toward the lazy whirlpool just around the next two bends, and ultimately, Lake Huron. The AuSable didn't meander. It swept. In a blur of cedar tree tops, my pink snowsuited body floated.

My father ran toward me through the water that was up to his thighs. He let the current push him downstream, his big strides clumsy with panic—the sound of water churning filled his ears. I was almost around the first bend when he hauled me out.

Years later, when my mother told this story, she said that I was gazing up at the low, gray sky with wide eyes. She and my father were surprised that I didn't cry or struggle—that, instead, on my face was a look of wonder as I bobbed down the river, a bundle growing smaller on the river's glassy surface.

One year after my immersion, my father died from a sudden heart attack. He was forty. The story is made of images, things sensed, dreamed: my mother's Tupperware party, her long dark hair, her late pregnancy, a snowstorm, a Catechism class that my father taught before he came home and shoveled the driveway, before he cried out in the darkness. My mother found him lying on his back, eyes open, gazing upward.

What if my father's heart was so full of love, so open, that his body couldn't take it? What makes a heart break open?

In the wake of my father's death, I fell in love with the muscle of the river, with nature, with life. The sky is a miracle from under the surface. The sun spreads out and down, penetrating the coldness. To feel the force of the river's current you have to attempt swimming across it, attempt paddling against it—to feel the cold rush in your ears. The river has its own gravity and yours is no match for it. This particular river—the landscape of the water--has taught me about how grief gently but persistently becomes part of who we are, the way the ancient currents shape everything from stones to plastic to bones to trees. My immersions within the river instilled in me a desire to further immerse myself fully into other places.

***

Inherent in statements that label a place as "ruined" is an assumption that there was once a "better time," or a time when things were somehow better. When we idealize a mythical past, we reveal our fear of the future and neglect the present, which is at the heart of bearing witness. Conversely, our dominant culture associates death with failure instead of resting in the wisdom that it is a necessary part of existence. Further, examining ruin always puts us in touch with the immediacy of the present. I think that is why a lot of people don't want to acknowledge the "invisible" ruined landscapes, in contrast to the ongoing fascination with and very visible lure of urban ruin. The challenge is not to try to analyze it away—but to abide with it. This is especially so in the world of academia, in which we are often convinced that we must observe from a distance, keeping ourselves removed from what we examine.

Sometime after I moved to Iowa, I asked my colleagues if it was possible to swim in the Cedar River. Unanimously they said, "No." The reason: farm run-off. Every town in Iowa has at least one community swimming pool, with slides and waterfalls: clear, chlorinated blue "lakes" surrounded by corn fields, hog confinements, and miles and miles of green, mowed grass. I could not imagine living in a region where I could not safely swim in the rivers and lakes. As a child, teenager, and adult I did so without question or hesitation. Hardly anyone had swimming pools. And even if they did, I still preferred the bracing, clear cold of north Michigan waters: from great lakes to the tiny, hidden spring-fed lakes that you could only reach by hiking—lakes that looked like the setting of a 1970s horror movie. It is a strange feeling, to be surrounded by water in Iowa, but not be able to swim in any of it. My stepdad , who was born in Flint, Michigan, told me that when Iowa gave itself completely over to agriculture, that was just one sacrifice that had to be made in the name of progress.

When asked to consider Iowa, people who have never been here might think of the films *Bridges of Madison County*, *Field of Dreams,* and the second half of *Sleeping with the Enemy*, set in idyllic Cedar Falls. In America's "breadbasket," home of apple pie and 4-H club, what does "ruin" really mean? On its bucolic surface, Iowa is green and rolling. On a summer day, the huge blue sky seems to crash down upon the fields. People don't come to Iowa to photograph the polluted rivers, dead pigs piled up in the driveway of a hog confinement, the absence of worms in the ground of over-sprayed fields, the bitter effects of Monsanto's Round-Up. Ruin becomes a much more contested idea in Iowa, when the sources of ruin are not as readily visible as they are in places like Detroit or Flint.

In the graphic memoir, *Imagine Only Wanting This*, which chronicles her exploration of ruined places throughout the world, Kristen Radtke describes both being from Iowa, where she went to university, and then leaving to find a career elsewhere: "Iowa was a place I began leaving constantly [to seek out ruin elsewhere]. Native Iowans told me about the dangers of all the state's rivers, the flat and modified land that flooded [in 2008] and formed lakes, roof peaks jutting from the surface like coastal boulders and forming currents across roads, the moldy basements when the water drained the closest thing they had to ruins" (110). Though her memoir is about her fascination with ruins—urban decay, in particular--Radtke does not explore the idea of Iowa as "ruined landscape." However, Radtke's memoir poses an important question that applies to the kind of ruin that characterizes Iowa's land: "What can be made of the spaces that we cannot witness?" (204)

On a drive on back roads one weekend, my husband and I passed a hog confinement that sits less than ten miles from our house. With a strong south wind, especially on a hot day, the smell is so powerful that we can't have the window open in the bedroom. The day we drove by the confinement, we couldn't see any pigs, just long, white covered buildings with ventilation pipes. Then we noticed, right in the front of the property, a pile of pig corpses stacked up in a concrete fenced in area. I didn't even think about taking a photo. I was too shocked. I thought, there are seven times as many pigs in Iowa as there are people (Schmidt 9C). I live in a world now where it is automatic, an instinct, even, for people to take photos and film everything. But there are still private spaces, where unspeakable things happen—where it is both impossible, and absolutely necessary, to bear witness, to bear the silence that both holds the story, and denies it.

When I first contemplated the notion of ruined landscapes, I thought about the science fiction and horror films I loved when I was an adolescent in the 1980s. I thought of John Carpenter films, and the strangely beautiful, apocalyptic and spare electronic soundtracks, which I still enjoy, that perfectly matched the seemingly empty, evocative spaces that filled my car window as I sat in the back seat looking out at endless fields and urban sprawl, plugged into my Walkman. I remember being mesmerized by the vastness of the crumbling houses, the still-apparent majesty of long-abandoned department stores, a train depot, a theatre, and a ghost mall. At one time an economic auto capital boom-town, then a bombed out, apocalyptic shell of a city, Detroit is now sought out for its glorious ruined buildings, photograph-ready decay, and its powerful urban history. Detroit's ruins exude a haunting beauty that now draws artists, musicians, writers, and hipsters, who are starting to re-inhabit the parts of the city once thought too dangerous to live in. Detroit is sublime. Its beauty has grown out of its ruin, and is part of its appeal now. One could say that its ruined status has imbued Detroit with a new kind of credibility, a richness of spirit that was always there, but has somehow been reawakened by the gaze of those who are drawn to ruined places. But what of ruin that is not as visible, let alone celebrated? Because its "ruin status" is not the same as, say, Detroit's, or Gary, Indiana's, people do not seek out a ruined landscape like Iowa's and take photographs, because they do not see it and do not look for it.

I think of this lack of ability (or willingness) to witness the space of Iowa whenever I see commercials for Round-Up. One ad is particularly disturbing: it features a smug, slender white man in a uniform—white, red, orange, green—wearing a baseball hat. He carries Round-Up spray bottles in both hands, holding them as if they are guns and he is a cowboy. This is a free-for-all, like the old west. This is war. To me, a Round-Up commercial signifies a powerful representation of ruin that goes deeper into the territory of grief than does a crumbling building in Detroit. When I see images of weeds drying up and turning to dust the instant they are sprayed, I think of the groundwater, of birds, of bees, of butterflies. I think of the soil—the literal foundation upon which our existence and all of our dramas unfold. I wonder, how on earth did we think up this awful power, to literally vaporize the life that sustains us? What kind of species does that? What claim on meaning or life can I make, let alone teach, with this awareness?

***

In the introduction to her 2017 epic poem, *Plenty*, which evokes the work of Walt Whitman and Rachel Carson, Corinne Lee chronicles the complex links between what happens to the bodies of all animals and how untold pollutions infiltrate everything we eat, drink, breathe and wear. She does not write about Iowa specifically, but focuses on the Midwest, where Monsanto (housed in St, Louis, Missouri) created Round-Up to be a powerful herbicide and desiccant, to kill weeds and facilitate early harvest by prematurely drying grain. Monsanto has genetically engineered 'Roundup Ready' seeds such as corn, soy, canola, alfalfa, sorghum, and wheat—these plants resist glyphosate and similar herbicides, remaining alive even when native grasses and other plants around them perish after a spraying. In response to widespread opposition, Monsanto withdrew its Roundup Ready wheat from production in 2004 (xv).

Over the past two years, class action lawsuits have been filed against Monsanto—and legal commercials airing in Iowa have been soliciting victims of Round-Up's effects to come forward and sue Monsanto. Lee goes on to point out that Round-Up's far-reaching impact cannot be underestimated: it is literally everywhere. It kills plants, but also destroys bacteria and damages soil, killing earthworms, who are obviously vital to the soil's health. Monarch butterflies have experienced an 81 percent decline, "because the chemical destroys milkweed—the only plant monarch caterpillars are able to consume" (xvi).

Speaking about ruin as an invisible force, Heather Swanson, in her 2017 essay, "The Banality of the Anthropocene," asserts that ""Iowa is objectively one of the most ruined landscapes in the United States, but its ruination garners surprisingly little notice." Swanson's chief argument is that Iowa's dominant demographic, the white and middle-class, do not see that the ruin lies in their lawns, their corn fields, their malls, and drainage ditches. Ruin is "the industrial pig farm. It is the 4-H county fair and eating hot dogs on the Fourth of July. It is precisely this banality, this routinized everydayness…that makes the Iowa Anthropocene so terrifying." Iowa's tallgrass prairie, its bees, butterflies, migrating birds, CSA/organic farms, and its maze of rivers, hardly receive any press. And they should. While urban, human-made ruins may be the stuff of great photographs, ruins wrought by irrevocable ecological imbalances are just plain scary, and put us in touch with a deep grief (and guilt) that most are not willing to face, and therefore discussions about Iowa's status as a ruined landscape often result in a troubled silence.

This is true of all quietly ruined landscapes. My thoughts once again turn to Flint, where silence shrouded that lead-poisoned drinking water until too many people were getting sick and it couldn't be ignored anymore. In Grayling, Michigan, where I lived from age four to eighteen, we drank well water. The house I lived in is situated in a subdivision built into a marsh-bordered forest of red pines, tamaracks, maples, oaks, jack pines, and white pines. The marsh is actually where the headwaters of the AuSable and Manistee Rivers end and where the East Branch of the AuSable flows, behind our house, toward the main branch. A mile to the west of our neighborhood is the Camp Grayling Military Airport. For years, our well water and soil have been contaminated by an invisible plume of perfluoroalkyl substances (PFASs), also called perfluorinated chemicals (PFCs). The investigation into these chemicals, initiated by the Michigan National Guard, is part of a nationwide Department of Defense effort to test military sites for PFAS contamination caused, primarily, by historic use of Aqueous Film Forming Foam (AFFF), a firefighting foam the military began using in the 1970s that was laden with PFAS chemicals that helped quash jet fuel fires. According to Garrett Ellison, reporting for Michigan News Live, as of September 2017, about 180 wells south and west of the airfield have been sampled. Of those, 83 tested positive for some level of PFAS compounds and four tested above the 70 parts-per-trillion, which is the Environmental Protection Agency health advisory level for two of the compounds, perfluorooctanoic acid (PFOA) and perfluorooctyl sulfonate (PFOS). How do we address the truth of a place, or a person, in a sea of silence? The chemicals contain stories, too, about ruin and restoration. How can we tell those stories, and provide our students with the language to tell them, as well?

Silence is the repository of everything we deny as individuals and as a culture. Silence is cancer, growing in my mother's body. Silence is also the ground of the capacity to behold the world, to rest a soft gaze upon it, to be still amid the trees, the birds, the prairie, the river. Silence can hold us back, and it can hold us up. *Silence*: around the military bases that pollute groundwater in northern Michigan: around the disappearances of frogs' songs, snakes sunning themselves on dusty trails: around dead zones at the mouth of the Mississippi: around dead bodies of pigs next to hog confinements. Silence is a civil defense against inconvenient truths, brokenness, and the necessary outrage and demand for change that must be voiced in the face of ruin.

I am coming to learn that maybe I can begin to acknowledge what is ruined, and at the same time nurture a love for the world while I cultivate a sense of curiosity in my students. I have discovered that, even more than when I taught in Michigan, students are more likely in Iowa to have come from farming communities and families—and at least one student I know has interned or worked for Monsanto. I have taught many students who have grown up on hog confinements. Still, they often seem to be, or feel, disconnected from the wider implications of such experiences—and how could they not be, if this is all they know, and they do not have a means for understanding their place and experience as part of a larger context? In teaching, it is a delicate balance: not to "lose" the student by demonizing what Monsanto stands for to a large part of the world, but to also give them the tools to find out more about where they come from, even, and especially, when it doesn't warrant much attention or curiosity on their part.

***

The mission of cultivating curiosity in students has always been a challenge for teachers. All we can do is provide the conditions that are favorable for sparking that curiosity: by teaching them how to ask good questions, and get in touch with what they *really* are afraid of, excited about, confused about. I often ask my students what changes they notice about their home place when they return periodically after they have left. I tell them about how I couldn't wait to leave my hometown—how college had been expected of me. I also remind my students that some stories are like tender shoots, and need the dark nourishment of the ground for a while—that it's okay not to share everything. I haven't told my students this story: that at the same time my stepdad and I witnessed yet more trees come down near Grayling, near the house I grew up in, to make way for the lumber industry, and other trees die from unexplained illnesses, we watched helplessly as ovarian cancer, commonly known as "the silent killer," ravaged the ecosystem of my mother's body. Ovarian cancer has one of the highest death rates of all cancers because it is notoriously difficult to detect—and when it is, it is very often too late.

My mother lived for two and a half years, from her diagnosis in 2015 to her death in November of 2017. Over those years, we felt time differently. It came in the form of vignettes: waking up that first summer of chemo and watching my mother brush out her thick dark hair and fling it into the wind, shouting, "It's for the robins' nests!"; seeing her hair grow back all salt and pepper curls; eating her homemade "gorp" trail mix as we talked in a Cincinnati hotel room and got ready to go to her sister's funeral; laughing in the back seat of a car with the windows down eating Boom Chicka Pop; or sitting at a picnic table at the Dairy Queen in late August—the last time I would eat with her. Just days before she would stop eating altogether, we sat shoulder to shoulder, savoring our Blizzards, our backs to the setting sun in late August.

That night I lay in my childhood bedroom with the window open and heard nothing—no crickets, no frogs, no rustlings of raccoons or deer. The silence frightened me. I was suddenly five again, panicked that my mother would die. At 2 a.m. I found her awake on the couch, as she was often too uncomfortable to sleep. I lay my head in her lap and cried. She rubbed my head and said, "Oh, honey. Everything is going to be all right."

***

What do we do when it all feels like too much—when we are frustrated by knowledge? When the more we know, the more paralyzed we feel to change anything? I try to stay present to the smallest things: the shape of a rabbit's silhouette in the bright silver light of the moon against melting snow; a goldfinch at my window looking in and chirping; the miracle of earthworms in my garden, a place unsullied by Round-Up. I want to cling to them as I wanted to cling to my mother. Even though I've never given birth, I have learned that being a mother means, among so many other things, to learn how to let go of what is beloved to us. If I am to be alive in this time, then how am I to live? How do I live without my mother?

***

Iowa, as Swanson and many writers have observed, like much of the Midwest, has been forever altered by agriculture. The ruined status of Iowa's landscape tends to be literally "underground"—but is visible in the clear loss of prairie: that between 1830 and 1910 Iowa lost 97 percent of its prairie acreage. According to Swanson, "Nearly every acre has been privatized. Ninety-nine percent of its marshes are gone. The level of its main aquifer has dropped by as much as three hundred feet since the nineteenth century, largely due to the extraction of irrigation water." Recently I spoke about this with a friend who has lived in the Black Hawk region of Iowa her whole life. She and her husband live in her mother's family farmhouse, where three generations have lived.

Twice they have had to change the place where to dig their well, due to high levels of nitrates found in the drinking water. I know that her situation is not unique; I know of other nearby farms who have had to completely re-design their water-retrieval system and dig even deeper wells.

These stories are small, in the bigger scheme of things—but they reveal both the silence that surrounds the state of Iowa's ruined landscape, because nothing has changed in relation to mono-agriculture and hog confinements; and they reveal the invisibility that continues to define much of the Midwest in general, despite its importance in food production. Swanson offers that "we are all implicated in Iowa. We are all entangled with the everyday violences of industrial agriculture and nationalist projects in a way that substituting an organic latte for the hot dog or shopping at Whole Foods won't solve." One way to address these entanglements, if we choose it, is to involve poets and writers in the crucial work that ecologists and biologists do. Amid the research that goes into sampling soil and cataloguing the decline of endangered species, we need poets, writers, and musicians to command an audience—to transmute data into storytelling. The writer-teacher, instead of looking sadly outside a shuttle bus window and proclaiming the local landscape a ruin, might need to ask how he can help—and maybe come to love this place that is now his home.

***

In late October of 2017, two weeks before my mother died, I drove back to Michigan and accompanied her and my stepdad to Traverse City, an hour west—to the new cancer center that attached to the complex of Munson Medical Center. We walked into the cancer center where over the last two and a half years my mother had received her chemotherapy, had liters of fluid drained from her body, clinical drug trials, and the invasive pelvic exams that she hated so much. It was late: the clinical trial was not working, and she hadn't eaten anything since August. I'd never been to this place before: finished in 2016, it was impressive—all glass and metal and Frank Lloyd Wright—like a spaceship standing near the gothic Victorian structure of the old state mental institution—once a ruin itself, now a maze of art galleries, hipster coffee bars, bakeries, fusion restaurants, and apartments for retired doctors.

The cancer center was housed with a café on the bottom floor; a Zen garden; art on the walls; a nursery; a chapel; it was modern, tasteful, with soft colors, wood, metal, and glass—as if the architects had consulted a *feng shui* book. There was no hint whatsoever of death, or dying—at least on the surface. You only saw it in the eyes of the patients, many of them, despite their street clothes, fleece North Face clothes and soft beanies, baggy on spare skulls, and bright colors against pale skin. Under their tasteful scarves and hats, some of them had the far-off look that I'd noticed developing in my mother's eyes since July. The research nurse greeted her with a cheery familiarity that I found bracing. She told my mother that she "looked good."

My mother thought she was going to have chemotherapy. But not fifteen minutes after she'd been called back to see the doctor, my mother, stepdad, and I were led into a small, triangular room. We sat in the three chairs that were spaced far apart. One wall was a window looking out over the colorful October trees. Cars swept by below, as if it was just a normal day. The sun was warm coming in the window, where two flies buzzed against the glass. I noticed a fitness magazine with an impossibly fit forty-something celebrity on the cover—her face carefully and obviously smoothed out by photo-shop, her hips narrow, her stomach flat and hard. On a small counter with a sink I saw a miniature plastic model of female body parts: uterus, ovaries, fallopian tubes, all packed into a disembodied plastic recess, like a puzzle toy. I thought about how we carve up the body like we carve up the world. I recalled the long vertical scar on my mother's abdomen, where just two years earlier the oncologist had taken out her ovaries, uterus, and cervix—how her scar had looked as if he'd just pulled the flesh together and sewn it up with the crudeness of Dr. Frankenstein. Days after the surgery she lay on the floor unable to stretch out from the pain, pulling her knees up as I covered her with a blanket and lay my hands on her belly and breathed with her.

After a few minutes, the oncologist burst in, harried, his face full of practiced concern, and oddly, embarrassment. He told my mother that she was too weak to have any more chemo. She nodded politely, her knees pressed together like a little girl. The doctor continued, "Your body is riddled with disease. You are no longer achieving quality of life. Go home, be with your family. Eat some chocolate, drink some wine. At this point you may want to contact hospice."

Then, he apologized on behalf of the flies, who kept bouncing off the window. "Oh," my mother laughed, "I hadn't noticed them." I thought, at least the flies are more honest than any of us. So far no one here had used the words "death" or "dying," much less the words "grief" or "cancer." But my mother *was* dying, and with a swiftness that surprised all of us more than her lack of pain. She hadn't eaten in a month, and every two or three hours she vomited bile, a bright, emerald green. She had no interest in food or water anymore, much less chocolate. She was, I realized, as I looked at her peaceful face, doing exactly what a dying person is supposed to do.

I never saw fear in my mother's eyes while she was dying. Her eyes were intense in her face, dark, and contemplating—but not afraid. Though faraway at times, her eyes were never drawn from the present. It was as if she was becoming *more* present, even as she was disappearing. One day, I asked her what she was thinking about when her gaze becomes so intent—when she looks so deeply into me, not unlike the way she must have when I was a baby.

She said to me, "I am just trying to take you in."

I knew then something I'd never considered—that the dying miss us, too.

***

We all witness something of the natural world disappearing every day—and this witnessing most often happens in silence and isolation. Even though I know others see it too, we do not discuss it openly, or if we do, it is with anxious humor or that fatalist, cynical, and protective language that reveals how isolated and helpless we feel in the face of what we cannot control. We stay silent, maybe because we can't bear how others might respond to us if we wept for a tree, or "roadkill," or the disappeared prairie. The language that heals may be the one that opens up this vulnerable part of ourselves—to admit that yes, it is sane to weep in the face of what is disappearing, or gone.

If part of our vocation is to teach students to think for themselves, to be "whole citizens" and educated, informed individuals who know how to engage in critical thinking and discourse, then the natural world, the landscape, the world under their feet, the air they breathe, the animals they share this planet with, absolutely must be part of this endeavor. This means that we have to tune in to our own limitations, to not rest in our authority on a specific subject, but to expand our awareness to the spaces around us. From the very beginning, Iowa has gently, slowly, but persistently claimed me. To be claimed by a place is not only about standing ground, or defending it, either. Iowa confirms at once its status as a "ruined landscape," but it also tells the story of how ruin is actually a process of transformation—and not a permanent state of being. We have seen this hypothesis come true as we witness what is happening in places like Chernobyl, Detroit, and Ohio, where in 1970 the Cuyahoga River caught fire due to pollutants.

Hogan writes, "Can we love what will swallow us when we are gone? I do. I love what will consume us all, the place where the tunneling worms and roots of plants dwell, where the slow deep centuries of earth are undoing and remaking themselves" (30). In a culture that is fixated on light, striving, achieving, and by all means, not failing, we don't have many opportunities to be still, to withdraw, to go into the dark and sink down into those places where we hurt so much. When the things we love die, they leave a hole that can never be filled again. Maybe a broken heart doesn't write despite these things, but alongside them, or even because of them. Maybe that means that we are called to have the courage to fill our hearts with our love for the very world that reclaims us.

Works Cited

Blevins, Brooks. "Back to the Land: Academe, the Agrarian Ideal, and a Sense of Place." *Black Earth and Ivory Tower: New American Essays from Farm and Classroom*, edited by Zachary Michael Jack, U of South Carolina P, 2005, pp. 303-12.

Ellison, Garrett. "DEQ doubles size of Grayling's water investigation area." *Michigan News Live*, 20 Sept. 2017, www.mnewslive.com.

Graves, Robert. *The White Goddess*. Edited by Grevel Lindrop. Farrar, Strauss, and Giroux, 2013. Google Books, books.google.com/books?id=hjUORTBSyIkC&printsec= frontcover&dq="white+goddess"&hl=en&sa=X&ved=0ahUKEwj4lcj8tuTfAhVQnOA KHePKBJwQ6AEIKjAA#v=onepage&q=there%20seems%20to%20be%20no%20 escape&f=false.

Harper, Lynn Casteel. "The Golden Hour." *North American Review*, vol. 302, no. 1, 2017, pp. 3-15, northamericanreview.org/2017/golden-hour.

Hogan, Linda. *Dwellings: A Spiritual History of the Living World*. Simon and Schuster Touchstone, 1995.

Lee, Corinne. *Plenty*. Penguin Poets, 2016.

Martone, Michael. "Pulling Things Back Down to Earth." *Black Earth and Ivory Tower: New American Essays from Farm and Classroom*, edited by Zachary Michael Jack, U of South Carolina P, 2005, pp. 120-33.

Radtke, Kristen. *Imagine Wanting Only This*. Pantheon Books, 2017.

Sayre, Laura. "Cultivating Georgic." *Black Earth and Ivory Tower: New American Essays from Farm and Classroom,* edited by Zachary Michael Jack, U of South Carolina P, 2005, pp. 84-192.

Schmidt, Mitchell. "Iowa taps 'abundant' biomass resources." *The Gazette,* 21 Oct. 2018, 1C, 9C.

Swanson, Heather Anne. "The Banality of the Anthropocene." *Cultural Anthropology,* 22 Feb. 2017, culanth.org/fieldsights/1074-the-banality-of-the-anthropocene.

Star Wolf, Linda, and Anna Cariad-Barrett. *Sacred Medicine of Bee, Butterfly, Earthworm, and Spider.* Rochester Bear and Company, 2013.

Zencey, Eric. "The Rootless Professors." *Rooted in the Land: Essays on Community and Place,* edited by William Vitek and Wes Jackson, Yale UP, 1996, pp. 15-19.

Teaching Animals in the Post-Anthropocene: Zoopedagogy as a Challenge to Logocentrism

Anastassiya Andrianova

Abstract: *This essay examines a theory and practice of zoopedagogy that encourages exploring non-logocentric mode(l)s of communication while promoting environmentalism, critical thinking, and empathy.*

> 'Do you really believe, Mother, that poetry classes are going to close down the slaughterhouses?'
>
> 'No.'
>
> 'Then why do it? You said you were tired of clever talk about animals, proving by syllogism that they do or do not have souls. But isn't poetry just another kind of clever talk: admiring the muscles of the big cats in verse? Wasn't your point about talk that it changes nothing? It seems to me the level of behaviour you want to change is too elementary, too elemental, to be reached by talk. Carnivorousness expresses something truly deep about human beings, just as it does about jaguars. You wouldn't want to put a jaguar on a soybean diet.'
>
> 'Because he would die. Human beings don't die on a vegetarian diet.'
>
> —J. M. Coetzee, *Elizabeth Costello*

Since Nobel laureate Paul Crutzen popularized the term "Anthropocene" in 2000, we have been hearing about the devastating effects of anthropogenic pollutants which cause the translocation and annihilation of wildlife species and have increased the species extinction rate in tropical rain forests by up to ten thousand fold (Crutzen 17). Factory farms are responsible for much of the anthropogenic impact on the environment and wildlife. Building on Peter Singer's *Animal Liberation*, Jonathan Safran Foer, in *Eating Animals*, urges us to end factory farming because that would also "help prevent deforestation, curb global warming, reduce pollution, save oil reserves, lessen the burden on rural America, decrease human rights abuses, improve public health, and help eliminate the most systematic animal abuse in world history" (257). We can intervene to help animals survive beyond the Anthropocene by redirecting our resources away from the rearing of animals for human use, slaughter, and consumption and toward a more ecologically sustainable model. This entails a radical reevaluation of the human-animal relationship and of human needs in light of those of nonhuman animals and the environment.

That this must be done is philosopher Donna Haraway's point in *Staying with the Trouble: Making Kin in the Chthulucene* (2016). Haraway insists that the name Anthropocene no longer fits our "transformative" age in which human exceptionalism, individualism, and other pillars of Western Enlightenment have been debunked; a "multispecies muddle" offers a better framework for thinking about the complex and messy ways in which humans are linked to other species (30-31). What others have labeled the Post-Anthropocene, she calls the Chthulucene wherein *Homo sapiens* is but one species enmeshed, like the tentacles of the *Pimoa cthulhu* spider, with multitudes of others. Anna Tsing opens her 2015 book, *The Mushroom at the End of the World: On the Possibility of Life in Capitalist Ruins*, with a similar critique of the Anthropocene, a misnomer for what has less to do with Anthropos' biological species than with the rise of capitalism—hence, the Capitalocene; the latter "entangles us with ideas of progress and with the spread of techniques of alienation that turn both humans and other beings into resources," while, at the same time, "obscuring collaborative survival" (19). Haraway and Tsing urge us to "stay with the trouble" and work together on strategies for "collaborative survival," rather than surrender to either faith in easy technofixes or bitter cynicism and despair, the two most common responses to "the horrors of the Anthropocene and the Capitalocene," and with a new focus on our "multispecies muddle," think not just about other critters, but also *with* them (Haraway 3).

In this article, then, I argue that as humanities teachers, we can help raise students' awareness of animal rights[1] and of the anthropogenic environmental degradation facing human and nonhuman beings alike, by promoting inquiry and writing which interrogate the human-nonhuman boundary, challenge human exceptionalism, and expose speciesism, which Singer defines as "a prejudice or attitude of bias in favor of the interests of members of one's own species and against those of members of other species" (6). Studies of animal life can help combat the so-called "anthropic principle," to use Victor Stenger's term, "according to which the universe is a purposeful creation uniquely suited for intelligent life, meaning us" (de Waal 22). A zoopedagogical approach that brings animal studies into the classroom can help students develop critical thinking and empathy; it can also help us think more broadly about the paradox of a humanities not dominated by human exceptionalism, but open to other(ed) voices.

Yet, how can we escape the limitations of (human) logocentrism and engage in collaborative conversation with (nonhuman) animals who do not speak and for whom words do not serve as an expression of external reality? Ludwig Wittgenstein's remark, "If a lion could talk, we could not understand him" ("Wenn ein Löwe sprechen könnte, wir könnten ihn nicht verstehen," 190), has been criticized by animal studies scholars for erroneously asserting the impossibility of understanding and communicating with animals. It is unfortunate that Elizabeth Anscombe's commonly accepted translation of "könnten...nicht" as "could not" supports such interpretations: that lions cannot speak or have nothing to speak of/about, their *umwelts*, or "surrounding worlds,"[2] being too different from ours or entirely nonexistent. What if, however, it is not lions but humans who are lacking in something? A non-speciesist reading points to human, rather than

---

1. I use animal rights, rather than animal welfare, as per the distinction outlined by PETA: whereas "animal welfare" presupposes the use of animals for human benefit provided humane guidelines be followed, "animal rights" implies "that animals, like humans, have interests that cannot be sacrificed or traded away just because it might benefit others" ("What is the difference").

2. This is Jakob von Uexküll's term for the individual ways in which each organism senses the environment (de Waal 7).

animal, deficient inability to understand. By combining critical pedagogy, as outlined by Paulo Freire, with animal studies and theatrical techniques, I have developed an in-class exercise that asks students to speak without using words (or ASL cues), as a challenge to logocentrism and an invitation to explore alternative mode(l)s of communication. By sharing this exercise with other teachers, my goal is to implement Haraway and Tsing's call to think-*with* and develop interactive, collaborative strategies that will not terminate in individual assignments or courses, but continue to shape students' ethics beyond the classroom.

This experiment in integrating academics with environmentalism is not without risks. In trying out zoopedagogical approaches in my literature classes, I have encountered both openness and resistance to animal rights, revealing cognitive dissonance in students' thinking about who they are and what—or *whom*—they eat. Yet, the most contentious, uncomfortable discussions are, perhaps, also the most conducive to students developing empathy and honing valuable skills of critical thinking and ethical decision-making. In an eristic conception of knowledge production, debate, not consensus, matters. While I focus on long-term changes, the short-term institutional fallout is also worth mentioning: in my own experience, student evaluations were lower than average, with comments criticizing the liberal environmental politics undergirding the course as well as the instructor's alleged promotion of vegetarian and vegan lifestyles. After considering the benefits of zoopedagogy, in the concluding section of this article, I will reflect on the challenges of engaging in this and other critical/radical pedagogies and suggest some solutions. I will also suggest how zoopedagogy might help us expose the academy as a speciesist enterprise and initiate a discussion about disciplinary and institutional change.

Like Elizabeth Costello's son, in the epigraph to this article, I am hardly naive about the idea that "poetry classes are going to close down the slaughterhouses" (Coetzee 103). Indeed, I think that reading poetry and prose about animals is not enough for students to move out of their proverbial comfort zones and imaginatively inhabit the mindset of the other. It is not enough, moreover, to create change. But by incorporating theatrical techniques, an embodied performative experience can make animal existence a bit more real. In describing a specific in-class activity, I invite others to experiment with zoopedagogy not only to help familiarize students with difficult theoretical concepts of animal-standpoint theory, such as logocentrism, but also to explore alternative mode(l)s of communication. I begin with a theoretical section outlining my vision of zoopedagogy as ecoliteracy, rooted in Freirean ecopedagogy and animal studies discourses. Next, I describe and provide a script with directions for an activity that builds on theatrical techniques to make this theory accessible to students, along with my own notes from facilitating such an exercise. This information will be useful to teachers of animal studies, but can also be adapted to suit other pedagogical objectives to give voice to the voiceless, powerless, and dispossessed, whether human or not.

Zoopedagogy as Theory: Where Critical Pedagogy Meets Animal Studies

My vision of zoopedagogy stems from Paulo Freire's definitive *Pedagogy of the Oppressed* (1968), which has also inspired ecopedagogical writings, such as Moacir Gadotti's *Pedagogy of the Earth*, Francisco Gutierrez's *Ecopedagogy and Planetary Citizenship*, and Richard Kahn's more recent and so far the only book in English on ecopedagogy, *Critical Pedagogy, Ecoliteracy, and Planetary Crisis: The Ecopedagogy Movement*. As Kahn writes, "Just as there is now an ecological crisis of serious proportions, there is also a crisis in environmental education over what must be done about it" (5). Kahn notes that while federal and state legislatures require that environmental education be part of public education, "most Americans continue to have an almost shameful misunderstanding of the most basic environmental ideas" (5-6). This may be because environmental education, unlike the broader and more pervasive environmental movement, remains a marginal academic discipline, most often confined to natural sciences departments, with little, if any, interaction with scholars in the humanities or in education (Kahn 6). Kahn calls, therefore, for a more critical, interdisciplinary form of environmental literacy with a stronger "ethical focus that is presently demanded by our unfolding planetary crisis"; we should present students not with idealized experiences, of, say, life on a family farm, as does the Apple Valley Zoo's Wells Fargo Family Farm program, but with an ecoliteracy that exposes questionable practices, such as the naturalization of a corporate "family farm," and also teaches them how to take responsible parties to task (7).

Critical pedagogy is, of course, most closely associated with the work of Freire and Henry Giroux. It is an effort, within educational institutions, to study inequalities of power and "the way belief systems become internalized to the point where individuals and groups abandon the very aspiration to question or change their lot in life" (Burbules and Berk). The main focus is on transforming "inequitable, undemocratic, or oppressive institutions and social relations" (Burbules and Berk). For Freire, who worked on adult literacy in Latin American peasant communities, the task of critical pedagogy was to bring the members of an oppressed group to a critical consciousness (*conscientização*) of their situation as a beginning point of their liberatory *praxis*. Revolutionary leadership, Freire insisted, cannot "merely 'implant' in the oppressed a belief in freedom"; this is, rather, something that must come from dialogue and be "the result of their own *conscientização*" (Freire 67).

The reason why animal rights, unlike broader environmentalism, have been largely excluded from discussions of critical pedagogy as well as ecopedagogy lies in anthropocentric and speciesist biases. That human and animal oppression are interconnected can be seen in the case of meatpacking factories and the fast-food industry employing minimum-wage workers in unsanitary and dangerous labor conditions, as exposed by investigative journalist Eric Schlosser in *Fast Food Nation* (2001), to name but one example. Nevertheless, the latter receives little attention in critical pedagogy, as confirmed by a 2005 doctoral thesis which surveyed the Critical Pedagogy Program at the University of St. Thomas in Minnesota. The program has no formal mention of animal rights even though it prepares doctoral students "to address economic issues of social injustice present in educational settings as well [as] the greater society" and focuses on "issues of inequality and oppression" (McGee v). When surveyed, more than half of the participants noticed some connection between animal rights and critical pedagogy, yet none requested that animal rights be included in their program of study (McGee 1, 174). A meagre 5% participated in any programs or classes which addressed animal rights and/or speciesism, and only 11% facilitated such discussions themselves (195).[3]

Added to this is the theoretical objection. Given Freire's insistence on bringing the members of an oppressed group to critical consciousness through literacy, animals, with their other(ed), nonverbal "literacies," do not seem capable of engaging in their own empowerment. Because animals, especially farm animals bred and reared for slaughter, are oppressed as much as, if not more than, their human counterparts, the choice to exclude their concerns is logocentric, that is, based on the notion coined by the German philosopher Ludwig Klages and central to Western epistemology, namely: that (human) words and language constitute the fundamental expression of an external reality. To counter logocentrism, compounded with the anthropocentric, or human-centered, bias also at work in the exclusion of animals from critical pedagogy and ecopedagogy, we can either speak on their behalf or redefine what we mean by language, so that they can speak for themselves. We can demonstrate that, since words are not an operative criterion given their species(ist) limitations, animals can, in fact, become conscious and voice their discontent by means other than narrowly conceived human language, and that, moreover, they can engage in the production of knowledge, with the latter broadly defined. Animals do, after all, have diverse ways of expressing themselves: they bite, kick, scratch when they disagree, oppose, or lack interest in something, but also nuzzle up, lick, or purr to show consent and affection. Then there is also the problem of domestication and animal consciousness: a farm animal may have internalized its captive status to such a degree that it cannot develop a consciousness (if, indeed, animals have consciousness[4]) critical enough to challenge the status quo. But this, too, can be at least in theory overcome through Freirean "dialogue."

The best option is to let the animals speak for themselves by expanding the meanings of language, literacy, and knowledge. In her research on nonhuman primate culture and language at the Great Ape Trust in Des Moines, Iowa, Dr. Sue Savage-Rumbaugh has shown that "language and personhood are simply not coincident with the human form" (qtd. in Bradshaw 22), and that meaning can be "cultivated…across species lines"

---

3. The data reveal conflicting views regarding animals: the majority of the participants (56%) believe that it is not necessary for humans to eat animal products (dairy, meat) to maintain their health, but only 5% describe themselves as vegetarian/vegan (McGee 195-196).

4. That nonhuman animals have consciousness is a debatable issue only insofar as acknowledging it would make carnivores uncomfortable. Charles Darwin, writing 150 years ago, recognized that animals had emotions. Recent research confirms that a neocortex (absent in nonhumans) is not essential to experiencing affective states, which, in his provocative book on the inner lives of fish, Jonathan Balcombe takes to mean: "you don't need a big, convoluted humanlike brain to feel excited about food or scared of predators" (83-84).

(Bradshaw 17). Great apes "[can] indeed learn to use and to respond to full sentences and understand the demands of grammar as well as of signs" (Weil 8). This challenges "humanity's monopoly on epistemic authority" inviting us both to assert "animal agency and embrace new modes of communication and models of knowledge that bring other species into dialogue and authority as equal partners" (Bradshaw 15). The problem with this radical, though admittedly irresistible, proposal is that we have yet to acquire the practical means of understanding what animals are saying, despite having made some progress with species who most resemble us but comprise a tiny fraction of the animal kingdom; with the sixth mass extinction under way, then, we might need to step in and serve as their proxies.[5]

Through a zoopedagogical approach to the humanities classroom, that is, through the teaching of animals, we can become effective spokespersons for animal rights. This is not a limitation, as critics might charge based on similar accusations made against postcolonialism as a Eurocentric "first-world discourse" (Sethi 20). Opposing the charge that all research on animals is unavoidably biased, Rob Boddice urges us to acknowledge that scholars begin their work "*because* they are human, with unique skill sets and marks of distinction" (12). Another related objection to animal studies is anthropomorphism—that is, ascribing human traits, forms, or attributes to a being that is not human. Kari Weil suggests that we address charges of anthropomorphism by adopting a "critical anthropomorphism." Building on Jill Bennett's "critical empathy," which is a "conjunction of affect and critical awareness" (10), Weil urges that "we open ourselves to touch and to be touched by others as fellow subjects and may imagine their pain, pleasure, and need in anthropomorphic terms, but stop short of believing that we can know their experience" (19-20). At the other end of the spectrum lies "anthropodenial," the term coined by primatologist Frans de Waal, which refers to "the a priori rejection of humanlike traits in other animals or animallike traits in us" (25). Ultimately, we can address such objections, as well as the paradox of a humanism not centered on humans, by recognizing, with Boddice, that we ask questions because we are human(ists), but that our answers must be qualified by the fact that we are *human animals*, both connected to and separate from our nonhuman animal planetary companions.[6]

One important aspect of critical pedagogy which zoopedagogy can emulate, so as to become a viable platform for the study and promotion of animal rights, is its contextual relevance: it is applied to "the specificity of particular contexts, students, communities, available resources, the histories that students bring with them to the classroom" (Giroux and Tristan). The animal turn seems particularly suited, then, to land grant institutions with historically strong agricultural programs, to which students likely come

---

5. This is analogous to Vladimir Lenin's notion of a vanguard party which, though inconsistent with Marxist dogma, nonetheless helped the Bolsheviks launch a successful revolution.

6. "Even the term nonhuman grates on me," de Waal admits, "since it lumps millions of species together by an absence, as if they were missing something." In his comments on student papers he wants to write (sarcastically) "that for completeness's sake, they should add that the animals they are talking about are also nonpenguin, nonhyena, and a whole lot more" (27-28).

from rural areas, having grown up on farms, to pursue veterinary and animal sciences degrees or seek careers in agribusiness. This situation carries "the specificity of particular contexts," to use Giroux's phrase, that, in effect, adds both relevance and potential resistance: especially in rural areas, students may see themselves as masters of the agricultural-industrial complex which places animals on the same plane as other utilitarian tools of agribusiness—as means to an end, not as sentient beings whose individual lives matter. They may have strong beliefs about animal welfare, rather than animal rights, very different from those of animal activists. While some may be able to conceptualize the various connections among animals, humans, and the environment, the knowledge and values these students bring to the classroom will likely make them see animals as commodities in economic more than ethical terms, welcoming provisions for animal protection so long as these do not interfere with material production. It is this attitude that should be brought into dialogue, though initially also into conflict, with a progressive zoopedagogy.

Nor is this impediment limited to rural areas or land grant institutions: students at urban universities may be removed from the natural environment and from the brutal realities of meat, poultry, and fish production, their engagement restricted to the digestion of processed, attractively packaged, faceless animal remains. Such intellectual distance may be as difficult to overcome as physical proximity: the latter requires reconceptualizing real violence to which one has become desensitized, while the former requires making symbolic violence real. We could think of this as the less obvious objective violence Slavoj Žižek describes as "systemic," "the often catastrophic consequences of the smooth functioning of our economic and political systems," the violence that goes into sustaining "a comfortable life": "not only direct physical violence, but also the more subtle forms of coercion that sustain relations of dominance and exploitation" (2, 9).

It is precisely such anthropocentric thinking that a zoopedagogical approach can expose and challenge. With co-production of knowledge and broadened, non-anthropocentric definitions of language remaining theoretically tempting but practically inaccessible, the route toward spokespersons seems the most prudent, albeit unorthodox, given Freire's insistence on not simply "'implant[ing]' in the oppressed a belief in freedom." An embodied performative exercise, beyond an abstract channeling of the other's mindset, is key to such engagement. In the following section, I describe a multi-phase in-class activity that can bring us closer to that end.

Zoopedagogy in Practice: Teaching Animals in Humanities Classrooms

The following in-class activity has been adapted specifically to the teaching of animal studies based on a professional development workshop I attended in Chicago in August 2016, during the annual meeting of the Association for Theatre in Higher Education (ATHE), a conference that brings together teachers, theorists, and practitioners of drama and theatre. Entitled "Theatrical Jazz Workshop" and facilitated by Omi Osun Joni L. Jones, professor of performance studies in the African and African Diaspora Studies Department at the University of Texas at Austin, the workshop was designed to explore various theatrical jazz techniques, such as "ensemble-building, non-mimetic movement, virtuosity, layering of elements, as well as writing that investigates the personal as political." The goal was to develop "the practice of being present and collective witnessing" (ATHE).

In spring 2017, I developed and facilitated my own zoopedagogical version of theatrical jazz exercises I had learned in that workshop in my split undergraduate/graduate course at North Dakota State, a land-grant, research university in the Midwest, where I teach in the English Department. I designed this Topics in British Literature course to focus on texts about animals from the British Isles and the Commonwealth, such as Anna Sewell's *Black Beauty*, the autobiography of a horse, which inspired Margaret Marshall Saunders' *Beautiful Joe: A Dog's Own Story*; Virginia Woolf's *Flush*, a charming imaginative biography of Elizabeth Barrett Browning's cocker spaniel; T.S. Eliot's whimsical collection of poems in *Old Possum's Book of Practical Cats*; Peter Shaffer's provocative psychoanalytical play *Equus*; the novel *Watership Down*, in which Richard Adams invents a special Lapine language spoken by rabbits; and Coetzee's *The Lives of Animals*, among others. Through the close analysis and discussion of animal-centered fiction, poetry, and drama, I encouraged my students to explore how animals and animal experience are represented in narratives, and how the material conditions of their existence are handled in theoretical and activist texts, such as Singer's *Animal Liberation*, Foer's *Eating Animals*, and Haraway's *The Companion Species Manifesto*. This was an interdisciplinary, reading- and writing-intensive course with an underlying philosophy that reading and writing about animals can help students become better critical readers as well as more empathetic, conscientious citizens capable of informed ethical decision-making with respect to animals and the environment at large. As I noted in my introductory lecture to my students, a recent study suggests that literary fiction helps readers become smarter and more empathetic individuals, as the latter is an integral component of socialization, thus supporting the view that literary fiction should be included in educational curricula. Of all the different genres assigned to the participants in the study, it was their reading of literary fiction that measured the highest in terms of ability to understand other people's thoughts and emotions because of its focus on the psychology of the characters, their intentions and motivations (Chiaet). And if it is difficult enough to understand what other humans and characters are thinking or feeling, animals pose a greater challenge, and hence present a great exercise to flex our creative and analytical muscles.

The multi-phase zoopedagogical activity, based on the ATHE workshop in theatrical jazz, was conducted in the first week of class so as to invite the students to think about how nonhuman animals "speak" by asking them to communicate without using words or verbal cues. This was reinforced at the end of the semester, when the students were asked to write letters to their future selves with expectations for three, six, and twelve months in the future, to promote a greater awareness of empathy and environmentalism beyond the scope of the 17-week course. Their letters were mailed to them six months after the course's completion, allowing them to evaluate their commitments halfway and adjust accordingly.

The purpose of the activity, more specifically, is to encourage those used to operate within and through human language to think outside its confines, relying on extra-linguistic communication, ocular, vocal, and gestural cues, and bodily movement to express not just basic needs but potentially also higher-order cognitive ideas. Here the logocentric trap presents itself. As Weil asks in her book *Thinking Animals*, "how do we bring animal difference into theory? Can animals speak? And if so, can they be read or heard?" (5). Evoking the title of Gayatri Spivak's essay "Can the Subaltern Speak?," Weil presses animal studies scholars to reconsider how they give voice to voiceless nonhumans, lest they, like Western postcolonial scholars, end up not only providing the terms for but effectively speaking on behalf of the dispossessed peoples whom they claim to represent, Spivak's warning against the critical establishment. Think about primatologists who, their best intentions notwithstanding, might "try to teach apes to sign in order to have them tell humans what they want" (Weil 5). By experimenting with nonhuman communication, however, we can challenge ourselves to think outside human language, an exercise that could get us closer to hearing, or at least learning to hear, what the animals are really saying.

Along with the theoretical hurdle posed by animal difference, some practical limitations include: the layout of the room, as space is needed to walk around; and accessibility for persons with disabilities, who might have difficulty moving freely about the room, or those with autism spectrum disorder (ASD) who might have trouble maintaining eye contact. For the latter, however, a critical discussion might replace Phase 1 of this activity, providing an opportunity to verbally interrogate the common association of eye contact with empathy, as well as the misconception that individuals with ASD who experience difficulty maintaining eye contact also struggle to identify with the thoughts and feelings of others. A recent study questions traditional theoretical accounts of ASD in which lack of eye contact and other social difficulties were seen as indicators of interpersonal indifference to others; firsthand reports from verbal people with ASD, on the other hand, suggest that "the underlying problem may be one of socio-affective oversensitivity": that is, lack of eye contact, when constrained gaze is tested with a dynamic face, has more to do with increased anxiety, not antisocial behavior or lack of empathy (Hadjikhani et al.). Difficulty with eye contact also poses an opportunity to explore affinities between animals and humans with autism, particularly having to do with attention to detail and pain perception, as described by Temple Grandin, professor of animal studies at Colorado State University, specialist in livestock behavior, stress reduction, and humane slaughter, and prominent spokesperson for autism.[7]

---

7. In *Animals in Translation,* co-authored with Catherine Johnson, Grandin argues that animals, like autistic people, see in detail whereas "normal" people see the large picture and draw inferences about these raw data and small details; the latter, in fact, experience what Arien Mack and Irvin Rock call "inattentional blindness," that is, inability to "*consciously* see any object unless they are paying direct, focused attention to that object" (qtd. in Grandin and Johnson 50). Noting that this difference between animals and humans has been corroborated by neurological research (by Nancy Minshew, among others), Grandin further insists: "When an animal or an autistic person is seeing the real world instead of his idea of the world that means he's seeing *detail.* This is the single most important thing to know about the way animals perceive the world: animals see details people don't see" (31).

One of Grandin's many insights involves putting human eyes on the same level as the animals', a notion that could provide further rationale for embodying the animal in a zoopedagogical exercise. When providing cattle plant owners with a checklist of items to handle cattle or hogs who refuse to walk through an alley or chute, Grandin describes "[getting] down on [her] hands and knees and [going] through the chute the same way the pigs did": "You have to get to the same level as the animals, and look for things from the same level angle of vision," she writes, because that is the only way to spot the "tiny, bright reflections glancing off the wet floor," which are causing the pigs anxiety (Grandin and Johnson 34). An even more radical experiment is Charles Foster's attempt, in his book *Being a Beast*, "to see the world from the height of naked Welsh badgers, London foxes, Exmoor otters, Oxford swifts, and Scottish and West Country red deer; to learn what it is like to shuffle or swoop through a landscape that is mainly olfactory or auditory rather than visual...a sort of literary shamanism" (1). Going beyond the theoretical assertion that "our capacity for vicariousness is infinite," and that we can "become one" with an animal by empathizing with it (216), Foster ventures out into the wilderness and, for example, instructs his children to spraint like otters and then try to reconstruct someone's life based on sniffing their fresh feces (83-85).

Short of tasking students with digging around in the dirt, we can bring embodied performative activities into the classroom and experiment with placing more emphasis on the body. "Within performative pedagogy bodies can be acknowledged, made visible, and moved to the center of pedagogical experiences," write Mia Perry and Carmen Medina in an essay investigating the role of embodiment in critical performative pedagogy. "Bodies are perceived as inscribed and inscribing people's relationships, engagement, and interpretation of multiple ways and histories of being, experiencing, and living, in the world" (63). By employing theatrical techniques and recognizing the ideological movement of bodies through space, "[s]tudents can be seen to be engaging their bodies in a negotiation of ideological and intellectual ideas, both of their own and of other participating and performing students," while also enabling both students and educators to reflect on how an awareness of our bodies can forge new modes of learning (Perry and Medina 70, 72). By redirecting attention from the mind to the body, in this zoopedagogical activity I aim not to re-assert Descartes' speciesist assumption that animals are soulless or mindless machines, but rather to re*mind* the human animals in my classroom that they, too, are em*bodied* subjectivities that can express themselves *sans* words.

Below is the script for the in-class activity, which can be provided orally or projected on an overhead screen.

Differences in vision, as explained by neurology and physiology, might also account for the differences in perspective between humans and animals. This has to do with the structure of the eye (humans have a fovea, or round spot, whereas domestic animals have a visual streak); and their respective perception of color and contrast, with humans' color perception being more developed and animals' contrast vision being sharper, as contrast is sharper in black and white, though along with better night vision comes "relatively poor color vision" (Grandin and Johnson 43).

Zoopedagogical Activity: Can the Animal Speak?

- **Phase 1**: Walk around the room, taking in your surroundings; pause when prompted and maintain eye contact with one person. No words.
- **Phase 2**: Walk around the room; pause when prompted and communicate to one person something about yourself. No words. Gestures ok.
- **Phase 3**: Walk around the room; pause when prompted and communicate to one person (someone new!) something about yourself. Words and gestures ok.

For Phase 1, I recommend allowing 15 seconds of eye contact the first time around, and then repeating the exercise several more times with 10-second intervals. The interstitial times allotted for walking around the room, getting to know one's body within that space and with respect to others, could range from 30 seconds to a minute or more. For Phase 2, I recommend a 30-second interval first, followed by several rounds of 20-second intervals, totaling, similar to Phase 1, about 3-5 minutes. The same for Phase 3 as for Phase 2. This should be followed by 10-15 minutes of debriefing, to be extended or shortened based on the enthusiasm of the responders. Free-writing and pair-sharing prior to sharing with the larger group will engage both oral and written skills in a collaborative context. A script for the debriefing session follows; this, like the steps above, could be projected on a screen.

Debriefing Questions

- **Eye contact**: describe your experience of maintaining eye contact with a person. What did you notice about the other person? What did you learn about yourself? Was it easy or difficult to maintain silence? Are all silences the same? What emotions did you experience, and which, if any, of these, did you express?
- **Saying without words**: describe how you felt telling a stranger something about yourself. Did saying this *without using any words* make it easy or difficult? What other kinds of extra-linguistic techniques or body language did you use to express yourself? Was this liberating? Frustrating? Both?
- **Describing yourself**: how does this linguistic experience compare to the previous one? Did you have any difficulty choosing how to define yourself or what "something" to express?
- **Conclusions**: Based on this activity, what can we infer about human *intraspecies* communication? What do we, in other words, rely on to define ourselves and tell our stories? What can we, in turn, infer about human-animal *interspecies* communication?

* * *

According to my notes from facilitating this activity in my animal studies class, during the eye contact exercise many students looked uneasy and somewhat anxious, and I heard several of them say, "this is so awkward" or "this is uncomfortable"; there was some audible laughter, and a bit of confusion in the room. During Phase 2, there was more confusion and uncertainty about how long to keep trying to communicate without words. At least one student started using (what looked like) ASL, but then switched to less familiar, more erratic gesticulation. Phase 3 was by far the smoothest, and there were conversations as well as stories audible. Although it might seem redundant, I do not recommend omitting this phase as it provides fertile ground for comparison, enabling the students to see how much we rely on stories told through words and human language while also learning alternative mode(l)s of communication for other(ed) storytelling.

In the debriefing following this activity, valuable insights were shared by the students themselves. When questioned about how long they thought they had to maintain eye contact, some of the students said 30 seconds, while others insisted it was 3 minutes (the actual intervals were 15 seconds first and 10 seconds thereafter); the intimacy and vulnerability that come with sharing someone's gaze made the experience seem longer, even unbearably long. One student commented on how uncomfortable it was to look at another person and not know what else to do or how to move; another admitted that she had trouble with eye contact when younger due to attention deficit disorder. One other student noted that eye contact was "aggressive," explaining that people of Scandinavian origin, so common in the Midwest, feel uneasy when forced to constrain their gaze. In contrast, someone else said about this phase, as about Phase 2, that not knowing how much longer to continue or what to do when finished provided the unease, rather than the eye contact or the gesturing.

When asked about Phase 2: "Saying without words," some students had trouble thinking of something to share. One person who immediately turned to ASL said she started to use "language," but thought it was cheating and stopped, and then added that this demonstrated the arbitrariness of language since even if she used ASL, she would have no idea whether the person at the receiving end was getting the message or (mis)taking ASL for "random gestures." The students came to a general consensus about how much they rely on words and how difficult it is *not* to say anything. Also, they shared their frustration at not knowing whether the message was conveyed and received accurately. This brings to mind Wittgenstein's notion of a language game, or *Sprachspiel*: with the rules of a specific game known to one but not to both players, it is unclear how to play or even what the game is, like an inside joke that only one of them is in on.

Such debriefing and post-activity discussions can, furthermore, stimulate discussions of linguistics, especially the contested identity between thought and language in the study of cognition, providing an opportunity to consider, for example, Jean Piaget's reluctance to deny thought to preverbal children and his subsequent declaration that cognition must be independent of language. "With animals," as de Waal insists, "the situation is similar. As the chief architect of the modern concept of mind, the American philosopher Jerry Fodor, put it: 'The obvious (and I should have thought sufficient) refutation of the claim that natural languages are the medium of thought is that there are non-verbal organisms that think'" (de Waal 102). The Dutch primatologist himself sees humans as "the only linguistic species," capable of rich and multifunctional symbolic communication; he calls it "our own magic well." However, de Waal also recognizes that other species not only have complex emotions, intentions, and other inner processes, but are able to communicate them through nonverbal signals, though "their communication is neither symbolized nor endlessly flexible like language" but "almost entirely restricted to the here and now" (de Waal 106). Even so, animals have developed ways to signify objects at a distance: honeybees signal distant nectar locations to the hive, monkeys utter calls in predictable sequences (akin to human syntax), and Kenyan velvet monkeys even have distinct alarm calls for a leopard, eagle, and snake (107).

The connection between language and intelligence is fraught, exposed through testing that has been shown to carry racial, ethnic, cultural, and class biases.[8] To these we can add speciesism. Rather than "testing animals on abilities that *we* are particularly good at—our own species' magic wells, such as language—why not test them on *their* specialized skills?," de Waal proposes (22). A zoopedagogical exercise in which the students find themselves unable to partake in a simple language game, which is not formally presented, but might still be perceived as a test of their intelligence, is likely to help them develop both humility and empathy toward others who are regularly not in on the inside joke, in areas outside the classroom's safe and contained environment, where this carries serious material and spiritual repercussions.

Conclusions: Teaching Animals in the Speciesist Academy

The purpose of the described zoopedagogical activity is, ultimately, ethical and political: to combat anthropocentrism and speciesism. By seeing ourselves as the masters of our planet, we tend to ignore and downplay the rights of other species. Whereas animals must rely on their natural skills for survival (fangs, claws, acute sensory organs), we have developed various technologies of domination and can enhance these with the use and abuse of our planetary companions. The ways in which we have justified our dominance over the animal world and the many arguments we continue to make (that animals lack consciousness, cannot feel pain, do not experience emotions etc., and hence deserve to be enslaved, owned, domesticated) echo those made throughout history about various others (non-European, non-white, non-male, non-cisgender)—hence, the connection between animal studies and women's and gender, queer, postcolonial, and critical race studies. The latter opens up this activity to teachers and practitioners in other humanities disciplines, including foreign-language and multicultural studies classes that would benefit from initial bewilderment as a stepping stone to confronting and embracing difference. We cannot read animals *in the original*, the way we can read the untranslated stories of other humans whose languages we can learn, but are left to read animal narratives ventriloquized by, however sympathetic, writers, poets, dramatists, and artists; yet, an embodied performative experience like the one described above, in which we have to rely on more than words, is still an animal leap in the right direction.

Added to our logocentric limitations and the epistemological difficulties of knowing the animal qua animal is institutional resistance to doing such liberatory work in the academy. I will conclude by reflecting on such hurdles, starting with one I have

---

8. For biases in standardized testing in particular see, for example, *The Skin That We Speak: Thoughts on Language and Culture in the Classroom*, edited by Lisa Delpit and Joanne Kilgour Dowdy, especially Asa G. Hilliard III's chapter on "Language, Culture, and the Assessment of African American Children" and Victoria Purcell-Gates' "'... As Soon As She Opened Her Mouth!': Issues of Language, Literacy, and Power." For a speciesist approach to language and intelligence, see Daniel C. Dennett's "The Role of Language in Intelligence."

experienced myself, that of lower student evaluation scores, which nonorthodox pedagogical practices and course designs might realistically incur. The following are institutional data from the Topics in British Literature course which I designed and taught as "Animals of the British Isles & Beyond." "The quality of this course," one of the criteria included in faculty evaluations, was rated by my undergraduates at 3.8 and by the graduates at 2.8, as compared to my two-year average of 4.0, which matches the departmental average. Anonymous student comments included: "This course was extremely political…you are wrong if you are a conservative, and you are wrong if you are not a vegetarian/vegan"; "We read…mainly about vegetarianism"; "This course is wrongly marketed, still trying to figure out why this has anything to do with British lit. Instructor promotes her democratic political agenda. Not cool"; "This class was very interesting, but I feel as if [the instructor] was concerned with pushing her beliefs on the topic onto her students." On the positive side, one student said, "I enjoyed this class as it taught me about a new topic in English studies. [The instructor] knows how to challenge her students which I think is very important." Student evaluations/ratings of instructors are, of course, notoriously unreliable and reflect gender bias, among others, as a growing body of educational research has repeatedly confirmed, with women and people of color rated lower than their white male counterparts by male and female students alike. The American Association of University Professors' (AAUP) Committee on Teaching, Research, and Publication studied this issue in 2014 and provides useful recommendations as well as other less biased ways to measure teaching effectiveness (Vasey and Carroll).

Still, the position of a liberatory practitioner is inevitably precarious and those most vulnerable (untenured, non-tenure track), who make up the majority of teaching faculty and whose retention and promotion are typically contingent upon such scores, might feel reluctant to engage in nonorthodox pedagogies. (In my case, the chair was supportive of innovation and aware of its perils, and I continue to contextualize the scores and comments as such.) I would suggest mitigating risks by incrementally implementing shorter, low-stakes activities and including individual animal-centered texts in surveys rather than revamping entire courses or curricula. Another suggestion would be to bring literary scholars together with scientists to team-teach cross-listed courses on animals in order to play up interdisciplinarity and innovation, which often figure in universities' strategic plans and would appeal to their various stakeholders, while simultaneously reinforcing Haraway's insistence on the inseparability of human and nonhuman worlds ("naturecultures"). Concerns over student enrollments, however, which would be divided between departments and colleges, and other institutional logistics might preclude such collaboration.

The moderate approach to zoopedagogy, moreover, falls short of an oppositional critical pedagogy's potential to expose the academy as a speciesist enterprise, one where the contributions of nonhuman animals are everywhere hiding in plain sight: from animal testing by animal sciences departments without the subjects' consent,[9] and the

---

9. The American Association for Laboratory Animal Science (AALAS) is "dedicated to the humane care and treatment of laboratory animals," but a search of its website produces references to human consent only, such as the consent I would need to obtain to "reprint, copy, electronically reproduce, or utilize any document on this web site."

speciesist handling and disposing of animal tissue by teaching and research facilities alongside cadaveric material,[10] to the operation of university meats laboratories carefully equipped for the theater of death: the slaughter, cutting, and chilling rooms and freezers that likely go unnoticed by most visitors to campuses. Although courses in animal studies or anthrozoology (focusing on science, ethics, policy, and animals in the arts and humanities) are currently taught at at least 25 U.S. institutions, there is still an underrepresentation of animals given their pervasiveness (The Animals and Society Institute).

A more far-reaching response to speciesism, informed by Haraway's critique and truer to the spirit of the Chthulucene, would mean reconceptualizing education to account for the labor power of all animals and effecting change through political demonstration (with other animals) against the institutionalization of speciesism in all its variants.[11] The zoopedagogical activity was part of a course designed to expose the exploitation and dehumanizing treatment of animals, to raise awareness of endangered species and mass extinctions, and to assist in forging an environmental ethics that recognizes and aims to combat such injustices. That the activity "spoken" of here means to challenge logocentrism may seem paradoxical, as is conducting such anti-speciesist Chthulucenesque work from within the speciesist academy. Similar charges have been raised against the discipline of postcolonial studies being embedded in elitist neo-colonialist institutions. Although, at the moment, our contribution as practitioners of radical pedagogies may be limited to pointing out this contradiction, our responsibility remains to outline a vision for a future academy that is more reflective of Haraway's "multispecies muddle."

As another small step in that direction, following Haraway's invitation to "[i]magine a conference not on the Future of the Humanities in the Capitalist Restructuring University, but instead on the Power of the Humusities for a Habitable Multispecies Muddle!" (32), in January 2018 I organized and chaired a special Modern Language Association session to discuss how, as scholars, teachers, citizens, and eco-ethno-feminino-vege-zoo activists, we can rewrite the doomsday ending to the anthropo-capitalo-progressive narrative. Building on Haraway's work and "thinking tentacularly" about multiple elastic, muddling, messy networks, the panelists proposed a critique of the academy as a neoliberal consumerist enterprise as well as a seemingly detached humanistic enclave with staunchly enforced disciplinary divisions, suggesting paths towards new diverse ontologies and emergent ecologies, and offering pedagogical applications for Haraway's conceptual reconfiguring of Humanities/humusities by proposing interdisciplinary theoretical models and curricula for experiential and sensual learning and knowledge production in and with nature. My hope for this work is to initiate similar conversations in humanities classrooms and beyond.

Acknowledgments

---

10. The differences in the treatment of animal tissues and human cadavers fall along species lines due to "differences in our perceptions of their respective intrinsic and instrumental values [with] [a]nimals [being] considered to have lesser intrinsic value and greater instrumental value than humans" (Kaw, Jones, and Zhang, abstract).

11. I wish to thank Reviewer 2 for this particular insight.

I wish to thank the editors and anonymous reviewers for their immensely helpful suggestions. I also wish to thank Omi Osun Joni L. Jones, my English 483/683 students, Ron Milland, and Alexander Champoux. Parts of this article were delivered at PAMLA 2016 and MnWE 2018.

Works Cited

The American Association for Laboratory Animal Science. Mission Statement. *The American Association for Laboratory Animal Science (AALAS)*, 2018, www.aalas.org/about-aalas.
The Animals and Society Institute. "Animal Studies/Anthrozoology Overview." *Human-Animal Studies: Animal Studies/Anthrozoology*, www.animalsandsociety.org/human-animal-studies/courses/has-courses-in-animal-studies-anthrozoology/.
Association for Theatre in Higher Education: Performance in Theory & Practice. *Association for Theatre in Higher Education* (ATHE), www.eventscribe.com/2016/ATHE/assets/2016-ATHE-Conference-Program.pdf.
Balcombe, Jonathan. *What a Fish Knows: The Inner Lives of Our Underwater Cousins.* Farrar, Straus and Giroux, 2016.
Bennett, Jill. *Empathic Vision.* Stanford UP, 2005.
Boddice, Rob. *Anthropocentrism: Humans, Animals, Environments.* Brill, 2011.
Bradshaw, Gay A. "An Ape Among Many: Animal Co-Authorship and Trans-species Epistemic Authority." *Configurations*, vol.18, no. 1-2, Winter 2010, pp. 15-30.
Burbules, Nicholas C., and Rupert Berk. "Critical Thinking and Critical Pedagogy: Relations, Differences, and Limits." *Critical Theories in Education*, edited by Thomas S. Popkewitz and Lynn Fendler, Routledge, 1999, faculty.education.illinois.edu/burbules/papers/critical.html.
Chiaet, Julianne. "Novel Finding: Reading Literary Fiction Improves Empathy." *Scientific American*, 4 Oct. 2013, www.scientificamerican.com/article/novel-finding-reading-literary-fiction-improves-empathy/.
Coetzee, John Maxwell. *Elizabeth Costello.* Penguin, 2003.
Crutzen, Paul J., and Eugene F. Stoermer. "The 'Anthropocene'." *Global Change Newsletter*, vol. 41, 2000, pp. 17-18.
Dennett, Daniel C. "The Role of Language in Intelligence." *What Is Intelligence? The Darwin College Lectures*, edited by Jean Khalfa, Cambridge UP, 1994. ase.tufts.edu/cogstud/dennett/papers/rolelang.htm.
Foer, Jonathan Safran. *Eating Animals.* Back Bay Books, 2010.
Foster, Charles. *Being a Beast: Adventures Across the Species Divide.* Metropolitan Books, 2016.
Freire, Paulo. *Pedagogy of the Oppressed.* Translated by Myra Bergman Ramos, Continuum, 2005.
Giroux, Henry, and Jose Maria Barroso Tristan. "Henry Giroux: The Necessity of Critical Pedagogy in Dark Times." *Global Education Magazine*, 6 Feb. 2013, www.truth-out.org/news/item/14331-a-critical-interview-with-henry-giroux.
Grandin, Temple, and Catherine Johnson. *Animals in Translation: Using the Mysteries of Autism to Decode Animal Behavior.* Harvest, 2006 (Harcourt, 2005).

Hadjikhani, Nouchine, et al. "Look Me in the Eyes: Constraining Gaze in the Eye-region Provokes Abnormally High Subcortical Activation in Autism." *Scientific Reports*, vol. 7, no. 3163, 2017, doi:10.1038/s41598-017-03378-5, www.nature.com/articles/s41598-017-03378-5.

Haraway, Donna. *Staying with the Trouble: Making Kin in the Chthulucene*. Duke UP, 2016.

Hilliard, Asa G., III. "Language, Culture, and the Assessment of African American Children." *The Skin That We Speak: Thoughts on Language and Culture in the Classroom*, edited by Lisa Delpit and Joanne Kilgour Dowdy, The New Press, 2008, pp. 87-106.

Kahn, Richard. *Critical Pedagogy, Ecoliteracy, and Planetary Crisis: The Ecopedagogy Movement*. Peter Lang, 2010.

Kaw, Anu, D. Gareth Jones, and Ming Zhang. "The use of animal tissues alongside human tissue: Cultural and ethical considerations." *Clinical Anatomy*, vol. 29, no. 1, Jan. 2016, pp. 19-24, www.ncbi.nlm.nih.gov/pubmed/26475721.

McGee, Kevin P. *Critical pedagogy and animal rights: The inclusion of humane education in the Critical Pedagogy doctoral program at the University of St. Thomas*. University of St. Thomas (Minnesota), 2005.

Perry, Mia, and Carmen Medina. "Embodiment and Performance in Pedagogy Research: Investigating the Possibility of the Body in Curriculum Experience." *Journal of Curriculum Theorizing*, vol. 27, no. 3, 2011, pp. 62-75, journal.jctonline.org/index.php/jct/article/viewFile/100/05PerryandMedina.pdf.

Purcell-Gates, Victoria. "'...As Soon As She Opened Her Mouth!': Issues of Language, Literacy, and Power." *The Skin That We Speak: Thoughts on Language and Culture in the Classroom*, edited by Lisa Delpit and Joanne Kilgour Dowdy, The New Press, 2008, pp. 121-41.

Schlosser, Eric. *Fast Food Nation: The Dark Side of the All-American Meal*. Houghton Mifflin Harcourt, 2001.

Sethi, Rumina. *The Politics of Postcolonialism: Empire, Nation and Resistance*. Pluto Press, 2011.

Singer, Peter. *Animal Liberation*. Harper Collins, 1975.

Tsing, Anna. *The Mushroom at the End of the World: On the Possibility of Life in Capitalist Ruins*. Princeton UP, 2015.

Vasey, Craig, and Linda Carroll. "How Do We Evaluate Teaching? Findings from a survey of faculty members." *American Association of University Professors*, May-Jun., 2016, www.aaup.org/article/how-do-we-evaluate-teaching#.Wt6jd9PwaHq.

Waal, Frans de. *Are We Smart Enough to Know How Smart Animals Are?* Norton, 2016.

Weil, Kari. *Thinking Animals*. Columbia UP, 2012.

"What is the difference between 'animal rights' and 'animal welfare'?" PETA, www.peta.org/about-peta/faq/what-is-the-difference-between-animal-rights-and-animal-welfare/.

Wittgenstein, Ludwig. *Philosophical Investigations*. Translated by G. E. M. Anscombe, 3rd ed., Blackwell Publishing, 2001.

Žižek, Slavoj. *Violence: Six Sideways Reflections*. Picador, 2008.

Writing about Wolves: Using Ecocomposition Pedagogy to Teach Social Justice in a Theme-Based Composition Course

Michael S. Geary

Abstract: *Elements of ecocomposition are employed to construct a course that uses the relationship between wolves and humans as a social justice metaphor. Students explore how mythmaking leads to dire consequences for any population being exploited. This approach to teaching first year composition allows students to acquire new knowledge about conservationism while focusing on developing their critical reading, writing, and researching skills.*

When my Composition I students enter my darkened classroom, they see stunning images of wolves chasing down caribou. They are perplexed. Are they late for class? Like patrons arriving late for a movie, they take their seats in silence, trying not to block anyone's view of the screen. The documentary *Wolves: A Legend Returns to Yellowstone* is being shown, and before I have even said a word about who I am or what the class will be about, they are having an "encounter" with wolves. This experience may seem fitting for a science classroom in the Western U.S. where the conflict between wolves and ranchers is front page news. Instead, this scene plays out in a writing classroom at Bristol Community College in Fall River, MA. We are far removed from the "wolf wars" of the West, so what is the purpose of bringing my students into this discussion? This course, which I have nicknamed "Writing about Wolves," came from my own interest in the design of thematic-based courses in composition studies as well as a lifelong passion for environmentalism.

I have always been interested in the idea of mythmaking and the role that it plays in shaping the way that people perceive the world. Particularly, I am fascinated by the way in which the written word persuades readers to adopt points of view that may often be inconsistent with the reality of the situation at hand. Given the current concerns about "Fake News," the study of mythmaking is all the more timely and relevant for first year composition students. While designing "Writing about Wolves," I wanted to create a course in which students could objectively examine the impact that written mythmaking has upon a particular population. As such, the class is divided into three segments that I have dubbed "Fiction," "Fact," and "Fallout." The "Fiction" section introduces students to the scope of the wolf mythology where they examine an assortment of stories from around the world. Here, we look closely at the way these stories are written with consideration given to the environment from which they come. The "Fact" unit explores writing done by biologists, naturalists, and scientists that represents what wolves are actually like in the wild. Close examination of these texts allows students to see how rhetorical conventions are used by professional writers and the way in which their writings speak to and against one another. The "Fallout" unit engages students in wolf conservation efforts and asks them to consider the value of beginning an effort in New England. Through this unit, students learn how to advocate for a specific population that is viewed negatively as a result of misinformation. For students, it is an opportunity to consider themselves as social justice advocates, which provides them with a skill set that can be applied to other social issues that they will address in other courses and in society at large. Through academic research, students will come to see the value and relevance of engaging in this type of discourse.

One of the challenges that we face as professors of writing is how to bring engaging content into the classroom to sustain our students' interest. I am frequently met with comments by students that they only want to write about what they already know, and I always find that reaction to be troubling. After all, the whole point in coming to college is to acquire new knowledge about topics with which they are unfamiliar, right? Yet, I think that reaction stems more from a lack of awareness of how much knowledge is lying dormant, buried beneath a wealth of other life experiences that are more vivid to them. So when I introduce a theme to a class, especially something more abstract to New Englanders like the relationship between wolves and humans, I need to find a way to access this dormant knowledge.

In this article, I will advocate that there are significant benefits for students to engage in a theme-based composition course that may on the surface seem to have no apparent relevance to them. While the theming of courses is a longstanding practice in composition studies, I will reference recent scholarship that defines the best practices for selecting course themes. Further, I will show how ecocomposition and its application for first year composition are vital for choosing these themes. Lastly, because of its ties to ecocomposition, I will also talk about how a wolf themed class can serve as a mechanism to explore other social justice issues that follow a comparable pattern of mythmaking and conclusion-drawing that is detrimental to the population being studied.

Course Themes: Relevance and Breadth

When considering a theme for a course, it is important that the "breadth and relevance to the age range of the students" are closely considered (Friedman 80). Further, it needs to be clear why the theme has been chosen, which places the burden on the professor to justify the curriculum to the students. After all, "if a course theme engenders any student resistance or hesitation about the public spiritedness that guides it, that theme can potentially hinder their development as writers" (Sponenberg 544). To make sure that this hindrance does not occur, professors need to consider the essential questions that "frame the intellectual inquiry of the course" (Friedman 80). The more focused the course theme is, the better. Choosing a maximum of 3 or 4 essential questions seems reasonable for a standard 15 week class.

In "Writing about Wolves," those questions are:

1. How has written mythology defined the wolf?
2. What have professionals written about wolves in the wild?
3. What are the consequences when the wrong information is believed?
4. How do we use writing to reverse the damage done by misinformation?

These questions establish a specific link between written texts and the impact that those words have on society while exploring how to reverse damage that has been done as a result of those texts. The course guides them from the mythical to the scientific to the political, social, and economic reality of wolves in the world.

While "Wolves" demonstrates breadth, there are many other popular themes that do so as well. "Monsters," "Sustainability," "Food," "Money," and "Happiness," are all themes that are broad enough to create Friedman's recommended 3-4 essential questions. I need to emphasize that "[n]o course theme for an academic writing course deserves priority as 'the best' or the only one that will facilitate transfer of learning" (Beaufort). In other words, there are different ways that written communication competencies can be achieved. Rinto and Cogbill-Seiders argue that "the literature recommends choosing themes that are flexible enough to capture the interest of an entire class of students and simplistic enough that little class time needs to be devoted to teaching the subject matter of the theme" (16). I am not at all comfortable with the notion of a theme needing to be "simplistic." That might call into question the relevance of even selecting the theme in the first place. However, I would argue that in choosing a theme, professors need to be sure that they do not spend all of their time introducing the topic to their students. If they do, then not enough time is spent on the teaching of writing. Therefore, I want to define a "simplistic theme" as a theme that students have already encountered, consciously or unconsciously, and should have their pre-existing knowledge of interrogated, challenged, and expanded. Simplicity speaks to the relevance of the theme to the students taking the class.

Kimberly Moekle says, "if a writing course is designed around important themes in students' lives, even a required writing course can offer a specific context in which to develop a rhetorical skill" (81). She agrees that the course content must be relevant, but sometimes it may not be obvious how it is. For "Writing about Wolves," I ask my students to consider their first encounter with a wolf. One of the things that students immediately wrestle with is what an "encounter" with a wolf actually is. Given the fact that my students are from an urban area where wolves are not a part of the ecosystem, they are sometimes perplexed with how to connect with the topic. This past semester, my students kept referencing coyotes that they encountered in their backyards as the closest parallel that they could make. There is an analogy to be made between wolves and coyotes. Both are wild canines that serve as major predators within their respective ecosystems. Yet, my students had defined "encounters" too narrowly.

I define "encounter" as any interaction (physical, textual, or virtual) that the student has had with the population being studied. Most of them have likely heard at least one fairytale that has involved a wolf, but they have not interpreted that as an "encounter." To illustrate that broader definition, I cite my first wolf "encounter" when I watched a film called *The Journey of Natty Gann*. In the film, a young girl flees an abusive nanny and travels cross country to find her father who is working for a logging company during the Great Depression. On her journey, Natty encounters a wolf that is being forced to participate in a dog fighting ring. She liberates the animal, and he becomes her fellow traveling companion until it hears other wolves in the wild. She encourages it to join them, but the wolf is hesitant to leave her. Ultimately, the call of the wild is too great, and the wolf runs off into the forest. At the end of the film, Natty finds her father, and in one of the final shots, the camera pans up to the wolf as he is witnessing the reunion of the father and daughter. Within the film, there are two different perceptions of this creature. The first is that he is a vicious animal that should be relegated to dog fights. The second is that he is a loyal creature that reciprocates love when he receives it. I tell my students that when I first saw the film, the duality of the perceptions raised questions in my mind about the animal. Those questions would linger until I became a wolf conservationist in my teenage years. In sharing this experience with them, I have given them a blue print to consider their own experiences. Here is what my first wolf encounter did for me; what did yours do for you?

With that model in mind, students now have an easier time identifying a wolf "encounter." With the additional prompting, students identify "The Three Little Pigs," "Little Red Riding Hood," *White Fang*, *The Jungle Book*, or *The Gray* as being their first encounter with wolves. When students begin to interrogate their reactions to these texts, they begin to realize the way in which the written word (including what has been written for the cinema) has influenced their perception of wolves. A number of them now identify their perception as being a negative one and link that to fears that they might have about coyotes in their own yard. While "Wolves" initially appeared abstract to them, through careful prompting and freewriting, students can unlock dormant knowledge and experience. By asking students to redefine what an "encounter" with a particular topic may be, professors can implement a variety of themes that challenge students to think more broadly about their experiences. This notion of the relevance of the theme is particularly important as we consider how ecocomposition can be applied to the selection of course themes.

The Role of Ecocomposition in Course Design

The concept of ecocomposition can be especially useful when engaging students with a theme that is unfamiliar to them. Sidney Dobrin and Christian Weisser's *Natural Discourse: Toward Ecocomposition* provides a thorough overview of the value of ecocomposition as a framework for composition studies. Their text suggests that ecocriticism, cultural studies, ecofeminism, and environmental rhetoric all play a role in the shaping of this theory. While ecocriticism focuses primarily on the interpretation of texts, ecocomposition "is concerned with textual production and the environments that affect and are affected by the production of discourse" (24). Furthermore, ecocomposition has two facets: "one concerning the complex and dynamic relationships between a writer, audience, and issue, and the other concerning the role of place within discourse" (Moe). This pedagogy asks students to see how the writing that they do and the topics that they consider relate to the environment in which they live at the local and global levels. In other words, how the micro theme discussed is representative of a macro issue in the world around them. Ecocomposition asks writers to move beyond simply responding to texts that may be about environmental issues and for them to think about their writing as being an agent for inspiring change. As Dobrin and Weisser contend, "Encouraging students to be critical of the very environments in which they produce discourse and the effects those environments have upon their writing affects change" (26).

Dobrin and Weisser also suggest that there is a significant parallel between cultural studies, another popular topic in first year composition studies, and ecocomposition. They argue that cultural studies "often investigates and analyzes the ways in which social forces and practices may construct a particular environment, environmental issue, or environmental moment such as a geographical, historical, economic, technological, racial, or other issue pertaining to environment" (28). While studies of race and gender are of significant importance, ecocomposition suggests that the environment that creates the foundation for those studies is more important. In other words, "environment precedes race, class, gender, and culture" (32). Ecocomposition rejects the notion that race, class, and gender are naturally occurring and concludes that "nature is a discursive construct" (33).

The authors further infer that ecofeminism plays an important role in the shaping of the theory. They say, "ecofeminism has provided important discussions of how environmental oppression are linked with oppression of women which underscores why environmental concerns are feminist issues as well as why feminist issues should be addressed environmentally" (35). The authors illustrate that an analogy can be made between environmental issues and other social justice issues. I will explore this analogy in more detail later in this article, but I want to emphasize here that ecocomposition contains elements of ecofeminism, which is an overriding philosophy in other theme-based composition courses. Like ecocriticism, "ecofeminists inquire into the ways in which literary, religious, theological, artistic, and other textual representations of women and nature often result in oppressive actions toward both" (39). Thus, there is a consistent value seen in interrogating the written word and the impact that it has upon the readers. As texts are products of the environment that produces them, we can explore the impact that the environment has on the texts and the texts on the environment.

Rhetorical studies, and environmental rhetoric in particular, also lay the foundation for the design of an ecocomposition course. Dobrin and Weisser argue that environmental rhetoric "raises student awareness of the ways that people use language to construct knowledge" (46). In doing so, "it allows students to see that language is a powerful tool that influences us, and in turn, can be used to influence others" (46). As a result, students can "better recognize ways in which different discourse communities structure the content, form, and rhetorical appeals of their language to better communicate with their intended audiences" (46). By environmental rhetoric, the authors are not just talking about arguments that deal with environmental issues, such as sustainability. Rather, they are arguing that any type of environment (cultural, geographical, social) uses rhetorical constructs to communicate its virtues and vices to those within and outside of itself. Environmental arguments (water pollution, deforestation, species endangerment, etc.) tend to be good sources for examining these devices because they are commonly products of the environment that is most impacted by the concern itself.

Dobrin and Weisser have a high expectation for what a true ecocomposition course should entail. While they agree that all of the aforementioned elements are a component of ecocomposition, they insist that students need to move beyond writing and interpreting texts and focus on the ways in which their own writing is constructed and influenced by the environments which they inhabit. Yet their theory does not fully take into consideration all of the factors that influence the way in which composition professors choose to structure their courses. First year composition courses that allow for developmental reading as a co-requisite course challenge professors to identify readings and writing prompts that are accessible for exceedingly diverse student needs. Further, the need for assessment and the fulfillment of written communication learning outcomes also influences the way in which courses are structured. Also, as Peter Wayne Moe points out, "When much of ecocomposition theory advocates rewriting curricula, redesigning assignments, and incorporating service-learning into a course, instructors who do not have the pedagogical freedom to design courses cannot easily implement ecocomposition theory in the manner most scholarship recommends." Realistically, to achieve all of the goals of ecocomposition, it would need to be embedded into a writing studies program and extended into a writing across the curriculum initiative. As professors of writing, we need to be realistic about what we can accomplish in a mere 15 weeks that we spend with our students. If students begin to utilize the various facets of the ecocomposition pedagogy and realize how writing shapes their perceptions of the world, then a lot has been accomplished in one semester.

Unlike some other courses designed to focus on environmental and ecological concerns, "Writing about Wolves" is not by definition an ecocomposition course. However, I will say that it borrows elements of the genre and is, at its core, a class that situates writing as a product of its environment, considers the way in which writers use language to shape their rhetorical appeals, asks students to consider how their environment has shaped the way in which they formulate their ideas, and makes them consider how writing has influenced their perception of the world. Any topic related to environmental studies can follow the particular model that I used because of several common threads that will be discussed a bit later.

In order for this class to accomplish its goals, there needs to be a close tie between critical reading and writing. Given the diverse perspectives about wolves that permeate both written text and visual media, it is essential that I teach students how to be good readers and to see how other writers organized their thought processes. Can they see within and between texts how observations about wolves agree and disagree with one another? In selecting my texts for the course, I subscribed to David Bartholomae and Anthony Petrosky's view: "Reading . . . can be the occasion for you to put things together, to notice this idea or theme rather than that one, to follow a writer's announced or secret ends while simultaneously following your own" (3-4). Their theory is consistent with the ecocriticism component of ecocomposition. In order for my students to be ecocritics, they need to think about the way in which they read texts and how their environment influences the way in which they do so.

Because students are reading a variety of sources (fiction, nonfiction, scholarly), they become critical readers by adopting diverse reading strategies in order to make the texts accessible. The environment that produces the text and the one in which they read it require them to adjust their strategies while making meaning of the language on the page. However, students need to be aware that they are shifting their strategies and should be able to articulate why they have done so. As Ellen Carillo states, "all reading approaches that are taught apart from a metacognitive framework intended to promote transfer are problematic" (108). For that reason, I endorse Carillo's theory of "mindful reading." According to Carillo, "mindfully reading involves enacting a theory of reading" (117). As part of this theory, students learn why and how a text works in a certain way and asks them to acknowledge when a particular approach is not working. When they read mindfully, they identify places within a text where they needed to adjust their strategies (Carillo 117). This mindful reading allows students to track their evolving relationships with texts. As they challenge claims made in the writing itself and they examine the way in which claims are structured, students are asked to consider how their shifting views of texts impact the overall credibility of the arguments that they make. These reading skills are transferable to texts in other disciplines and lead students to consider the environments from which the texts have emerged. The most important part of the pedagogy is increasing student awareness about the situation in which they read the texts.

Early in the semester, my students examine stories about wolves from around the world. In doing so, students are not introduced to literary theory or the value of literary genres. Rather, they look closely at the way in which wolves are written about and consider what that tells us about the environment from which these stories emerged. For example, why does a Germanic story like "Little Red Riding Hood" depict the wolf as being a sexual predator that devours helpless women? Does the geographical isolation of members of that society influence the mythmaking? Putting the wolves to the side, what does it say about the way that women are thought of by that society? By examining how the author uses words to illustrate both wolves and women in the story, students are opened to broader questions about the environment that crafts these stories. As the length and complexity of these literary texts vary, students are asked to identify and critique their critical reading strategies and to consider other scenarios in which they may be applied. There do not necessarily need to be longer analytical essays that are written about the strategies that they use. Journaling or other forms of metacognitive reflection should be embedded in the daily routine in the course. So the classroom becomes the place for the written reactions and reflections to take place and, hence, an environment in which writing is produced.

As we shift toward nonfiction and academic texts, my students engage in a close analysis of environmental rhetoric by closely examining the appeals that are used by authors with diverse academic backgrounds. However, students are asked to consider how texts make both inter and intraconnections. In doing so, students get to see how writers influence one another and also how texts can function as part of a larger arena of argumentation. Bridging the gap between the fiction and the nonfiction is key. To illustrate, let us again consider the vicious wolf in "Little Red Riding Hood" that my students encounter first. When my students read Farley Mowat's *Never Cry Wolf*, a text used for examination of rhetorical appeals rather than nature writing emulation, one of the first things that they discover about the small Canadian town that Mowat has arrived in is that the inhabitants believe that "wolves reputedly devour several hundred people in the Arctic Zone every year" (Mowat 24). The claim shows an alignment between the fairytale and the established belief of the population that deals with wolves regularly. As the memoir unfolds, Mowat's experiences show that the wolf is not quite as threatening as its reputation says. Mowat summarizes his early encounters with the animal: "On three separate occasions in less than a week I had been completely at the mercy of these 'savage killers'; but far from attempting to tear me limb from limb, they had displayed a restraint verging on contempt, even when I invaded their home and appeared to be posing a direct threat to the young pups" (76). Within Mowat's text, students can see that there are different perspectives: one formed from a mythology and a second formed from observation in the natural world. These points of view emerge from two different environments. Mowat is an outsider who objectively comes into the landscape to record his experiences while the townspeople are limited to the knowledge that has been passed along to them by others. Whereas Mowat is a seeker of information, the townspeople are consumers of what is offered. Students can interrogate the rhetorical situation in which these claims are made and supported. They see both an inter-connection between the literature and the memoir, followed by an intra-connection made between contrasting ideas within the text.

Further inter-connections are made when texts speak against each other. For example, in one of the selections from the Mech and Botani text, we are told "The book *Never Cry Wolf* (Mowat 1963), a mostly fictional work (Banfield 1964; Pimlott 1966; Mech 1970; Goddard 1996), was the first positive presentation of wolves in the popular culture" (Fritts et al. 294). Mowat acknowledges in the text's "Preface," which was written in 1993, that "Some dedicated wolf haters including the far-flung network of those who kill for sport, went so far as to claim it was an outright work of fiction. Others brushed it aside, claiming it was invalid because its author was not a bona fide scientist with at least a doctoral degree" (v). He then goes on to claim "that almost every facet of wolf behavior described by me has since been rediscovered by the selfsame scientists who called my studies a work of the imagination" (vi). While it is clear that Fritts et al. are not "wolf haters," it is a curious thing that they reference a number of articles written decades before Mowat's "Preface." Further, is Mowat making generalizations about his opposition? Which of his claims have been proven, if any? This exchange allows students to explore the importance of sourcing, while also investigating the *ethos* of the authors. From this activity, students are empowered to question, rather than blindly accept, the statements made by more experienced authors. While Fritts et al. are published biologists who have extensively researched wolves, students should still question the information they provide and consider the rhetorical appeals used by the authors to substantiate their claims. Likewise, the agreeable nature of Mowat's lighthearted prose should not prevent them from challenging what he claims to have witnessed as he is using rhetorical appeals differently than Fritts et al. are. In the era of "Fake News," students need to learn the importance of asking questions of anyone who claims to be the authority on a particular topic. Under what circumstances were these texts written? How do the environments that shaped these authors influence the way in which they communicate their ideas? How do the ways that these authors write impact the way in which students make meaning of the texts? This is ecocriticism, and students need to respond as ecocritics to the texts that they encounter.

When selecting an appropriate theme for a composition course, professors should choose a sequencing of texts that approach the topic from wide perspectives. Choosing texts from across a set period of time and from diverse populations is key for students to fully analyze the ways in which authors use writing to make meaning of abstract topics. Any of the themes mentioned earlier can be addressed rhetorically with emphasis placed on how students read texts. Formal writing assignments in the course should ask students to articulate the ways in which these texts have shaped their reading experiences as well as the way in which they perceive the theme. The first step in creating an eco-composition course is to allow students to become ecocritics. However, while doing so, professors also need to be aware of the transferability of the skills that they are teaching. Carillo's mindful reading is an essential part of teaching to transfer. Having addressed ecocriticism and environmental rhetoric that is embedded in "Wolves," I now want to turn to a more complex aspect of the pedagogy: ecofeminism and cultural studies.

Ecofeminism, Cultural Studies, Social Justice, and Wolves

As Farley Mowat says in his "Preface" to *Never Cry Wolf*, "We have doomed the wolf not for what it is but for what we deliberately and mistakenly perceive it to be: the mythologized epitome of a savage, ruthless killer" (viii). In my course, we explore the truth behind Mowat's statement, and we look at the way in which that "ruthless killer" is established and facilitated by society. "Violence" and "domination" are recurring aspects of the complex relationship between wolves and humanity. Fear of wolves led to their near extinction in the twentieth century, yet it is not just out of fear that they were hunted in mass numbers. It is also the fact that humanity encroached upon their territory and claimed it for its own. But in this configuration, facts that challenge humanity's assertion of power are repressed. As a result, if given the choice between the cattle industry and the preservation of a natural ecosystem, big industry will win out. That isn't just true about wolves and humans. We can also look at the pursuit of fossil fuels in natural preserves, over-fishing and whaling, and deforestation as other examples of how this conflict between the natural world and humanity plays out. Humanity will dominate the environment simply because it can. This dynamic between nature and humanity illustrates the ecofeminism and cultural studies pedagogies of ecocomposition.

There is a clear analogy that can be drawn between nature as an oppressed entity and other oppressed populations in society. Dobrin and Weisser contend, "ecofeminism seeks to end all oppression and recognizes that any attempt to liberate any oppressed group – particularly women – can only be successful with an equal attempt to liberate nature" (34). In addition, ecocomposition "agrees that the very power structures and ideologies which incur oppressions over women and other groups are responsible for the oppressive actions taken over nature" (37). In other words, if we want to understand why certain populations are oppressed and how those social structures are built, we should look at how we exploit the natural world. We can use our treatment of nature as a metaphor for our treatment of any minority population. Further, ecocomposition, "pairs ecocolonialism with ecofeminism in its quest to undermine dominant paradigms that portray 'Nature' as an exploitative resource for human use and consumption" (37). If we seek to overthrow the social structures that allow certain populations to be oppressed, then we should start by considering the way in which we interact with the environment. We can mean this to be the natural world, but also the "environment" that surrounds the oppressed population. Paul Walker says when considering ecocomposition, "The close analysis of environmental discourse . . . can provide students the opportunity to identify and critique the tacit societal values to which we adhere and how accepted language and labeling contribute to and inform the continuation of those values" (70). Therefore, through the close examination of the ways in which we label nature as something that can be dominated with violence, we can transfer our understanding of that labeling to other populations, particularly our fellow humans.

Because wolves have been labeled as a menace and representing the untamed natural world, their problematic relationship with humanity can be used as a micro metaphor for a macro environmental problem. Their exploitation parallels that of other environmental resources, which, according to ecofeminism, aligns with the way that women and other racialized and ethnicized minority populations have been exploited by society. We need to understand the social structures that allow the exploitation to occur. By considering the way in which one population is rhetorically written about, we create an entry way to extend our study across other populations. If we consider how myths are written and examine the consequences that they bestow, we can begin to find ways to rewrite the myths and attempt to end the domination of minority populations that are met with violence daily. Because wolves are more abstract, we can approach the study of their oppression more objectively rather than directly discussing racial discrimination. As professors, we should realize that not every student is going to feel comfortable discussing these race relation issues directly. Given the fact that race is a hot button issue today, some students may be less inclined to engage in the discussion out of fear of offending a classmate. Because the demographics of individual sections of courses will be different, if we select race relations as a theme, we are not sure about our students' attitude toward an especially polarizing issue. Thus, wolves become the "micro theme" to the "macro issue" of discrimination in society. Wolves, or the natural world by extension, become a safe space to discuss the same factors that contribute to the more controversial issues that impact our society today.

As part of the class, I introduce the notion that there is a metaphorical value for exploring wolves as a theme through critical reading of images. Near the beginning of the semester, I show my students a sequence of images that depict various interpretations of the wolf (vicious, kindly, etc.) The final image, originally published on a huntsman group webpage, shows a cohort of hunters whose faces are covered with white sacks with slits cut for eyes, nose, and mouth. One of them is holding the carcass of a dead wolf while several others are grasping shotguns. To the left of the hunter with the carcass, several others are holding up an American flag. We examine the rhetorical appeals of the image, and my students are surprised by the imagery used. The hunters remind my students of Klansmen, and a discussion about the role of the KKK in society today usually arises. The brandishing of the firearms and the American flag suggest that there is something patriotic happening here. Yet, my students view the image as the opposite of that. This activity introduces the idea of natural world as a metaphor for larger social issues. While I don't press the issue further, students will sometimes come back to this metaphor throughout the semester. For example, a discussion about the repression of women logically emerged from a discussion of Mowat's text when the Kavanaugh hearings were occurring. Activities like these allow students to ask questions about the information that they encounter and to consider how the texts that they are handed are products of the environments from which they emerge.

Dobrin and Weisser conclude, "Ecocomposition seeks to overturn conceptualizations which demarcate natural environments as entities which may be mastered and ruled. In turn, ecocomposition resists oppression of all living organisms – human or other – and their environments" (40). As such, the adaptation of the ecocomposition pedagogy is to embrace the notion that social justice can be taught through writing.

The most important aspect of the pedagogy is for students to take their writing beyond the classroom. They need to start thinking about how their writing can have an impact on the environments in which they live. Furthermore, they need to perceive that the stances that they adopt have consequences. That is why students need to consider wider and more diverse audiences when they write in a composition class.

Considering Audiences beyond the Classroom

Students instinctively believe that any writing done in the classroom has a single audience: the professor. They tend to overlook the fact that peer reviewers, writing center tutors, or even family members with whom they share the writing are also members of their audience. Yet all of those individuals are part of a controlled population; they are immediately accessible to the writer. How can we get students to consider a wider audience?

Dobrin and Weisser suggest that it is best to have students compose documents that break the mold of the academic essay. They offer an assignment for designing a flier and another for designing a web page as ideal examples of true ecocomposition (143-44). However, as previously mentioned, professors are typically bound by course outcomes, departmental assessments, and limitations on academic freedom which collectively make it difficult to implement less conventional assignments. At many colleges, fliers and web pages are inconsistent with the outcomes of a first semester composition course.

A compromise is to provide students with hypothetical scenarios of real world writing situations that target specific audiences. In "Writing about Wolves," my students engage in such a scenario with their end of semester research paper. They are asked to consider whether or not a wolf conservation effort in New England would be appropriate. To reach their conclusion, they need to identify the specific geographical area where the conservation effort should happen. I ask them to synthesize what they have learned about the needs of wolves and of the population that would be living with the animals on a daily basis. The intended audience for this paper is the governor of the state where the effort should commence. They are asked to make use of the rhetorical appeals that they have seen other writers use throughout the semester to advocate for their conservation movement. Conversely, students may also opt to argue why a conservation effort should not happen. While the scenario is hypothetical, it asks them to consider the implications of their advocacy and to determine what types of information a politician would need to be convinced that the cause is justified. Having discussed the role of rhetorical appeals during the semester, they are now able to show that they can apply them. Even though my students have never sent their essays to the governors of the states that they have identified, I have never discouraged them from doing so. As the class continues to evolve, that seems like an appropriate next step. If not sending a paper via e-mail to the governor, then the designing of the web linked documents referenced by Dobrin and Weisser definitely would be.

Conclusion

Designing theme-based courses is an engaging, challenging, and rewarding way to invest students in their first year writing experience. The elements of ecocomposition that I have referenced here are essential guidelines for achieving established course outcomes. A theme that is broad enough allows students to remain invested in a single concept and to see how their knowledge of it evolves over a period of time. Finding the relevance of the theme for the students is key. As Moekle says, "When students care about a topic, they are eager to participate in the discussions that characterize that field of study, and they want to have an impact on their audience" (81). One of the challenges we face is finding the right themes for our unique student audiences. As we all interact with the natural world in some way, starting with an environmental theme is a good option.

However, we also should remember that the natural world provides us with a safe place to discuss the violence and domination that humanity bestows upon the planet. Ecocomposition allows us to explore the metaphorical similarities between the natural world and exploited minority populations in society. It begins by teaching our students to be ecocritics. Dobrin and Weisser argue, "studying textual representation of nature is critical to understanding how textual production occurs" (41). When students consider the environments that help to construct the texts that they read, they can begin to consider how their own environment influences them.

"Writing about Wolves" is just a single example of how elements of ecocomposition can be employed to teach critical reading and writing strategies, social justice awareness, academic research, metacognition, and environmentalism. Using a theme-based approach while keeping the written products as the central goal of the class can both engage students in the course and help them to grow as readers and writers. If students can truly understand the mechanisms through which mythmaking impacts the belief systems of a society, then they are on their way to making sense of the "Fake News" era and the associated consequences of spreading false information. In the process, they may also learn how the environment that they live in now is primed for the spread of misinformation. In the end, that environmental awareness may help to relegate the "Fake News" era to the history books where it will hopefully never be repeated.

Works Cited

Bartholomae, David, and Anthony Petrosky. *Ways of Reading: An Anthology for Writers*. 6th Edition. Bedford, 2002.

Beaufort, Anne. "College Writing and Beyond: Five Years Later." *Composition Forum*, vol. 26, 2012. compositionforum.com/issue/26/college-writing-beyond.php.

Carillo, Ellen C. *Securing a Place for Reading in Composition*. Utah State UP, 2015.

Dobrin, Sidney I., and Christian R. Weisser. *Natural Discourse Toward Ecocomposition*. SUNY P, 2002.

Friedman, Sandie. "This Way for Vampires: Teaching First-Year Composition in 'Challenging Times.'" *Currents in Teaching and Learning*, vol. 6, no.1, Fall 2013, pp. 77-84.

Fritts, Steven H., et al. "Wolves and Humans." *Wolves: Behavior, Ecology, and Conservation*, edited by L. David Mech and Luigi Boitani, U of Chicago P, 2003, pp. 289-316.

Journey of Natty Gann. Directed by Jeremy Kagan, Disney, 1985.

Mech. L. David and Luigi Botani, editors. *Wolves: Behavior, Ecology, and Conservation*. U of Chicago P, 2003.

Moe, Peter Wayne. "Composition: Ecocomposition, Aristotle, and the First-Year Writing Course." *Composition Forum*, vol. 24, 2011. compositionforum.com/issue/24/ecocomp-aristotle-fyc.php.

Moekle, Kimberly R. "The Rhetoric of Sustainability: Ecocomposition and Environmental Pragmatism." *Teaching Sustainability/Teaching Sustainably*, edited by Kristen Allen Bartels and Keely A. Parker, Stylus, 2012, pp. 76-83.

Mowat, Farley. *Never Cry Wolf*. Back Bay, 2001.

Rinto, Erin E., and Elisa I. Cogbill-Seiders. "Library Instruction and Themed Composition Courses: An Investigation of Factors that Impact Student Learning." *The Journal of Academic Librarianship*, vol. 41, 2015, pp. 14-20.

Sponenberg, Ashlie K. "Course Theme and Ideology in the Freshman Writing Classroom." *Pedagogy: Critical Approaches to Teaching Literature, Language, Composition, and Culture*, vol. 12, no. 3, 2012, pp. 544-49.

Walker, Paul. "(Un)earthing a Vocabulary of Values: A Discourse Analysis for Ecocomposition." *Composition Studies*, vol. 38, no. 1, 2010, pp. 69-87.

Wolves: A Legend Returns to Yellowstone. Directed by David Douglas, National Geographic, 2007.

Relational Literacy

W. Kurt Stavenhagen

Abstract: *In this paper, I propose literacy practices that further shift us from subject-object dichotomies and exclusive language practices to a focus on relationships and multimodality. Based in large part upon Indigenous Scholar Shawn Wilson's concept of relationality, I define a relational literacy wherein we counter an undue abstraction of the environment by mapping interspecies relationships and placing them within kinship narratives.*

In his comedy special, *Cinco*, Jim Gaffigan jokes, "Remember 15 years ago when they were like, 'Stop buying SUVs, everyone. They're wasteful and bad for the environment. And we were like, 'Okay (pause). I'd like to buy an SUV.'"

Gaffigan gets at a cultural meme – that abstract prescriptions and knowledge alone don't trump personal desire. We all know that by 2050 literacy and life will be largely shaped by climate change. Migration of climate refugees will have mushroomed, coastal cities will be compromised if not under water, and we'll be in a maelstrom of powerful hurricanes, tornadoes, snowstorms, rainstorms, and fires. Tesla SUVs, anyone?

Though a tremendous amount of scholarship on materiality has been recently pursued among rhetorical scholars,[1] a default within textual studies is to critique and theorize systems models without parsing literacies that prompt more direct care for the natural material world. As communications scholar David Maxcy disturbingly implicates, "the human capacity for linguistic communication alienates humans from the material-physical reality of nonhuman nature" (331). In this essay, I consider further the recasting of the entity of environment as a series of relationships between nonhumans and humans as a way to address the disconnection between our lifestyles and concern for the environment, and more pointedly, disconnections between writing instruction and student care for the environment. With what follows, I review some shortcomings of ecocomposition. I then review Deborah Brandt's call for particularism, Robert Brooke's idea for "dwelling in place," and Derek Owens's definition of place as neighborhood as means to conceptualize and acknowledge the environment in literacy[2] classrooms. Turning to the work of Michael Salvador, Traceylee Clarke, and Shawn Wilson, I then survey the role nonhumans might play in such a reconceptualization of the environment. To

---

1. See Kerry Banazek's "Carpentry in Context: What Does It Look Like to Be an Ethical Materialist Composer?" (2018) for a helpful overview of the field. Also, to limit the scope of this paper I will not address object-oriented ontology.

2. I define literacy as knowledge making practices that promote particular relationships. I draw from Kim Donehower, Charlotte Hogg, and Eileen Schell's definition of literacies as "the skills and practices needed to gain knowledge, evaluate and interpret that knowledge, and apply knowledge to accomplish particular goals" (4) and Deborah Brandt's call for "communicative competence" (507).

complement and supersede other approaches to the environment, I propose multimodal[3] literacy practices that prompt us to narrate our relationships[4] with nonhumans and more fully realize our interconnectivity with them.

From Bifurcation to Place and Distributed Agency

In a 2018 article on how specific places serve as premises of writing, Madison Jones provides a succinct and helpful history of ecocomposition. She notes that for over thirty years, compositionists have discussed the study of ecology and writing. Some have focused on its application in first-year courses, others on the locations of writing, while still others have reconceived of rhetoric and systems of composition as ecologies. Challenging the field to situate writing as interactive with a particular place, she pointedly cites David Grant's and Tim Taylor's works for charting two prevalent approaches to the environment: one as treating it as a metaphor, and the other as using it as a subject. Jones helpfully sets up other discussions by pointing out disjunctions between discourse and materiality. According to Jones, the terms environment and ecology often get applied as metaphors or constructs without acknowledgment of specific materiality outside the classroom. Notwithstanding the recent and perhaps corrective uptake of New Materialism[5], ecology has been often used as a construct for writing with minimal consideration on how textual practices and pedagogy affect nonhumans. Donald A. McAndrew's "Ecofeminism and the Teaching of Literacy" from 1997 serves as a representative example. McAndrew helpfully argues that ecology and feminism belong in the composition classroom together because they vividly reveal the "patriarchal power grab" and exploitation of nature "bound to social processes that oppressed people" (368). He also brings to light the problematic binaries of man versus culture, and mind over women, nature, and the body. Yet in his collapse of these binaries, he only applies ecofeminist insights to composition practices, missing an acknowledgment of ecology beyond humans. De-centered classrooms and readers and writers get "interrelated in an ecology of communication," but surrounding interchange between humans and non-

---

3. Beyond "linguistic pathways." (See Patricia Dunn's *Talking, Sketching, Moving: Multiple Literacies in the Teaching of Writing*, 2001).

4. See Malea Powell and the Cultural Rhetorics Lab for their definition of knowledge as constellations of relationships, and their tradition of naming the places of writing and conversations in their texts. I define relationships both as subjective realizations and objective realities. The purpose of the literacy of naming human and nonhuman relationships is to move from a separation of ontology and epistemology toward a realization and honoring of relationships, often by experiencing and storifying them.

5. Here I am thinking of its emphasis on distributed agency, ambient rhetoric, and Paul Lynch's push to make the classroom less a place of critique and more one of chronicling and mapping concrete problems. See again Kerry Banazek's recent (2018) helpful overview of the field and proposal for rhetoricians to envision themselves as ethical materialist composers. See also Lynch and Rivers' edited collection *Thinking with Bruno Latour in Rhetoric and Composition* (2015), Thomas Rickert's *Ambient Rhetoric* (2013), and Lynch's article, "Composition's New Thing: Bruno Latour and the Apocalyptic Turn."

humans is not acknowledged. As Grant notes, "environment-as-metaphor" approaches helpfully "posit an ecology of information" but often do so by sacrificing consideration of the natural environment (209).

The problem seems to be rooted in how discourse and the natural environment are conceptualized as dualities. Though much of Sidney Dobrin and Christian Weisser's work weaves together strands of place as discursive iteration and place as situated locale, as Matthew Ortoleva and David Grant critique, Dobrin and Weisser's separate semiosphere and biosphere is problematic. In *Natural Discourse*, Dobrin and Weisser foundationally define ecocomposition as the study of relationships between environments (natural, constructed and even imagined places) and discourse (speaking, writing, and thinking) (8). As such, they claim the relationship between discourse and place is dialogic and reciprocal. Furthermore, ecocomposition "foreground[s] the fact that discourse always occurs within particular environments, that these environments are integral to the construction of language and knowledge, and that particular acts of communication have their own nature according to the circumstances and locations that precipitated them" (14). In these instances, Dobrin and Weisser clearly underscore that nature or environment shapes and is shaped by discourse, and that particular locations influence human communications. Yet they further define ecocomposition as drawn "from disciplines that study discourse (chiefly composition, but also including literary studies, communication, cultural studies, linguistics and philosophy)" merged "with work in disciplines that examine the environment (these include ecology, environmental studies, sociobiology and other 'hard sciences')" (6). Here and elsewhere in their work, the environment is defined more as a biological entity and domain of science, and discourse estranged from it. Grant critiques similar moves of bifurcation by Dobrin and Weisser as keeping nature "separate from discourse" and theorizing it "mainly as a tool representing external reality" (202). Ortoleva concludes that Dobrin and Weisser's dual semiosphere and biosphere risks loss:

> Ecocomposition is a generative concept and can result in critical practice; however, its broad treatment and bifurcated nature can remove it from the ecological exigence currently affecting all levels of the biosphere, micro and macro. As a result, the focus on the human habitation of the biosphere is lost, as is the connection between the semiosphere and the biosphere originally suggested by Dobrin and Weisser. (69)

As Grant and Ortoleva helpfully delineate, the definitions of the environment as a metaphor or biological entity risk externalizing nature and severing writing and communication from the environment. What are needed are more holistic means to account for humans inhabiting nature and the role and construction of language within an environment. Recommending ecological literacy supersede ecocomposition, Ortoleva further states we need to address "the way language is networked across dimensions of human activity, and also the way these networks of language affect the ecological communities to which we belong."

He suggests bioregionalism as one way toward developing such ecological literacy. Particularism and bioregionalism offer an initial means past the impasse of considering the environment as metaphor or mass impersonal entity. In an essay collection on the future of literacy studies in the February 2018 issue of *College Composition and Communication*, Deborah Brandt claims Shirley Brice Heath's ethnographic approach marked a significant turn in literacy scholarship whose adopters continue to refute the idea of the "university as some sort of new, replacement society that offers abstract socialization into universal abstract discourses" (506). Brooke also critiques mainstream education that often "points elsewhere: to history happening in other parts of the world, to migration as the means of personal advancement in the corporate industrial complex, to an ineffective form of citizenship" (163). Like Brandt, he emphasizes a robust locale of learning that reverberates with global influence but has within it a sense of dwelling in place.

Derek Owens's *Composition and Sustainability: Teaching for a Threatened Generation* defines the environment in ways that complement both Brandt's advised particularism and Brooke's idea of dwelling in place by revisioning the environment as neighborhoods. Taking up Ellen Cushman's challenge of envisioning rhetoricians as agents for social change, Owens has students question all aspects of their home neighborhoods—social, economic, and environmental—and then explore ways to "make them more livable" (76). In the process, he exposes a false reification of nature as sanctum apart from our daily living[6] and exposes the false binary between human welfare and the welfare of nonhuman species. Complementing Brooke's idea of dwelling, Owens demarcates nature/environment as more than a scientific domain, metaphor or even a place of social bidding. The environment is considered a place of habitation and desire.

In this sampling, Brandt, Brooke and Owens invite literacy practices that thoughtfully regard human inhabitance. One can sense in the establishment and interrogation of place as neighborhood an engagement with what about a place makes for affect, attachment and commitment. Rather than engage the environment as an abstract entity or metaphor, we engage ourselves and language as resident. This appeal to a sense of "home" within language has much to offer, yet the capture of a more robust sense of place within the literacy classroom is still elusive. Notwithstanding Owens's uptake of place as neighborhoods, as Brandt makes apparent, most colleges are perceived as transient by faculty, students and the public. Unlike Owens's university, many other universities do not draw students from nearby communities. In enacting even parts of Owens's pedagogy, instructors must often contend with the reality that many students have not lived in the university neighborhood long and as such are not deeply tied to places on or around the college campus. As Brandt further notes, universalism still thrives in universities because students are "disconnected from families and home communities" and faculty are often "transplants too" (506). While Brandt, Brooke, and Owens offer ways to invigorate place as more than an abstraction of the environment, mutual material and discursive engagement remains a challenge.

Nominalism as a Root Cause for the Abstraction of Nature

A further answer to this dilemma may lie in examining the methods of our naming of the environment and the occlusion of its inhabitants. In his posthumanist treatise

---

6. Michael Pollan's book on "second nature" is especially a helpful text to expose this idea with students. See also William Cronon for a full history of how nature was made a park, "free" from the contamination of human influence.

From Nature to Creation, Duke Professor of Theology and Ecology Norman Wirzba argues that John Duns Scotus's rules of naming still inhibit our understanding of the environment. Medieval philosophers John Duns Scotus and William of Ockham propagated nominalism: the claim that the names we give things are independent of the reality they represent. Wirzba contends nominalism superseded a naming of nonhumans based upon experiential understanding.[7] As he chronicles, naming used to be based on the Latin *sappere,* "having a taste for something in one's mouth." Since the Enlightenment, however, concepts get named more so by human cultural convention rather than by a responsiveness to nonhumans. He shares the example of being handed baby plants and being told one is a flower, another is a weed, and a third is a vegetable. For most, the labels will prompt us to treasure the flower, plant the vegetable, and discard the weed (18). The upshot is that nonhumans get categorized into scientific names and predicated by other names that demarcate their usefulness and value relative to dominant, mercurial human sensibilities. How we label nonhumans predicates our relationship with them and our comprehension of the "environment."

Take the honey bee, for another example. When I was growing up, my Dad, my brother and I had a sideline business wherein we kept 120 hives, and harvested about 5000 pounds of honey per year. I earned an allowance and bought my own hives. I then sold honey harvested from the hives to help pay my way through college. My brother took it even further—he studied apiculture at Ohio State University, and now manages 4000 hives as a commercial beekeeper. Since 2006, in the U.S. we've lost about a third of our honey bees every year, up from previous losses of 15% per year prior, a problem that has greatly affected my brother. The phenomenon that burst on the scene was labeled CCD—short for colony collapse disorder—a mysterious occurrence wherein thousands of bees abscond the hive to leave only a handful of young bees and the queen to subsist and eventually die. In part, my doctoral dissertation addressed the lack of thorough representation of bees in this crisis.

Soon after the crisis erupted in the U.S. in 2007, documentaries and full-length nonfiction books pummeled the point that without honey bees' pollination, we'd lose a third of our food supply. Apocalyptic rhetoric reigned. Rowan Jacobsen ends the first chapter of his nonfiction work *Fruitless Fall: The Collapse of the Honey Bee and the Coming Agricultural Crisis* with this warning: "The losses threatened an ancient way of life, an industry, and one of the foundations of our civilization" (5). The documentary *Silence of the Bees* (Shultz) ends similarly with an emphasis on bees as pollinators: "The future of our food supply rests on the tiny honey bee. . . Scientists warn that the steady decline of pollinators could trigger a crisis bigger and more immediate than global warming." And a key EPA memo, written in the early stages of the crisis, prioritizes bees as pollinators:

---

7. See also Carol K. Yoon's *Naming Nature: The Clash between Instinct and Science.* Yoon chronicles her amazement at how folk taxonomies around the world, regardless of language or culture, follow a remarkably similar form of order (her naming of it with the German word *umwelt*) and how scientific classification had waged a "two-hundred-year-long battle" against such natural order. Nominalism and scientific classification can both be defined as potent forces occluding nature.

"exposure through contaminated pollen and nectar and potential toxic effects, therefore, remain an uncertainty for pollinators" ("Clothianidin Registration").

In this discourse, bees become abstract, pluralized functionaries. Labeling them as "pollinators" reduces them to a functional economic input for agribusiness that renders them machines rather than biological entities. In *Network*, Clay Spinuzzi exposes how the consignment of human labor strips agency from people, a point that applies to nonhumans too. He states in the construct of generic labor one is "assigned a given task, with no reprogramming capability" (168). Such assignments, according to sociologist Manuel Castells, "presuppose the embodiment of information and knowledge beyond the ability to receive and execute signals" (qtd. in Spinuzzi 168). As such, laborers can be conveniently replaced with machines. What is true for the human is as true for the nonhuman. Just as such a label defines knowledge not as residing in us but getting moved through us, when bees are labeled as pollinators, knowledge is understood as not residing in them but getting moved through them. As forced laborers to act the role of machines, bees get stacked in square boxes, hauled on flatbed trucks, and plunked down in the center of a monocrop desert.

While one could argue that labeling bees as pollinators rhetorically plays to human bias, the point remains: lost in this agribusiness representation is a more full and informative representation of honey bees' embodied communication. What of their mass genocide, numbering in the billions? What of their individual shaking in pain, falling off of flowers, and absconding from the hive to leave behind "healthy bees" in a last-ditch effort to save it? What of the loss of the brilliance of a superorganism's mind? What of their resiliency and amazing resistance to dozens of chemicals over the last forty years? Given that language has historically "alienated" humans from the material reality of nature, language scholars have an important role in narrating the emotional experiences we have with nonhumans and identifying names and metaphors as valid approximations of nonhuman communication. "Science cannot tell us about the screaming" (Maxcy 331; 334).

Toward Relational Literacy

In their landmark award-winning article "The Weyekin Principle: Toward an Embodied Critical Rhetoric," Michael Salvador and Tracey Clarke specifically propose "both a different way of listening to and a different way of speaking about the environment" (245). Based upon their lengthy study with the Nez Perce, Salvador and Clarke advocate we adopt principles from their practice of *weyekin*—a responsive caring for a species of animal or plant who is a manifestation of a virtue. Like Maxcy, they claim humans cannot "socially construct" the world through discourse. Constitutive theories of language denigrate nature as having no value "beyond that assigned through symbols" and instantiate a dualism between humans and nature, and between linguistic and nonlinguistic communication that perpetuates "the subjugation of the nonhuman world" (244). Claiming that both nature and bodies speak, they propose nonhumans be understood through embodied listening and time spent observing and chronicling the "lifeworld" of an animal or plant; that organism's symbiosis with their watershed, weather, and other flora and fauna. Salvador and Clarke emphasize that in advancing the *weyekin* principle, the researcher does not ignore critical rhetoric but rather attends to the "corporeal experience of the nonhuman world so as to articulate the symbolic-material tensions obscured by predominant systems of meaning" (248).

This attending to corporeal experience is squarely affective. When I show to students YouTube excerpts of bees falling off of flowers due to pesticide poisoning, things get personal, even confessional. Students express their loneliness and loss for their home pets. One said they felt guilty for missing their cat and asking about them more than their parents (to which others laughed and agreed). Another shared how from years of working at a stable, she observed horses had complex social orders and references to each other. Another almost sheepishly admitted to loving to sit and watch the black squirrels scamper about on campus. These presumed "side point" confessionals brought up cultural scripts of what is deemed acceptable knowledge-making (literacy) about animals in the academy. We discuss U.S. culture and the university culture that make it unintellectual or militant to acknowledge animals, animal suffering, and our affections for them. Many thought it was because we kill so many and we don't want to admit it; others said we don't want to admit that we too are animals; still others discussed the duality between the mind and body that makes us uncomfortable with discussing affections; that the academy is the province of rational discourse, and that discussion about animal welfare would mire us in subjectivity. Yet, is there any other way? Ecology is more than a systems theory for writing or an analog for compositional practices, and the environment is more than the domain of science or one more category added to that of gender, race, and class within our field—categories that already suffer from undue separation.[8] Mapping relationships with nonhumans is an opportunity for the language arts to realize the environment afresh and address its imminent demise.

Key to this project is recognizing relational literacy as a communal process and a way of building knowledge. In *Research is Ceremony*[9], Indigenous (Cree) Scholar Shawn Wilson shares stories and dialogues to invite readers to experience "a process of relationships that form a mutual reality" (71). Furthermore, there is "no one definite reality but rather different sets of relationships" (73). Similar to systems theory models proposed by New Materialists (for example, Bruno Latour's *Politics of Nature*), agency gets distributed. The difference is that in this case, ontology and epistemology get blended as a communal act; reality gets configured (and reconfigured) by the ongoing process of relationship. Subjects only take shape in relationships. They cannot be independent and still maintain their shape (8). Wilson shares, for example, how in his Cree language there is no word for chair. Rather, there is a word for the phrase "the thing you sit on." There is also no word for grandmother; only the phrase "your grandmother" or "my grandmother" (73). In Cree culture, you can't be a grandmother without being attached to someone. One cannot define the essence of a human or nonhuman without reference to a relation.

According to Wilson, the land grounds these relationships, often making time perceived as relative to a place and its inhabitants. In a transcript of a talking circle between Wilson and his Indigenous co-researchers, Lewis Cardinal shares how he desires schools

---

8. See Dobrin for a lucid, almost eviscerating critique of how ecocomposition had been taken up by the field (124).

9. Cited in Google Scholar 2088 times as of 23 December 2018.

expose students to more experiences in the outdoors. Having hunted and fished in the bush for a month, he remembers how "time slows down" and "you have a relationship with a black bird, a bear," and "suddenly the whole reality is different. You feel plugged in; you feel part of everything" (Wilson 105). The upshot? One then becomes a "guardian" for the "intergenerational relationship that forms between Indigenous people and sacred knowledge and place" (114).

This taps a deep memory for me. As first-generation German-American, I often felt in between worlds since my parents were not always accepted in mainstream American society. Going on long bird walks with my Dad and then long walks with my dog in the woods became a way of processing difference by way of communion with nature. I still take long walks and find myself often in similar suspended states of reflection that Cardinal describes, one complemented by the German concept of *Waldeinsamkeit*. *Waldeinsamkeit* parallels Wilson's idea of relationship that goes beyond a subject-object relationship and is grounded in appreciation and a sense of timelessness. The word cannot be fully translated from German but roughly means the personal and reciprocal sense of deep connection in the woods. As my father told me, the word means a personal form of abiding solitude *with* the woods; "they are woods that know your imprint."

A relational literacy invites this process of knowing from deeply abiding with nonhumans in a locale. It presupposes respect and defines that we affect and are affected by a constellation of named and unnamed relationships. When I come home from walks in the woods, I notice I'm almost always less talkative and more meditative. Perhaps in part this is because though I seek moments of communion with nonhumans, I can't predict how and to what extent that will happen. Perhaps too I more fully realize that the trees don't have to be explained as much as they have to be valued for their ongoing interplay of exchange. I get the privilege of walking into a world that can exist often fine without me, even as it beckons a reciprocal relationship.

Coexisting Constructs to Further Define Relational Literacy

Rather than the dialogic between environment and discourse often purported in ecocomposition, I propose some coexisting constructs[10] to inform a relationality between us and nonhumans and encourage further definition of relational literacy.

- *Writing—Speaking—Embodiment.* One aim here could be to discuss how physical presence-based communication and virtual reality differ. Another could be to chronicle and interpret communication between species. Following those in the field that cite New Materialism, how might we further theorize and chronicle presence-based languages of embodiment, pheromones, sights, sounds, and touch?
- *Biology—Socialization.* Reminding ourselves that we are objectively related to every sentient being grounds relational literacy. Yet also noting that subjective loyalty to kin is a natural predilection of many species helps us realize "nature" as a personal form of relationship. As relational quantum mechanics suggest, objects have location only relative to other objects. By defining our kinship with parts of nature we better locate ourselves. In his book on bioregionalism, landscape

---

10. With indebtedness to Robert Yagelski's *Writing as a Way of Being* for inspiration.

architect and professor Robert L. Thayer states we often contemplate three questions: "Who am I? Where am I? What am I supposed to do?" yet we fester on the question "Who am I?" in isolation. As a result, "we substitute shallow awareness of the entire globe for whatever deep wisdom and affection we might have had for a specific place" (2). When instead we settle down, and "stop searching for the hyperreal elsewhere," we come to terms with nature and culture (xiv). We can then probably better ask how global awareness of interconnectivity can co-exist with place-based culture.

- *Reception—Action.* Thanksgiving roots many Indigenous People's sense of place and action. How might a cultivation of gratitude for specific relationships ground our activism? For example, a food activist might first chronicle her/himself as receiving organic food, the relationship with the CSA farmer, and the offerings of the soil as gifts, much like the Haudenosaunee open their meetings by citing a Thanksgiving Address and realizing themselves as a community of one mind with the Earth.[11] How might cultivating thanksgiving for nature make its ownership as resource relative?

- *Time—Place.* Asking when and where helps define the environment in concrete, narrative, phenomenological terms. Climate change for me is the fast warming of neighborhood hardwood forests in the spring, causing great harm to maple trees. Realizing climate change in my neighborhood (place) in spring (time) gets me to more readily realize climate change. Experiencing time and place helps define nature. A sunset dictates how the landscape is experienced. In turn, the contour of the land and water dictate how the sunset is experienced. As humans, we are wired to respond to the interplay of the phases of sun and moon in relationship to land, water, plants, and animals. How might we further chronicle and demarcate experiences of time and place?

- *Emotions—Thought.* As a binary, this has been well-debunked by scholars and scientists, yet how often does this construct of "emotional flexibility" (Wenger 27) still get undercut in curriculums? Is it ok to be joyful about our discoveries in the academy? What does it mean to "chase an idea"? Conversely, can we just sit and chat about an idea without always arriving at answers? This coexisting construct also addresses the false belief that if we only share enough facts with enough intensity, people will do the right thing, and it challenges the belief that critique (building critical minds) is the main job of the academy. How might we borrow from the wisdom of religious traditions that have long defined the "heart" as the impetus of the mind?

---

11. The Haudenosaunee is the oldest living participatory democracy. Their central fire is in Onondaga Territory just south of Syracuse and they have a longstanding tradition of sharing a Thanksgiving Address at their gatherings. Their storifying place has deepened my relationship to their original lands, and I am grateful to have experienced the Thanksgiving Address as given by Onondaga Clan Mother Frieda Jacques.

Pedagogical Practices of Relational Literacy

To conclude, I offer three pedagogical practices of relational literacy. One is to invite Indigenous experts as guest lecturers, create talking circles, or take students on field trips to sacred Indigenous sites. Ceremonies might be scripted and conducted to lament and right the intentional erasure of Indigenous people and their wisdom. To build sustainable knowledge cultures, we need to regularly acknowledge the failure and intentional genocide of humans and nonhumans propagated by European colonization. The literacy classroom can lead

Another practice we might prioritize is deep-mapping places. English, Irish and Osage William Least Heat-Moon's *PrairyErth* still has resonance.[12] How might we recover the layers of stories in a place by researching and using paper, ink, and digital recorders to weave autobiography, history, archeology, weather, folklore, and interviews? Observing small plots and producing wonderful "mash-ups" of human and nonhuman culture regularly yields a rich sense of place.[13] Digital video can chronicle the relationships. Using a GIS (geographic information system) online map, one can link to media of a location, thus inviting spatial narratives. One of my students produced a video that featured such mapping after realizing that a family of raccoons regularly pillaged the dumpster adjacent to his dorm. Not only did he come to appreciate their territorial aggression, but he learned train tracks become corridors for the migration of raccoons, deer, and coyotes (among others) into and out of cities in the northeastern U.S. and Ontario, Canada. Deep mapping serves as a form of deep listening for the interconnections between species.

Concept mapping offers yet a third possibility. Drawing webs of the subjective relationships construed between ourselves and nonhumans makes the chronicle of our perceptions visual and offers a basis for self and group analysis. Whether paper or digital, concept mapping can help us identify the relationships we hold with humans and nonhumans. Similar to deep mapping, it invites multimodal language practices, but in this case, more forwardly identifies what we might label as causal and requisite relationships. What gets mapped? What doesn't? Concept mapping can open us to a discussion about the distance we place between ourselves and others, and how we might establish new relationships that nurture mutual environmental health.

Finding Home in Kinship

In relational literacy, the environment gets configured as a set of presence-based relationships. In kinship, we furthermore realize and name the roles individuals play within the web of a community. In kinship narratives, relationship gets baked in. Honoring sentient beings as kin breaks the false binary of humans vs. nonhumans at the core of environmental crises. At times I call one of our family cats, Cosette, "my kid." At other

---

12. See also Robert Brooke and Jason McIntosh's "Deep maps: teaching rhetorical engagement through place-conscious education."

13. See Bridie McGreavy and Tyler Quiring's archival story-telling of folk clamming on the coast of Maine as one example: http://nest.maine.edu/clamcam/

times, when she's frisky and needs space, I'll call out, "hey, girl" or "you go, girl." She's a pet, her own being, and a mother's daughter. Tracing and admitting these relationships, especially that of honoring her original kin, helps me realize the roles I play and the power dynamics I am prone to acknowledge or not acknowledge. It invites me to respect her presence. At best, we experience each other as truly and honorably as we can, calling forth affection as I admit power dynamics. We coexist; we share space, air, earth, and resources. We share energy and embodied minds – the fierce intelligence of wit, and a will to live. And we honor sentience as the heart of knowledge.

Considering kinship, inviting dialog, and mapping relationships help move us past the impasse of subject/object dichotomy and the abstraction of the environment as a field of objects outside ourselves. Experiencing and defining relationships with nonhumans also address a disconnection between our values and actions, shifting us from the merely pragmatic question of "what can they teach us?" to the wonder of "Who are we here with?" and "What kinds of minds populate this world?" (Safina 20).

Works Cited

Banazek, Kerry. "Carpentry in Context: What Does It Look Like to Be an Ethical Materialist Composer?" *Enculturation,* no. 26, 2018, enculturation.net/carpentry-in-context. Accessed 15 Dec. 2018.

Brandt, Deborah. "Awakening to Literacy circa 1983." *College Composition and Communication*, vol. 69, no. 3, 2018, pp. 503-10.

Brooke, Robert. "Voices of Young Citizens: Rural Citizenship, Schools, and Public Policy." *Reclaiming the Rural: Essays on Literacy, Rhetoric, and Pedagogy*. Southern Illinois UP, 2012, pp. 161-73.

Brooke, Robert, and Jason McIntosh. "Deep Maps: Teaching Rhetorical Engagement through Place-Conscious Education." *The Locations of Composition*, edited by Christopher J. Keller and Christian R. Weisser, SUNY P, 2007, pp. 131-50.

"Clothianidin Registration." Memo to Branch Registration Division, EPA, Washington, DC. 2 Nov. 2010.

Cronon, William. *Uncommon Ground: Toward Reinventing Nature*. W.W. Norton & Co., 1995.

Dobrin, Sidney I., and Christian R. Weisser. *Natural Discourse: Toward Ecocomposition*. SUNY P, 2002.

Dobrin, Sidney I. *Postcomposition*. Southern Illinois UP, 2011.

Donehower, Kim, et al. *Rural Literacies*. Southern Illinois UP, 2007.

Dunn, Patricia A., *Talking, Sketching, Moving: Multiple Literacies in the Teaching of Writing*. Heinemann, 2001.

Gaffigan, Jim. *Cinco*. *Netflix*, www.netflix.com/watch/80117811.

Grant, David M. "Toward Sustainable Literacies: From Representational to Recreational Rhetorics." *Rhetorics, Literacies, and Narratives of Sustainability*, edited by Peter N. Goggin, Routledge, 2009, pp. 202-16.

Heat Moon, William L. *PrairyErth: A Deep Map*. Houghton Mifflin, 1991.

Jacobsen, Rowan. *Fruitless Fall: The Collapse of the Honey Bee and the Coming Agricultural Crisis*. Bloomsbury USA, 2008.

Jones, Madison Percy. "Writing Conditions: The Premises of Ecocomposition." *Enculturation,* no. 26, 2018, enculturation.net/writing-conditions.
Latour, Bruno. *Politics of Nature: How to Bring the Sciences into Democracy.* Harvard UP, 2004.
Lynch, Paul. "Composition's New Thing: Bruno Latour and the Apocalyptic Turn." *College English,* vol. 74, no. 5, 2012, pp. 458-476.
Maxcy, David J. "Meaning in Nature: Rhetoric, Phenomenology, and the Question of Environmental Value." *Philosophy & Rhetoric* vol. 27, no. 4, 1994, pp. 330-46.
McAndrew, Donald A. "Ecofeminism and the Teaching of Literacy." *College Composition and Communication,* vol. 47, no. 3, 1996, pp. 367-82.
Morton, Timothy. *Ecology without Nature: Rethinking Environmental Aesthetics.* Harvard UP, 2007.
Ortoleva, Matthew. "Let's Not Forget Ecological Literacy." *Literacy in Composition Studies,* 2013, licsjournal.org/OJS/index.php/LiCS/article/view/25.
Owens, Derek. *Composition and Sustainability: Teaching for a Threatened Generation.* NCTE, 2001.
Pollan, Michael. *Second Nature: A Gardener's Education.* Dell Publishing, 1991.
Powell, Malea. "Our Story Begins Here: Constellating Cultural Rhetorics." 25 Oct. 2014, enculturation.net/our-story-begins-here.
Safina, Carl. *Beyond Words: What Animals Think and Feel.* Holt, 2015.
Salvador, Michael, and Tracylee Clarke. "The Weyekin Principle: Toward an Embodied Critical Rhetoric." *Environmental Communication,* vol. 5, 2011, pp. 243-60.
Shultz, Doug, dir. "Nature." *Silence of the Bees.* PBS. 28 Oct. 2007.
Spinuzzi, Clay. *Network: Theorizing Knowledge Work in Telecommunications.* Cambridge UP, 2008.
Thayer, Robert L. *LifePlace: Bioregional Thought and Practice.* U of California P, 2003.
Wenger, Christy I. "Writing Yogis: Breathing Our Way to Mindfulness and Balance in Embodied Writing Pedagogy." *Journal of the Assembly for Expanded Perspectives on Learning,* vol. 18, no.1, 2012, pp. 24-39.
Wilson, Shawn. *Research Is Ceremony: Indigenous Research Methods.* Fernwood Pub, 2008.
Wirzba, Norman. *From Nature to Creation: A Christian Vision for Understanding and Loving Our World.* Baker Academic, 2015.
Yagelski, Robert. *Writing as a Way of Being: Writing Instruction, Nonduality, and the Crisis of Sustainability.* Hampton P, 2011.
Yoon, Carol K. *Naming Nature: The Clash between Instinct and Science.* W.W. Norton, 2009.

BOOK REVIEWS

Present and Feeling

Irene Papoulis

I imagine that most readers of *JAEPL* have at least some experience of meditation. You've probably sat for two minutes at least, taking some deep breaths and noticing your thoughts. Maybe you've done so more formally, sitting or chanting with other people, or maybe you are a serious meditator with a decades-long daily practice.

If you're a teacher, you've probably at least toyed with the idea of bringing contemplative practices into your teaching. Or maybe you've fully incorporated them into your classroom practice. Insisting that students move away from their phones and into their own inner experience, you might believe, could be a balm to students who surely long—doesn't everyone?—for more access to the depth of their own, and others', minds.

Or maybe contemplation somehow embarrasses you. Even if you might want to engage students in inner reflection, you might not be able to imagine how you could make explicit mindfulness work in class, maybe, or how it could fit with the things you're "supposed" to be teaching.

These books will meet you wherever you are. Two are concerned with emotions—embarrassment and rage---both insisting, without necessarily mentioning contemplative practices, on the need for self-examination. The others are explicitly concerned with bringing contemplation into the classroom.

Paradoxically, looking inward makes us more capable of looking outward with more clarity. Those who are wary of an explicit cultivation of the practice of looking deeply at oneself, especially in the classroom, often seem to worry that time spent thinking of ourselves is time away from exploring the intricacies of our social and cultural surroundings. However, in fact, as these books demonstrate, the more aware we, and our students, are of who we are—through the contemplation of the inside of our own heads and the examination of our own emotions--the more able we become to meet and change the world.

But self-knowledge is not easy. It can be quite embarrassing to look at, say, what makes us embarrassed as teachers. We've all participated in those faculty-room conversations in which colleagues gush about how wonderful their class was, how highly achieving their students have become. "That's *wonderful*," we might say, fretting privately that our own classes might not measure up. But admitting to embarrassments, to ourselves, and ideally to trusted colleagues, can help us move beyond them --an idea that Daniel Mrozowski explores in his review of Tom Newkirk's *Embarrassment*.

Contemplative practices can offer profound help with confronting our own embarrassments and rages, and three of our reviewers write of books that explore how. Jacquelyne Kibler writes about how Shinzen Young's *The Science of Enlightenment: How Meditation Works* can help teachers both understand and develop a relationship with the idea of reaching enlightenment. Christy Wenger looks at Alexandria Peary's *Prolific Moment: Theory and Practice of Mindfulness for Writing* with an eye to the complexities of "the self" and to the practicality of truly integrating mindfulness into classrooms and writing programs. Mary Leonard, reviewing Geraldine De Luca's *Teaching toward Freedom: Supporting Voices and Silence in The English Classroom*, brings us into a teacher's personal as well as academic journey as she incorporates mindfulness into her classroom.

Finally, Sharon Marshall's review of Brittney Cooper's *Eloquent Rage* brings us back to raw emotions with a "'homegirl' intervention," insisting that we look beyond ourselves at the interconnected social, cultural, and political realities that can rob us of freedom. Contemplative practices can help us do that. As they invite us to examine our own and others' emotions, they encourage us to be open to the interconnectedness of feminism, race, and politics, and, as Marshall is inspired to do after reading Cooper's book, to "focus [our] rage to accomplish good everyday."

✢

Newkirk, Thomas. *Embarrassment and the Emotional Underlife of Learning*. Heinemann, 2017. 207 pp.

Dan Mrozowski
Trinity College

In the humane spirit of Thomas Newkirk's new book, I'll start with my own story of embarrassment: my very first day teaching as a graduate assistant at the University of Michigan in 2003. I was just a year removed from my undergraduate days at a regional state school in Western Pennsylvania, and the night before was miserable. I desperately wanted to be a great teacher, but I had no idea how to become one, so I clung to my lesson plan scripting every single second of the 60-minute discussion section. Still, I was literally shaking, from nerves and coffee, as I walked into the classroom. I barely glanced at the students as the attendance sheet went around. I started reading my syllabus, staring at the words, hoping my voice wouldn't crack. Just as I was getting into a rhythm that might signify some semblance of authority, I noticed a bright drop of red on the paper in my hands. Another drop. A third. I was so nervous that my nose was bleeding.

The panic was almost total. I sped through the syllabus at an auctioneer's pace, dismissed the class with fifty minutes left in that first hour session, and somehow teleported to the nearest bathroom, where I staunched my bleeding, betraying nose. I don't know how I summoned the courage to leave that stall. I felt ruined as a teacher.

Thomas Newkirk's *Embarrassment* is about that exact type of feeling as it erodes our confidence in pedagogical moments. As Newkirk suggests, those experiences, underlined by unspoken and often unspeakable emotions, are fraught with power, from the simple act of raising one's hand to the immense "complexities of help seeking" in an office hours visit (56). Embarrassment is everywhere, across disciplinary lines and departmental allegiances, and Newkirk poses an elemental question to all educators: "how can we create conditions of support so that students can fail publicly without succumbing to embarrassment, or more likely, finding ways to 'hide' so they can protect themselves?" (15). His answers are woven from a broad range of approaches and sources: school psychology, composition studies, sociology, disability studies, self-help, coaching narratives and behavioral science. This interdisciplinary work, expertly introduced and connected, becomes animate through Newkirk's writerly voice, so warm and genial that one feels accompanied by a fellow traveler or a teaching mentor.

The first three chapters help to define what Newkirk calls "the emotional underlife of learning," particularly those ways in which genuine awkwardness and vulnerability —devoid of pessimism or defeatism—are vital to the kind of growth we hope to foster in education. The sensitivity to definitions here is deft, as Newkirk carefully positions embarrassment as a fundamentally evolved emotion that is profoundly inflected by social forces such as racism and poverty. Chapter Three, on stigmas, parses out those factors that alter our experiences of embarrassment, from segregation to labeling, particularly how deeply those influences can drive us into the more morally disruptive emotion of shame. After these definitional efforts, *Embarrassment* moves into two chapters of speculative solutions. Some are more student-driven, as in the development of empathetic introspection and familiarity in educational settings, while others include the elusive qualities of great teaching and coaching, like "soft hands," Newkirk's pungent name for the ability to listen, reflect, and guide conversation in an inclusive fashion.

Chapter Six, "Math Shame," recognizes how specific disciplines enable specific types of feelings of embarrassment, as in the titular emotional paralysis occasioned by failed math equations, while the next chapter situates the role of remembering and forgetting as particularly powerful prompts for embarrassment. Chapters Eight and Nine will be of special interest to teachers of writing, as Newkirk describes both responsive commentary and coaching narratives as means to tell a "better, more generous story about the writing process" (137). This spirit of generosity becomes a clarion call in his final chapter, as he summarizes the problems and potential solutions in terms of habit formation—breaking the cycles of embarrassment for our students and for ourselves.

I was unequivocally charmed and inspired by this book, but there are two elements that warrant particular praise. The first is how deftly he approaches the provisional, contextual nature of embarrassment. Risk is not the same for everyone, he reminds us, as students come to the classroom with different resources and reserves in terms of their own accumulated or inherited emotional capital and their own familiarity with or estrangement from competence. His description of the more fortunate, privileged student who may have picked up academic conventions through a "network of supporting adults," comfortable with professional hierarchies and with expectations for expressed opinions and disagreements, registered immediately with my own experiences teaching at a small liberal arts college (70). But this book is unabashed in its attention to those students who bear the burden of embarrassment with the fewest supports, those who have been inescapably marked by stigmas, and those who have been systematically segregated. Newkirk implores us to recognize how race, class, sex and gender situate the impact and fallout of embarrassment differently for different students.

Relatedly, *Embarrassment* actively resists and frequently attacks the banal pabulum of corporatist self-help that now passes itself off as pedagogy in some circles. I found myself doing a mental fist pump as Newkirk savaged a culture that fetishizes and reifies failure as a pathway inevitably leading to greater and greater success. As he deftly suggests, this rank celebration and even enshrinement of failure ignores its provisional nature for those privileged few who cannot fall very far or very fast. In turn, Newkirk defends praise with the sort of warm generosity one would expect from a writer so clearly in the wake of an Elbow or a Murray.

I wasn't ruined by my bloody nose. I've taught for sixteen years now, and that first day story has been molded into a quirky anecdote, the edges worn away by years of professionalism. Had I read Newkirk beforehand, I would have been kinder to myself. I was, of course, passing on that first day: sporting what could generously be called a professorial beard, wearing my dad's hand-me-down dress shirt, rocking the cheapest approximation of the shiny black leather shoes and thick black glasses my effortlessly cool undergrad mentor wore. I was unaware of my own unearned signifiers of authority and ease as a white, cis-gendered man in a tie and jacket (however ill-fitting and old); I was only conscious of what seemed the doom of failure, signaled by the revolt of my own body in a moment in which I wanted so much to evince control.

But I was able to break the silence of that embarrassment almost immediately. As I managed to hustle myself out of the bathroom to slink back to the English department, I ran into a friend from the MFA program, and I told the first rushed version of what had just happened. He listened, and by the magic of story and laughter, my embarrassment diminished. So I told it to everyone; I sought help processing it. And out of the general kindness of my cohort and professors, my experience transformed from damning indictment to foundational story. It wasn't just time or distance, but the active conversion of the experience into a narrative for a generous audience that buoyed me up. Newkirk calls this "self-generosity"—the alchemy of asking for help and getting it, in spite of embarrassment and not because of its absence.

Beyond the network of interests and evidence Newkirk so expertly weaves together here, perhaps nothing is so useful as the continual, thoughtful act of naming embarrassment itself, to counter what he sees as a pernicious, even systemic silence about a fundamental emotion embedded deeply into our professional and pedagogical systems. I found no claim more thrilling than a kind of existential gasp: "Enough silence. Enough" (13). This is a modernist slogan I can get behind. *Embarrassment* is a great starting note to counter this silence, filled as it is with such richly connected discourses, such frank and funny advice. We need more books this raucously readable on the fundamental emotions of learning.

✦

Young, Shinzen. *The Science of Enlightenment: How Meditation Works.* Sounds True, 2016. 264 pp.

Jacquelyne Kibler
Arizona State University

Right around the publication of this book, I attended a week-long silent retreat led by Shinzen Young in Oracle, Arizona. Before the silence began, Shinzen, in a white t-shirt and cargo-like shorts, spoke with the group. Our chairs encircled in the cafeteria area of the property. He laid out essential info for the retreat and asked us to introduce ourselves. As part of this introduction, he asked what our intentions were for our practice and for the retreat and included the pursuit of enlightenment as an example. That seemed rather lofty to me. I have long considered myself a bare-bones practitioner with a renegade meditation practice—five minutes here, twenty minutes there. The intentions of my practice tend toward a series of "nots." I practice mindfulness and meditation to *not* yell at my kids, to *not* be indifferent to my partner's needs, to *not* be a disconnected and unpleasant human being. The idea of pursuing enlightenment had never occurred to me. When it was my turn to share, I described a gentler version of those previous ideas, ending with something like "I had not considered enlightenment as a goal, but sure, why not?"

Reading this text three years later, I understand why Shinzen casually included enlightenment as a goal of practice. In *The Science of Enlightenment*, Shinzen systematically works to dissolve the ethereal and exclusive connotation around the concept of enlightenment. He claims it as something inherent in our beings, as an activity fostered by, but not absolutely contingent upon, Buddhist meditation practices. Shinzen acknowledges that defining enlightenment is "notoriously tricky," but he offers the reader a "a place to start," inviting the reader to "think of enlightenment as a kind of permanent shift in perspective that comes about through direct realization that there is no *thing* called a 'self' inside you" (2). However, there is an *activity* called a self, he clarifies. Meditation unblocks the mind-body sensory experiences, so that one realizes "that the thingness of the self is an artifact caused by habitual nebulosity and viscosity around your mind-body experience" (3). In other words, the thingness of the self might be described as the collected clutter from our life experience, from the nuances of living in the particular body we do, so like the other humans around us but "unique in its becoming" as I have heard Michelle Marks, a yoga instructor and mental health practitioner, describe. We often attach stories to our pains and joys, perhaps ones that exonerate us from blame or plunge us deeper into self-loathing, or, in joyful moments, stories that quantify our happiness, transform it into something we can cling to and store, like a type of currency. These habits can cloud or thicken the space around the naked emotional or physical experiences that circulate through our days. Meditation, then, fosters skills to connect with the emotional or physical sensation just as it is, without the stories that obscure its core manifestation. As these sensations are always changing, meditation also encourages a connection to this sense of change or movement, the "activity" rather than the "thing" as Shinzen states. Shinzen further claims his definition of enlightenment is a bare minimum one and acknowledges that each perspective on enlightenment "has its own characteristic hazards" and that his "chosen" perspective "is to explicitly describe enlightenment and present it as a feasible goal for ordinary people" (4).

In his foreword, Michael W. Taft, the editor of this book who spent a decade compiling and revising hundreds of hours of Shinzen's talks and evolving teachings, claims the text is not intended for the beginning practitioner (xiii), and that is somewhat true. The book contains little information on how to begin a meditation practice. However, I argue it is a fitting gateway text for academics. Taft describes Shinzen as "a classic nerd, the kind of guy who wants to talk about arcane minutiae of word etymologies, and is highly conversant in science and math," and "he relates such topics [science, meditation, and spiritual practice] to each other, interweaves them, and shows them to be interconnected facets of greater and deeper ideas and teachings" (x). The text skillfully puts in conversation ideas from science, philosophy, Buddhism, poetry, and fiction, all in an accessible yet sophisticated structure, incorporating the cognitive puzzlement and heavy lifting that we in academia enjoy as part of our professional playground.

Shinzen first offers his own experience in "My Journey," describing how he arrived in Mount Koya, Japan to write a dissertation on Shingon Buddhism and instead began initial steps, reluctantly at first as he describes himself as "by nature an agitated, impatient, and wimpy sort of guy" (11), toward studying with several masters, circulating through the three main forms of Buddhism: mindfulness (Theravada), Zen (Mahayana), and Tantra (Vajrayana) (20). In "The Most Fundamental Skill" and "Mysticism and World Culture," Shinzen grounds meditation in its basic effects and how it works in ourselves and in the world. Following that, he discusses major religions, focusing on the "high cultivation of concentration" (52) that is involved in the minority feature of main religions, mysticism. These opening chapters provide a baseline for the headier chapters to come. From there, Shinzen weaves, unpacks, and humorously and poetically punctuates the very largeness of science and the very ephemerality of enlightenment. Pulling from etymology, T.S. Eliot, the periodic table (87), a theory of meditation (103), general relativity (207), emptiness, no-self, and impermanence, Shinzen diffuses divides between spirit and science, constructing a platform for analysis and exploration.

As a writing instructor, I was impressed by his consistent attention to audience. He thoughtfully and thoroughly addresses various viewpoints that might engage this text. This is most notable in his final chapter "My Happiest Thought" where he describes the three life goals he set for himself upon returning to the United States from Japan. His first goal was to "reformulate the path to enlightenment in a modern, secular, and science-based vocabulary" (206). His second goal was to "develop a fully modern delivery system that would make the practice of that path available to any person in the world . . ." (206). His final goal was "to help develop a technology of enlightenment powerful enough to make enlightenment readily available to the majority of humanity" (206). In this discussion, he includes an "Objections" section that begins with, "Sometimes, my happiest thought causes people to freak out" (210). He then proceeds to lay out a continuum of possibilities, conceding concerns and describing the goals of his happiest thought in terms of probabilities, of the likelihood of positive outcomes.

The most salient take-away from this book is enlightenment is accessible to ordinary people through the "systematic cultivation of concentration, clarity, and equanimity" (138). All three elements are strengthened through meditation. Concentration is described as "extraordinary focus" (27), clarity includes "observing, analyzing, and deconstructing sensory experience" (68), and equanimity is "the ability to allow sensory experience to well up without suppression and to pass away without identifying with it" (10). Shinzen states, "The goal of meditation is to gain insight, to know that spirit energy is simply what happens to ordinary experience when it is greeted with extraordinary attention" (123).

The overall claim is that the systematic practice of meditation can make enlightenment possible for everyone, but "spirit energy" can be intense, which could cause ethical issues with integrating meditation into education. Shinzen elaborates on what some of these more intense experiences might look like. For instance, he includes a chart outlining the three levels of the spiritual journey: Everyday Consciousness, The Subconscious, and The Source (enlightenment, nirvana), showing the spiritual journey as being like the "geological strata of the earth" (135). He posits that we make ninety degree turns, turns toward the earth, to move forward in our spiritual journey. Shinzen discusses the subconscious or "intermediate layer" as being conditionings or blockages that obstruct our everyday experience from being in contact with the Source, or enlightenment. He claims that while not typical, unusual things can happen in the intermediate layer such as "weird images, monsters, or skeletons" or the experience of physical sensations of hot or cold or emotional or hypersensitive states without cause (140). After five or six years of practice, Shinzen states he experienced visions of large, vivid insects, visions that popped up in everyday life as well as during meditation. Therefore, if enlightenment is accessible to all *and* meditation brings us closer to enlightenment *and* it is possible to experience some disconcerting visions and sensations, then incorporating meditation into the classroom suggests some risks to students worth taking into account.

Studies examining meditation in higher education, such as Shauna Shapiro et al.'s "Toward the Integration of Meditation into Higher Education: A Review of Research Evidence," for instance, contains no mention of monsters or skeletons or other scary archetypes as outcomes of student experience. In fact, many current studies show positive benefits in self-regulation, anxiety, and executive functioning. However, as we progress in our use of meditation in the classroom, it would be helpful to understand the scope of experience, the complexity, and the variation of meditation practice. Shinzen Young presents a structure helpful to these efforts.

On the sixth and final day of the retreat, I wrote of feeling parallel to where I began, unfinished in my initial hopes of growing my practice. The term "retreat" seems a poor fit with what seems to happen there. Like Shinzen's description of taking a ninety degree turn toward the earth rather than a one-eighty away from it to experience enlightenment (135), a retreat can be a pulling in rather than a pulling away as the term "retreat" implies. While I may have staggered a few steps toward the deeper strata of the earth, I simultaneously felt agitated and clear, as if I'd been half-dipped into an undercooked enlightenment fondue.

In re-experiencing Shinzen's teachings through *The Science of Enlightenment*, I found myself going through some of the same phases as I had on retreat—blissful enthusiasm for attainable enlightenment, despair at its complexity, and frustration with my own practice as I stagger and sway toward the next geological stratum of spirituality. Then, finally, a sort of huffy settling in of something new, a kind of shift or expansion. In my notes from one of Shinzen's dharma talks, I quote him as saying, "you don't become enlightened, the world becomes enlightened to you." This statement reinforces a key element of Buddhist practice. It's already there, simply breathe and allow it a clear path. In finishing the book, I understood the messiness of my retreat experience and meditation practice a little better. Giving up the practice, renegade as it is, has never seemed an option. So with hope and despair, I found myself settling into the same phrase I began the retreat with—enlightenment, sure, why not?

Work Cited

Shapiro, Shauna L., et al. "Toward the Integration of Meditation into Higher Education: A Review of Research Evidence." *Teachers College Record*, vol. 113, no. 3, 2011, pp. 493–528.

Peary, Alexandria. *Prolific Moment: Theory and Practice of Mindfulness for Writing*. Routledge, 2018. 202 pp.

Christy I. Wenger
Shepherd University

The doctrine of *anatta*, or "no self" is central to Buddhist teachings. One such teaching, the parable of the chariot, is presented through a dialogue between King Milinda and a monk named Nagasena. To promote Nagasena's enlightenment, King Milinda encourages a rethinking of the self by comparing it analogously to the chariot in order to illustrate the lack of the permanent, inviolable presence of either. Of the chariot, King Milinda asks, "Is the pole the chariot?" to which Nagasena replies, "No, Reverend Sir!" (Buddha Sasana). The dialogue between King Milinda and Nagasena continues by cataloguing each piece of the chariot:

> "Is then the axle the chariot?"
> "No, Reverend Sir!"
> "Is it then the wheels, or the framework, of the flag-staff, or the yoke, or the reins, or the goad-stick?"
> "No, Reverend Sir!"
> "Then is it the combination of poke, axle, wheels, framework, flag-staff, yoke, reins, and goad which is the 'chariot'?"
> "No, Reverend Sir!" (Buddha Sasana)

As evidenced by this dialogue, a chariot, standing in for the self, is a "conceptual term, a current appellation and a mere name" (Buddha Sasana). We are left to consider how human beings are similarly aggregate collections without individual egos. We too are not our legs, or arms, or names or heads: none of our parts, like the chariot's, integrally constitute our beings. The parable urges us to release attachment to the idea that we are freestanding with a solid presence and to accept the nonpermanence and essential emptiness of self. We are, in turn, freed from the suffering of our individual egos and open to see our connections and relations to everything beyond and yet within ourselves.

Alexandria Peary's recent book serves as a meditation on the nature of the writer's "no self" and the consequences this lesson of impermanence has for the teaching of writing. When we approach writing with the goal of composing for a future audience, Peary argues, we approach it as if it were the inviolable chariot, a predictable entity with a fixed form, and accordingly we silence the integrality of factors like intrapersonal rhetoric, the preverbal, and preconception. We become attached to writing's outcome, limiting our approach to process, and, like all attachments, this can cause undue suffering because it hides writing's inherently transient nature. Through analogy, Peary sets up an entry point for mindful writing, attained through present-centered awareness, which can liberate the writer from suffering by creating conditions where detachment can occur: "A pedagogy and theory of mindful writing can alleviate writing struggle and stress and diminish aversion to writing while bolstering interest, confidence and fluency" (1). If practicing mindfulness through meditation creates a habit we can apply to the whole of life, practicing mindful writing helps us to detach from the product-based outcomes toward which we too often skew our practices, pedagogies and national policies.

The lesson of the no-self from King Milinda is the ultimate transience of being. Impermanence is a lesson of interest for first-year writers and their teachers, according to Peary, because it leads them to the practice of mindfulness, or moment-to-moment, nonjudgmental attention (Kabat-Zinn 4). The perspective of the meditator, who encounters the present through every inbreath and outbreath, focused only on what is unfolding in that "now" moment of meditation, can be applied to the rhetorical situation of composing, what Peary chooses to call the more present-focused "rhetorical moment" (3). It invites writing to take on the characteristics of meditation and the similar outcome of awareness. Like meditation, mindful writing increases students' awareness, so that mindfulness becomes "synonymous with the development of rhetorical and metacognitive awareness" (3). The connection between mindfulness and metacognition is key for Peary.

For readers wary of introducing spiritual beliefs into the teaching of writing, Peary is quick to point out that while she theorizes mindful writing on the precepts of Buddhist philosophies, she does not propose a practice of writing synonymous with Buddhism. Hers is instead the more pragmatic goal of getting writers to fluency, or helping them develop mindfulness as a writing strategy with the goal of composing always in mind. Indeed, Peary persuasively claims that "inspired mind*less*ness" or undirected thinking (63, my italics) is an important balance to the mindfulness for which she advocates. And while Buddhist mindfulness is typically seen as an end in itself, the process and the reason for engaging in meditation or yoga, Peary suggests "mindful composition operates with a goal that is antithetical to Buddhism: to help students reach a state of full absorption in a writing task with a possible outcome up ahead…this pedagogy favors a mix of directed and undirected thinking" (63). By separating the pragmatism of mindfulness from its historical connections to spirituality, Peary echoes the contemporary mindfulness movement—advanced by practitioners such as Jon Kabat Zinn, founder of the secularized mindfulness-based stress reduction method, and scholars like Robert Boice and Ellen Langer, who import mindfulness into the territories of writing and educational philosophy—and capitalizes on the recent surge of interest in contemplative practice advanced by compositionists like Donald Murray, Ellen C. Carillo, Gesa Kirsch, Irene Papoulis, and me.

Though she anticipates an audience mostly unfamiliar with mindfulness, Peary's commitment to the present rhetorical moment to promote student's invention, engagement, and fluency is one to which I suspect many who teach first-year writing can relate. Her book therefore offers us ways to revisit the significance of some of the "low stakes" writing we may already be doing with our students. I, for instance, often use a freewriting "snowball" prewriting activity. Like a standard freewrite, students document their moment-to-moment ideas; unlike a standard freewrite, they then wad up their freewrites and throw them like snowballs—in the recycling bin. Students are often resistant to throwing away what they created, but quickly find it liberating to detach from their words, a skill they have little guided practice in developing. The first time is usually marked by student surprise, but when we repeat the activity, students tend to write fearlessly—after all, they won't be bound to their words or be judged by an audience. The activity is a lesson in writing's impermanence, as Peary might suggest, one that leaves only their *experience* of writing intact and purposefully refuses questions of audience at the earliest prewriting stages where first-year writers' ideas are most vulnerable. Rather than using such activities as present-centered pauses in otherwise future-oriented curricula, Peary presents an important challenge to our pedagogies by having us consider these pauses, these moments of mindfulness, to be part of the central work of our classes.

Peary adeptly critiques current discussions of metacognition for too easily normalizing the processes of retrospection and forecasting without taking stock of the present rhetorical moment, the only moment in which we can compose. Peary theorizes the present moment *as* the writing moment, correcting a future-minded outlook on writing that includes "premature audience consideration, anticipation of criticism, and unreasonable expectations of outcome" (25). Guided by the Pali Sutra from "The Foundations of Mindfulness," Peary argues that mindfulness furthers metacognitive insight by making us aware of our attention and awareness and teaching us how to detach from our self-talk and ruminations. The difference, as I take it, is one between metacognition as rumination, a projecting forward or looking back, making stories about where we were and where we want to go, versus mindful metacognition as an abiding in the present moment as the moment of invention and the embrace of ambiguity and acceptance without attachment (27-31). As she later notes, the practice of mindfulness generates a "bare attention [that] fosters metacognition through realization of the otherwise obscure workings of the mind, providing critical thinking capacities" (91). I remain surprised that outside of a few general references Peary does not do more to explicitly connect mindful writing to transfer, even as she ends her book by exploring mindful writing's connections to writing policy. How mindful metacognition impacts our development of transfer theory is certainly an area that future scholarship might address.

With mindful metacognition in place, Peary asks us to revisit widely-accepted conceptual metaphors of writing as a process and the rhetorical situation, "two vehicles of mindlessness in composition pedagogy" (31). Ellen J. Langer's work on the importance of context within mindful learning helps Peary build an exigence for her own argument about the place-based situatedness and temporality of writing. When we strip the present moment from the process or the rhetorical situation, we gear it toward an eventual written product, taking away the immediate conditional context---taking, as it were, part of the chariot for the whole. New rhetorical factors that emerge from a present-centered focus are impermanence, intrapersonal talk, the writer's "interior river" (31; 37), and the writer's and writing environment's materiality, which "stimulates invention, sets up a realistic audience interaction, and allows the writing moment to become a source for connection with others" (40).

Peary follows Chapter One with an interchapter that works to flesh out her theory and show how she enacts mindful writing within her first-year classes. By that first interchapter, I was indeed craving some practical import to the classroom, so I found it helpful that Peary spends time detailing specific mindfulness activities she uses with students, from a version of open awareness meditation called "The Mind List," to an embodied freewrite called "yoga for hands" that asks students to pay attention to the physicality of writing and generating ideas, activities I would love to try in my own application of mindful writing pedagogy. This interchapter, along with the others of its kind, is short but pulls a great deal of weight for the book's development of mindful writing. Peary's format of chapter-interchapter works well to give space to her theories of mindful writing; however, I sometimes wish for more specific examples within the chapters themselves to help develop and illustrate her concepts.

Chapter Two takes a closer look at intrapersonal rhetoric, the rhetoric of the present moment. Peary heads off critique by addressing constructivist concerns regarding how the intrapersonal is intertextually constructed by the material of the social. Awareness of this intertextuality is a fundamental goal of Buddhist mindfulness as outlined by the chariot dialogue in my introduction: the no self is recognized through the self's dissolution within a larger network of other beings and connections. Even so, the inner talk of intrapersonal rhetoric is often devalued within writing studies, and Peary approaches this chapter admitting that she is swimming upstream as she attempts to reclaim its value for her theory of writing. What stands out about Peary's discussion of the intrapersonal is her effort to make it rhetorical, to argue for its internal discursivity.

The goal of claiming intrapersonal rhetoric for mindful writing is to loosen the grip audience has on writers so that they can open a receptive space for self-dialogue. When writers invite self-dialogue and value the persuasive nature of self-talk, Peary suggests, they develop an "advanced" mindful writing practice during which they can attend "to those passing, unrecorded bits of intrapersonal to return [their] awareness to the present" (59). Such practice not only validates the intrapersonal as a form of rhetoric, it also develops mindful metacognition as the writer learns to see and accept the internal river.

At this point in Peary's book, I found myself wondering about the students who resist her present-focused methods. While her second interchapter overviews the difference in word output depending on whether students are writing for an audience or not—anticipation of an audience restricts output (77-78)—students conceivably struggle with more than establishing their authority to write. In my decade of teaching mindfulness to student writers, I've encountered students challenged to find the present because previous (and concurrent college) educational experiences have trained them to focus on anything but the present moment. They are habituated to mindless writing behaviors, and these are difficult to break in a one-semester class. Others find it easier to remap behaviors with the help and guidance of mindful pedagogy, but for myriad reasons find the present frightening because of its unpredictability; they often see the inner talk of intrapersonal rhetoric as a daunting "river" (35), where a toe plunged in means getting pulled under. To continue my framing metaphor, they have no desire to grapple with the ambiguity of the chariot's presence. Peary's self-interview assignments (wherein students question themselves about the composing process in self-study form) and her internal rhetorical analysis papers that engage students in analysis of the ways the rhetorical appeals function intrapersonally to shape the writing experience and outcome are certainly tools that could be used to help such wary students find control over the rivers of their self-talk; I'd love to see more developed and diverse examples from Peary's students' in their own voices.

Chapters Three and Four argue for the discernment of no self and verbal emptiness as a metacognitive skill. Peary engages further with the Buddhist views on emptiness, particularly as represented within the Heart Sutra. She suggests that we encourage students' radical acceptance of verbal emptiness by spending much more time on prewriting for its own sake rather than persistently treating it as a means to the end of producing a final draft. The third interchapter offers an interesting variant on freewriting, "momentwriting," during which students are not instructed to simply keep writing for a designated period of time but are told to dwell in the present moment and observe, which may include a kind of freely written documentation of their thoughts and self talk but may also account for pauses in the process: "[m]omentwriting allows people to track impulses and sensory experiences and to honor them as part of their writing experience" (111).

Peary encourages students to come to terms with two types of mental formations that she calls "mind waves" and "mind weeds," borrowing from Shunryu Suzuki's classic treatise on Zen meditation, *Zen Mind, Beginner's Mind*. Mind waves are fleeting, nonverbal moments driven by urges such as shifts in position, body responses like clearing one's throat, or movements at outside noises (117). Mind weeds are discursive nets that entangle thoughts with narratives, storylines that root our attention away from the moment (117). Mind waves and weeds help writers identify the affective dimensions of writing, those feelings that may take them away from the present writing moment. Labeling these moments helps writers develop a mindful metacognition of the writing moment (119). Peary's focus on these two mental formations allow her to attend to the students' affective experiences of writing as an act occurring in real time, what she calls "real-time pathos, or the emotions students feel as they write, emotions about needing or wanting to write the project at hand" (121). Acceptance of waves and weeds also helps writers examine their self-talk to see how self-pathos impacts how and what they write.

In her final chapter, Peary loops back to her first chapter's argument about the importance of reclaiming the present rhetorical moment to address more pragmatically how writing studies at a national, disciplinary level might better support mindful writing. Of course, traditional metaphors of process and rhetorical situations don't just underlie classroom pedagogy; they are used as a foundation for national writing policies like "The WPA Outcomes Statement for First-Year Composition" and the "Framework for Success in Postsecondary Writing." Peary faults these documents and others for their future-forward thinking, which propels teachers and students out of the present moment and shifts the focus of writing on anticipated future audiences and writing products and away from "the real-time, fluctuating experiences and perceptions of writers" (145). Large scale institutional change must be accompanied by revisions to these national policies: "[m]indlessness in writing policy can be redressed through learning outcomes that emphasize process and rhetorical theory based on the present rhetorical moment" (147).

As a writing program administrator, I am struck by Peary's critique of the unaddressed gulf between the individual classroom and our national standards. I see promise for the average reader inside that gulf. Individual readers can react faster than national policy can change. One promise-filled middle ground might be the administration of writing programs. WPAs are always adjusting curricula to better represent national trends and growing ideas; programs therefore are inherently more flexible and responsive to new perspectives on writing than national policy. As someone already practicing mindful writing pedagogy who is also a WPA, I accordingly take from Peary's book a renewed commitment to apply mindfulness at the programmatic level and am encouraged to engage my writing colleagues in discussions of creating mindful writing programs and rethinking the future-oriented rhetoric of writing program curricula. Perhaps instead of always being focused on what students "will" be able to complete by the conclusion of our courses, we might spend more time on what students are already encountering in the present.

Works Cited

Anson, Binh. "Questions of King Milinda." *Buddha Sanana.* https://www.budsas.org/ebud/ebsut045.htm

Kabat-Zinn, Jon. *Wherever You Go, There You Are: Mindfulness Meditation in Everyday Life.* Hachette, 1994.

Suzuki, Shunryu. *Zen Mind, Beginner's Mind.* Shambhala, 2006.

✣

De Luca, Geraldine. *Teaching toward Freedom: Supporting Voices and Silence in the English Classroom.* Routledge, 2018. 118 pp.

Mary Leonard
Bard College M.A.T. program

In her introduction, Geraldine DeLuca points out that ever since the Common Core was introduced students are being tested continually. However, that program is being challenged in many states, which to DeLuca is liberating (3). In her resistance to assessment culture, De Luca does not claim to be writing anything original, but her passion is clear and her stories are useful and inspiring. She reviews the research and the pros and cons of "rigor" vs. "process" approaches to teaching, and finally explores a solution that grows out of her own contemplative practice and the use of meditation in classrooms. Thus her book takes us on a useful journey with a satisfying destination.

DeLuca begins by questioning the practice of college teachers who compile charts for evaluation—syntax, punctuation, grammar, etc.—and presents the story of a college teacher who kept failing an immigrant student's papers because of poor results on those charts. The student was finally transferred to a colleague's class who claimed the student was a poet. This story presents a question that underlies DeLuca's explorations: how do teachers have a right to stifle students' creativity in the name of "correctness?" Of course in the corporate or academic worlds students need to be literate and write in standard English. However, De Luca argues, standard English can productively be balanced with students' desires to be expressive.

In a dynamic section of her book, De Luca recounts June Jordan's story about assembling an "in your face" paragraph composed of student responses after the murder of a classmate's brother by the police. The paragraph was sent to various journals and television news shows but was not published. De Luca reminds us of Jordan's question about whether the paragraph would have been published if it were in "standard" English (18). She goes on to raise questions regarding race and class in the elusive race to the top and acknowledges that Peter Elbow was way ahead of his time in the seventies when he encouraged freedom through freewriting and resistance to Standard English. Acknowledging Lisa Delpit's questions regarding exploratory writing vs. preparation for the writing standards required in the "real world," De Luca suggests including students in an initial conversation about what they need from a writing class (49). This resonated with my own teaching: just recently one of my MAT students suggested a similar idea—a conversation among teachers and students about the needs and wants of all involved before beginning any college composition class. It could be revolutionary in its resistance to traditional teacher-student hierarchy.

De Luca moves from there to the confusing message we all give students: do research on others' work but be original. She claims that even in writing this book her mind became "a tissue of stuff." It's fortunate that she has shared some of that "stuff" with us; the book is valuable for her summary of the academic theorists underpinning her ideas. However, in keeping with her point, I would have liked to hear more about DeLuca's own mind and her experiences as a teacher.

In her sixth chapter DeLuca makes an interesting analysis of original thought versus plagiarism. She tells the reader that she submitted her own essay on plagiarism, co-written with a colleague, to *iThenticate*, a plagiarism detection program. It was deemed 11.06 percent deliberately plagiarized, with a note that since it was under 15 percent it was acceptable (78). The absurdity of such an assessment is striking and points to the dangers of a world in which writing is seen not as expression of thinking but as a quantifiable product.

In the final section of *Embracing the Contemplative Life,* we finally learn what is central to De Luca's thinking and teaching. However, even when she arrives at that useful moment of contemplation she feels the need to be scholarly, presenting the reader with lists of the many Buddhists who have influenced contemporary meditation practices. As someone who has read quite a bit about meditation, I had the impulse to skip another section of lists. However, I was really pulled in when De Luca wrote about her own journey into contemplative practice, which started for her with yoga. I found this section to be very engaging, especially her preparation for doing a headstand, which took years, and her insight: "I can't rush it. ...But I don't have to give up" (87).

Although she uses meditation practices in various ways in her classroom, DeLuca's final thought about teaching is this: "My yoga experience dramatically supports my belief that my students are already okay. Their sentence fragments, their various vernaculars, their second language influences--whatever they got going for time, it's all okay. ... yet yes they should learn the standard. Of course I hear you Lisa Delpit" (91). De Luca then goes on to explain how she uses meditation practices in her classroom and does give us lists of *how to*. She also journeys outside the classroom and acknowledges the importance of a contemplative practice for world-awareness as well as self-awareness.

While reading *Teaching Toward Freedom* I was engaged in DeLuca's academic and personal journey and found the process liberating. This book is useful as a reference for theories of learning and as a guide for teachers. Perhaps most importantly, though, it is useful as the story of how one teacher has used contemplative practice as a guide for her life and work.

Cooper, Brittney. *Eloquent Rage, A Black Feminist Discovers Her Superpower*, St. Martins, 2018. 288 pp.

Sharon Marshall
St. John's University

A Black Girl's Magic

Tyler Perry's movie version of Ntozake Shange's *For Colored Girls Who Have Considered Suicide When the Rainbow is Enuf* ends with the eight women whose stories have been dramatized in the film and narrated through their respective poems, gathered together on a New York City rooftop in a colorful group embrace that follows the revelation of the she-ness of the god that has been missing in their lives. I watched the movie on Netflix while I was reading Cooper's book, and that scene reminded me of a statement Cooper makes in her chapter devoted to Beyoncé, whom she calls *her* feminist muse, "One of feminism's biggest failures is its failure to insist that feminism is, first and foremost about truly, deeply, and unapologetically loving women" (26). After reading *Eloquent Rage*, I'm thinking that the feminist love for women and for freedom—Cooper says, "Freedom is my theological compass and it never steers me wrong" (143)—may well be the she-god whose power is missing from all our lives.

Cooper, who describes herself as "fat, black and Southern," is a professor of Women's and Gender Studies and Africana Studies at Rutgers University. In the preface she says the book is for "women who know shit is fucked up" and who want to change things but don't know how to begin. She writes, "Black women have the right to be mad as hell. We have been dreaming of freedom and carving out spaces for liberation since we arrived on these shores" (4). She tells the story of her student Erica who upset her when she pointed out how angry Cooper appeared in class, but who went on to say that her rage was "eloquent." Cooper explains that Erica helped her realize that focused with precision, her anger could be a powerful force for good—that it, in fact, could become her superpower.

Eloquent Rage is intended as a "homegirl" intervention for readers, similar to the ones that saved Brittney Cooper over the years, when her mother, grandmother and friends called her out and "demanded that I get my shit together, around my rage, around my work in the world, and around my feminism." "America," she says, "needs a homegirl intervention in the worst way. So in this book, I am doing what Black women do best. I'm calling America out on her bullshit about racism, sexism, classism, homophobia, and a bunch of other stuff. And I'm using feminism to stage [it]" (5).

For Cooper, feminism is far from being an historical abstraction or platform reserved for white women in pussy hats. She asks, "Why is it so easy for Black women to ignore how important feminism is to our lives?"(34). Then she shows us how her own Black feminist identity, politics, and praxis are a direct response (sometimes prompted by interventions) to lived experience—or that, as she might say, this shit happens to real people. In this way the book is a memoir, one I often found poignant and that resonated with me personally, as when her mother is shot by an ex-boyfriend while she is pregnant with her, or when young Brittney is rejected by other Black girls who do not understand her intellectual ambition in middle school, or when she tells her mostly absent father she doesn't love him because he hurts her mother, or when she graduates from Howard without having had a single date. However, these stories are not sentimental, especially when they become the basis for an almost surgically precise code-meshing, signifying critique of sexism, white supremacy, and neoliberal agendas that have so constricted and often taken the lives of Black women and men. In eight chapters Cooper analyzes, among other things,

- Black women's rejection of feminism
- Black men's lack of solidarity
- White women choosing race over gender
- Toxic masculinity
- Black women who stand up to white male authority and pay the price, like Sandra Bland
- Christian theology that "sets up a false binary between flesh and spirit, mind and body, and sacred and secular" (140)
- Respectability politics
- The danger of "white-girl tears" to people of color
- Hatred among Black men for Black women
- Rape and power
- The obsession with curtailing reproductive freedom in this country
- White fear ("cultural refuse of white supremacy" 210) and violence against people of color
- The requirement that Black people manage their fear
- Black women and marriage
- The myth of Black exceptionalism

It's been a long time since I've been a Black girl, but reading Cooper's book took this Black woman back to early encounters with feminist thought in the 1960s when I discovered Betty Friedan, in the 1970s when I read Alice Walker, and the 1990s when bell hooks changed my life. Brittney Cooper's twenty-first century "homegirl" intervention has allowed me to share in her story and has given me insight into the ways current social, cultural, and political realities impact Black women's lives and rob us all of freedom. She has helped me reconnect cherished beliefs with my righteous anger and reminded me that, "My job as a Black feminist is to love Black women and girls" (35) and to put that love into action by focusing my rage to accomplish good everyday.

CONNECTING

Finding Meaning in our Work and Writing

Christy I. Wenger

I've been thinking a lot about meaningful writing this semester—the kind we fully invest in because we find it personally significant, pragmatic and useful, and resonant with the identity markers of who we are or who we want to become. Of course, what is "meaningful" is slippery: for students, it's hard to pin down in some generalizable way but easier to retrospectively identify as connected to a particular assignment, one that allowed their voice to shine through or their decisions to shape the outcome. For teachers, it's somewhat more encompassing, an adjective used to describe the purpose of much of what we do. Teachers in my program, for instance, see just about every writing project they assign as "meaningful" when queried, even including the humble summary paper, projecting a wider continuum of meaning than the students I've informally polled in my classes.

Michele Eodice, Anne Geller and Neal Lerner trace the question of meaning in higher education writing instruction across the disciplines by posing the research question, "What was your most meaningful writing project, and why was it meaningful to you?" to 700 seniors at 3 universities. What they found was needed for meaning was, in sum:

1. Opportunities for agency
2. Engagement with instructors, peers and materials
3. Learning that connects to prior experiences and future aspirations. (4)

I'm drawn here to the first finding, the importance of agency, for the ways it brings together the seeming divergence in student and teacher descriptions of meaningful writing. What teachers and students seem to be coming to, albeit from different directions, is that meaning is a function of inviting writers to take control of their writing and actively construct their learning (34). Students see this most obviously when they are given new freedoms in their writing and are asked to approach novel tasks. For teachers, the novel and the routine both have meaning, and scaffolding takes on a heightened importance for cultivating agency.

When I shared Eodice's findings with students in my upper-level writing seminar this semester, they had plenty to say to support the importance of fostering agency among writers. Meaningful writing, according to my students, makes them feel heard when so many of their writing assignments ask for other voices to drown out their own and gives them space to see themselves reflected back in the finished product. This kind of writing materializes them in some all-too-often-neglected manner: "reflecting" and "representing" them in ways that helped them feel in "control" of their learning. This is what agency is all about.

Of course, agency is not something that can be simply "given" to students, like a gift at Christmas. Instead, agency is best delivered by choreographing the conditions for it to emerge.

Agency is emergent and a product of our effort as teachers to facilitate student learning and engagement, but it is also gained through the actions of students together with their peers as well as students' own uptake of ideas and topics. As Eodice et al. note, "[a]gency is strengthened by offering experiences that get students to notice they have the capacity to direct energies for themselves, in and beyond classrooms" (53). Students experience writing as agentive when it is immersive and when it helps them connect their academic and personal identities and interests.

The authors in this section provide an array of methods we might use to choreograph the conditions of agency in our writing classes and the ways teachers and students can co-construct meaningful writing experiences. Together, they offer a response to these findings on agency, a way of articulating how we might work to help students feel the control and newness they desire while still scaffolding the learning process, using our expertise as teachers to open the space for agency to emerge.

Monica Mische provides a poignant reflection on the importance of encouraging students to write for public audiences, an effort to expand the borders of the writing classroom from the university to the larger community. Her story recounts a pedagogical experiment that engaged students in writing for the *Washington Post Magazine*. Unexpectedly, Mische finds herself a subject of her own experiment when the model writing she produces for students is accepted for publication by the *Post*. Her teaching reflection not only exposes the ways we might cultivate assignments that invite students to take agency over their writing in hopes of finding meaning, but also illustrates how meaningful writing is co-constructed by teachers, mentors and students as we find ourselves moving fluidly between these roles.

Kristina Fennelly's piece that follows traces the question of student agency to the digital communications that permeate our students' literate lives outside of the classroom and shape the ways they understand their literacy and discuss it in our writing classes. Fennelly suggests that training students in rhetorical listening will help them command their communicative power in those digital spaces, transforming them into empathetic listeners. Agency here is contingent on not only the ability to voice our own ideas but also the ability to truly listen to other voices both in-person and in online environments. Fennelly's digital listening assignment asks students to help construct bridges between their informal online writing and academic writing, offering an example of a writing project invested in the very type of agency Eodice and her peers target and my students reiterate as key to finding meaning in their writing.

The stakes of agency become fuller when we understand how writing projects are a function of their learning environments: they are living artifacts of a meaningful writing *pedagogy* invested in the individual student bodies in our classes and not simply in abstract pedagogical principles. Laurence Musgrove's poem, "Sunday Before Midterms," underscores this point and starkly reminds us that students' material learning conditions include a host of mental and physical factors that follow students' into our classrooms. Lindsey Allgood reflects on how pauses, by pushing us to meaning, can help students produce "more satisfying and authentic writing," another illustration of how meaningful writing is connected to student bodies, not just their minds. Student bodies are a host of meaning for Allgood, who recounts her experiences working with student writers to discover meaning in writing center consultations. Allgood's lyrical narrative encourages us to question if agency itself has an embodied pattern or rhythm for the writer that we miss when we ignore the embodied dimensions of writing.

Together, the pieces in this section provide useful ways of approaching agency through personal connection, embodiment, and listening. They help us to pause over the idea of agency as emergent from the writer's body and incorporative of the teachers' presence. They invite us to embrace the ambiguity of what counts as "meaningful" to help us stumble upon it in our classes.

Work Cited

Eodice, Michele, Anne Ellen Geller, and Neal Lerner. *The Meaningful Writing Project: Learning, Teaching and Writing in Higher Education.* University Press of Colorado, 2016.

✢

Response from Beyond

Monica Mische

In my developmental English classes, I often encourage students to submit their writing to "real-world" venues. So often lacking confidence, these students need to feel that their words carry weight, that their voices matter, that they—beyond the walls of our insulated classroom—have something essential to say. To this end, we've mailed letters to authors and political representatives, sent op eds to newspapers, and submitted memoirs to anthologies. Sharing our work lends energy, focus, and inspiration to our writing. However, one interchange stands out as especially impactful, affirming for us the power of words, the profundity of "ordinary" lives, and the gift of empathetic listening.

For several years, the *Washington Post Magazine* ran a column called "Mine," for which readers wrote in about treasures they own. Capped at 250 words, these mini-essays focused less on describing objects than on relaying their significance—on describing the relationships that impart meaning to our experience. How beautiful, I thought. Determined to try this in class, I distributed past "Mine" columns. Then, we all brought in objects we valued. I presented an assortment of treasures, and students selected one for me to write about—a can of soup bequeathed to me by a dying friend. At home that night, I labored to capture my decades-old experience, but as much as I tried, I couldn't squeeze my story into the allotted space. At class the next day, students workshopped my draft and helped me make the brutal cuts. "Ok! Thanks to you, I think it's ready," and they watched as I emailed the *Post*: "I'll probably never hear back, but, see, I'm giving it a try!" Surprisingly, within days, I received a note from the editor David Rowell about publishing my piece. My heart sank a little, and I thought about declining, explaining this was just an activity for my students and, really, I wasn't seeking a by-line. However, something in David's phrasing gave me pause. He'd said the piece had "moved" him. I relented, thinking, "I'm asking my students to be brave; I should do the same".

The next week, I ventured to the *Post*'s offices to get my soup can photographed. David greeted me warmly, and as we walked the halls, we discussed my story—its resonance and themes. "We don't quite have the ending yet though," he conceded. I knew he was right, and over the next two days we exchanged a flurry of emails, devoted to reworking just the last couple of lines. He was patient and gentle and motivated me to probe more deeply. Finally, I was able to voice an epiphany, a realization I'd never seen before. Soon thereafter, two of my students also heard from David (that he was "moved by their stories") and embarked upon their own journeys of collaboration. Those students had lived such heartbreaking and inspiring lives; I felt David had somehow divined this, had traced through their writing to see who they were. Touched by his encouragement, I reached out to him for further insight. He kindly agreed to meet and share his thoughts about editing and writing.

Growing up in North Carolina, David was a natural story-teller who loved the movies. He'd dreamed of studying film and television, but in college he became captivated by a more tightly-woven form of expression—the short story—and determined to be a writer. Upon graduating, David worked first for literary publishers, then was offered a job with the *Washington Post*. He'd never edited journalism, never been to Washington, but they felt David understood storytelling and could bring out more literary elements of their pieces. That was nineteen years ago. Back then, the magazine was known for long-form journalism. David could craft articles with tremendous scope and insight, highlighting "ordinary people doing incredible things." However, the magazine had also developed a reputation of being dark and heavy; new publishers desired lighter themes; word-counts were slashed. Still, David pushed to make the stories "live" and to illuminate the beauty of individual lives.

When we met, David discussed some favorite recent stories: Muslim scout troops exploring what it means to live in a democracy in the shadow of Trump; and the longest serving keeper at the National Zoo (a man whose remarkable sensitivity allowed him to forge incredible bonds with the animals). Readers were so moved by the latter that the story was read aloud in the U.S. House chambers so that it would become part of the congressional record. Indeed, David sees his work that way—as "adding to the record of who we are, of how we live with the consequences of our decisions." And he believes this surfaces most keenly in the stories of people we've never heard of.

David has taught writing in an MFA program and understands how student writers (like most writers) are nervous about what their readers will think. He likens teaching to editing: "both require real dialogue and collaboration." No matter how weak the story, he finds something hopeful to say. "This is going to be great by the time it's done." If a piece is troubled, he'll start with good things but then carefully lay out steps for improvement: "This is where the pivot doesn't work. This is where the character drops off." He admits that some drafts are not ready for comments; that writers and editors must first talk it through. "This story's lost its way but we can re-imagine it and find its path." When asked whether such an affirming attitude is unusual in an editor, David admits he's known for the effort he puts into a story. For example, he'll help staff writers whittle down an 18,000 word draft to 3,000—something most editors would never consider. David knows how hard it is to write; thus he tries to be encouraging:

> My mother was a teacher, and my father a teacher for many years, and the people who played the most important roles in my life were also teachers—English teachers who encouraged me in my writing and made me feel confident about what I had to say. I think teachers are always the most important players in a person's life. Being an editor is not quite like being an English teacher, of course, but there are some similar aspects, and I try to never lose sight of that—the power of what we have to say about someone's story, the way we talk about how someone has told it. I guess I go about my life believing words are everything, and I know the wrong teacher can have a terrible, long-lasting influence, just as the right teacher can really shape who we are and what we go on to do.

Some months after our meeting, David relayed that "Mine" had been cancelled—a top-down decision, too few clicks on the web. Feeling my disappointment, he suggested that although he could no longer publish them, my students could send him "Mine" drafts anyway. And the next semester, for my new batch of students, David not only read their work, but invited us to visit the *Post* headquarters. On a beautiful spring morning, twenty of us took the metro downtown. Most had never read a newspaper, but there we were, sitting in white leather chairs in a glass walled conference room, just blocks from the White House. David, at the head, discussed the profundity of my students' keepsakes: a locket with strands of hair from a student's mother who had died too soon, a grandfather's army tags sewn into his grandson's belt; a cake-topper from a *quinceañera* a father couldn't attend. As David shared the profundity of their pieces, I saw nods and shivers of recognition. He had made each one feel special, each one feel inspired. At the end of the semester, the students reflected on their most significant experience. Every one of them said it was David—visiting the *Post* and hearing his words, hearing the beauty he'd found in their own.

✦

Reflecting on Arguing and Listening in Digital Spaces

Kristina Fennelly

Recent examples of Gamergate in 2014, various presidential and political tweets, and collective social organizing for activist-based protests by Black Lives Matter, white nationalist groups, and women's rights organizations via Facebook and Twitter all testify to the opportunity but also to the personal and intellectual risks of arguing in digital spaces. The form our students' writing takes in online spaces significantly shapes their lives and affects their academic writing. I'm interested in how students gain rhetorical power via exchanges in spaces typically not associated with academic writing like blogs, messaging exchanges, and Facebook discussion forums. Online, students think critically, question others' ideas in relation to their own, and arrive at new ideas via social discourse. Though perhaps unknowingly, they practice such skills in these digital forums on a near daily basis, yet they often do not value such exchanges or connect these practices to their academic writing since these skills are not as concrete as form and grammar, nor are they readily embraced in some academic settings.

I believe students can harness the rhetorical power inherent in online exchanges by developing their skills in listening rhetoric, which can in turn produce a more empathetic approach to how they argue. This approach privileges cooperation over agonism and is applicable to a variety of assignments, but especially those framed with public deliberation in mind. My call to action for students and instructors alike is to explore listening rhetoric in order to actively practice listening as a skill and to explore the process of deliberating ideas in online forums. Here, I want to explore two questions that drive this call to action: how do we "listen" when writing, and how do we listen in digital spaces where face-to-face interaction is minimized?

One crucial step in evaluating the role listening can play in rhetorical situations is to define goals for the listening-oriented writer as he/she sifts through competing viewpoints. Listening-oriented writers should be reflective, inquisitive, and curious: consider first, ask questions second, and respond last by acknowledging (though not necessarily agreeing) with a genuine understanding of other points of views. The over-arching goal is to understand other positions and interests cooperatively, *not* to aggressively convince the audience that this position is right. With this goal in mind, listening-oriented writers learn to suspend judgment in order to cultivate an empathetic approach to those who hold diverse and even conflicting views.

Exploratory essays are one way I've worked with students to develop such listening skills. In preparation, my students practice the believing and doubting game, an exercise made popular by Peter Elbow. As John D. Ramage, John C. Bean, and June Johnson note in their textbook, *Writing Arguments*, the believing and doubting game is the foundation of dialectic thinking (44). Through this process, students actively seek out alternative views and test those ideas against one another. This exercise develops students' skills in self-reflection, critical and sustained inquiry, and intellectual curiosity—skills they hone by evaluating online exchanges where they can witness the deliberation of a variety of views in a public forum. For their exploratory essays, my students are invited to write about an issue of their choosing. However, there is one important caveat: they must choose an issue that they are *open* to changing their mind about. Such assignments often give students the much-needed opportunity to break free from thesis-driven monologues and instead practice investigative dialogues. Indeed, students are often surprised when I encourage them not only to read primary source material but to also look at comment threads attached to contemporary news articles. Doing so allows them to read unfiltered public responses to key issues of the day, such as gun control, abortion, immigration, LGBTQ rights, etc. They quickly see how reading collective deliberations by citizens like themselves can prove just as meaningful and insightful as reading traditionally-published texts.

Another one of my writing assignments invites students to choose a current issue that has drawn close attention and great scrutiny. Then, they practice composing a content analysis based on the same criteria followed by Brian Jackson and Jon Wallin in their seminal study "Rediscovering the Back and Forthness of Rhetoric in the Age of YouTube." Jackson and Wallin's study serves as a model for instructors and students to realize the potential available in Web 2.0 applications such as YouTube, Facebook, and other online social network spaces that feature comment threads and discussion forums. Jackson and Wallin focus their attention on a YouTube video that captured the arrest and assault of Andrew Meyer, a University of Florida senior, at a town hall meeting with Senator John Kerry. The video provided "an opportunity for ordinary citizens to make arguments about free speech, police force, civility, ethos, and the normative standards of public forums" (386). I share this video with my students before we read and consider Jackson and Wallin's study. My students respond to this lesson because these are the kinds of videos and online content they engage with on an almost daily basis. Their interest is piqued because Jackson and Wallin's study involves a content analysis of a comment thread related to issues of free speech on college campuses. Students grow excited to see how public voices similar to their own can be read and interpreted in socially significant and meaningful ways in relation to contemporary issues with direct applicability to their lives.

Through discussion and informal writing assignments, students have the opportunity to follow Jackson and Wallin's lead, evaluating comments and arguments on a YouTube or news thread much like a "content analysis." In doing so, they draw on the same criteria Jackson and Wallin use to determine the effectiveness of dialogue in online forums. As Jackson and Wallin explain, these questions prove useful because they serve as the foundation for effective dialogue, a "back and forth" which they denote as "a procedure involving critical listening and responding, and then receiving, listening, and responding again" (385). The back-and-forthness of rhetoric is what I hope students will take from this assignment so they will treat argument as an exchange of ideas with the primary goal of apprehending a new perspective. This exchange lies at the heart of listening rhetoric. It allows students to break free from dichotomous thinking and develop empathy as our positions evolve, change, and grow.

One of my students, a Pennsylvania resident, in writing about the contentious topic of fracking, a prevalent practice in the state, exhibited such empathy in her balanced response. Her conclusion points to the ways in which listening rhetoric—when practiced by the careful evaluation of competing claims and when considered with the goal of empathy in mind—can yield great insight:

> Whether you support fracking or not, there is a clear imbalance between the will of companies and the will of individual citizens. The companies have the power and influence to get their way, which puts the democracy of society at stake. Even if the economic benefits are undeniable, do they really outweigh the safety of citizens who happen to be living on top of one of the country's most valuable shale deposits? Do they make it acceptable to potentially taint fragile aquatic ecosystems with poisonous chemicals? The humanitarian answer should be no. Companies need to be held accountable for their actions. Citizens should be able to make decisions for their own communities.

As my student argues, by seeing this issue from another's perspective, we can understand more and are thus less inclined to fight in counterproductive ways. If we can reason more as this student writer does here, then we are less inclined to act in our own self-interests to the exclusion of what might benefit the greater good. This ideal of empathy can, in fact, help students hone their role as writers situated within a moral community—a community intent on treating actual arguments in more complex ways than simply as a win, lose, or draw situation.

Listening to what others have to say in asynchronous communication invites us to slow down the pace of rhetorical exchanges in virtual spaces; we can provide students the opportunity to more thoughtfully consider responses they might offer in a comment thread, rather than issue an immediate reaction. A sustained commitment to listening thus distances the writer from hot-tempered reactions, impulsive shouting, and antagonizing tactics. I agree with Krista Ratcliffe that rhetorical listening is different from reading closely and carefully—the same way we might imagine listening closely and carefully to another speaker. I want my students to practice that level of attentiveness. Yet I also remind them what Ratcliffe argues: "listening does not presume a naive, relativistic empathy, such as 'I'm OK, You're OK,' but rather an ethical responsibility to argue for what we deem fair and just while simultaneously questioning that which we deem fair and just" (203). An empathetic understanding of the stakes involved seeks to uncover and identify more common ground, not just winning ground or giving up ground. Many of my students suggest the last strategy, disengaging from arguing online all together. They believe that if they somehow refuse to "take the bait," then they will solve the problem of the argument culture. Indeed, some websites, such as *Popular Science*, have adopted a similar mindset by eliminating their comment sections "due to 'trolls and spambots' who overwhelmed those who were actually 'committed to fostering intellectual debate'" (Sebastian). Yet shutting down comment threads and/or discouraging students from participating in online forums does not seem realistic or particularly useful. Instead, it is imperative for students to learn how to recognize positions in a factious argument in order to participate in debates in ethical and productive ways.

With Ratcliffe's context in mind, I urge them to see listening in asynchronous communication, which allows opportunities for purposefully pausing—opportunities that are not always available in face to face communication when we may feel a greater urgency to respond immediately in unfiltered ways. Some may find online exchanges also allow unfiltered responses afforded by the relative anonymity of posting and contributing to a comment thread. Yet if we treat listening as both a teachable and learned skill, instructors and students alike can embrace listening as a rhetorical act: one imbued with empathy and a conscious refusal to engage in agonism.

It is our duty as teachers to practice ethical dissent as responsible and active citizens and to teach these skills of listening rhetoric to students. Such ethical dissent involves locating potential solutions among disparate views and promoting collaborative wisdom over adversarial discourse. We must recognize how communicating in digital forums, namely Twitter and Facebook, necessitates a new way of approaching argument in a more constructive fashion. If we can identify, understand, and learn from both the potentials and pitfalls of social media exchanges, then we can revive the ethical elements of communication like dialogue, conversation, community, and cooperation.

Works Cited

Jackson, Brian and Jon Wallin. "Rediscovering the Back and Forthness of Rhetoric in the Age of YouTube." *College Composition and Communication*, vol. 61, no. 2, 2009, pp. 374-96.

Sebastian, Bailey & Scott R. Stroud. "No Comment: Online Comment Sections and Democratic Discourse." Media Ethics Initiative--The University of Texas at Austin Center for Media Engagement. 31 Aug. 2018: 1-3. https://mediaethicsinitiative.org/2018/09/04/no-comment/

Ramage, John D., John C. Bean, and June Johnson. *Writing Arguments*. 9th ed., Pearson, 2012.

Ratcliffe, Krista. "Rhetorical Listening: A Trope for Interpretive Invention and a 'Code of Cross-Cultural Conduct.'" *College Composition and Communication*, vol. 51, no. 2, 1999, pp. 195-224.

✢

Sunday Morning Before Midterms

Laurence Musgrove

I try to convince myself
That I shouldn't
Check my school email
Over the weekends.
But this before noon:

> *I was recently discharged*
> *from the hospital*
> *following a suicidal overdose.*
> *Because of this*
> *I have a mandatory*
> *psychiatrist appointment*
> *on Monday.*
> *Due to the severity*
> *of the overdose*
> *I will still be recovering*
> *from the side effects*
> *on Tuesday*
> *and will unfortunately*
> *miss your class.*
> *I apologize*
> *for the inconvenience.*
> *Thank you.*

I write no

You're welcome

To the student
Who sits closest
To the door.

+

Honoring Impulse, Attending to Gesture

Lindsey Allgood

Every Wednesday afternoon this past spring, I sat in a plastic chair in silent meditation with 12 strangers in a chilly, bare hospital conference room. This was Mindfulness-Based Stress Relief training at The University of California Irvine's Susan Samueli School of Integrated Health. Our task was to notice our thoughts but remain still as stone. The typical result: hot tears dribbled down my face. I felt like my body would explode with nervous energy if I didn't adjust my cramped leg, arch my back, or crinkle my nose, which was always overwhelmingly cold. I wanted to throw my chair across the room. Every class period, I panicked because when I forced my body into stillness, my mind raced, emotions boiled, and I was reduced to a state of overheated, agitated uselessness. Lately, I worry that students sitting in my office chairs feel the same.

Perhaps I didn't give motionless meditation a fair chance (I've always been a fidgeter). But I believe our bodies want to tell us how they need to move—or not—to function, express, and compose effectively. Stillness should never be imposed on invention. I've realized certain postures, twitches, habitual stretches, and seemingly mindless gestures lubricate my creative faculties. Most importantly to my professional life, un-stillness unclogs writers' block.

As a professional writing specialist, I often find myself sharing with students how, when I honor my intuition and impulse to move, I find deep satisfaction in the final product, be it an entire essay or simply a choice of this word over that. And as an artist, I think of that moment after a dancer lands a satisfying jump, but before her mind and muscles negotiate the next move and when and how to get there. In this split second (which can feel endless) a natural knowing occurs when we as composers of all kinds trust our bodies and their coded beckonings to twitch, turn, and shift.

But stillness is not the enemy; it incubates. Intentional reprieves polish and amplify intentional action. As Peter Elbow tells us in *Writing Without Teachers*, ideas need to simmer. We must literally walk away sometimes, meaningfully pause for meals, stretches, and naps to allow ideas to continue "bubbling, percolating, fermenting" (48). When our bodies take needed breaks and move how they naturally need to, our subconscious takes over as cook in the kitchen, where an enigmatic chemistry occurs that I'm not comfortable calling science. Composing—in and of my own mind and body—feels more like an art because I can't explain how when I pause to pop my knuckles on a beat, one by one, and pace in imaginary concentric circles, the sticky, frantic claws of anxiety and rumination are lulled into suspension for a time, and I can write in a way that feels "well." I want my students to feel this wellness, too.

During Writing Center consultations, I attempt to articulate how, as writers, our idiosyncratic cadences noted by actions and respites of varied lengths and intensities can help us produce more satisfying and authentic writing. I am reminded of a conversation with Anne[1], a multilingual art major who visits me often. In a recent consultation, I witnessed her slam into a mental wall. The prompt asked her to creatively explain how she relates to the word black in 140 characters. She shot backwards in her chair and threw up her hands.

"Ugh...I don't know the word," she grunted.

I believe Anne is comfortable with me because I understand as a fellow artist how she envisions the sentiment, color, and texture of a sentence far before the actual words. She is not only learning English, but her body's instinctive manner of kinesthetic scripting in a new language. She remains perfectly still for ten seconds or so. I intentionally mirror her silence. Her eyes lift to my bulletin board where I pin found poems, campus event flyers, and eclectic magazine cutouts of famous artworks juxtaposed with odd sayings. A black and grey illustrated turtle, courtesy Cézanne, catches her eye. Her frame droops and eyes narrow. She leans forward, outlining the turtle's shell with her finger.

"It is how black outlines the turtle." She caresses the print with a fingertip.

---

1. This student's name has been changed to protect privacy. Permissions are IRB approved.

Figure 1.

"Oh? What else?"

"And how black keeps in a screen." She traces a finger around her MacBook's black rim.

Figure 2.

"Why?" I ask.

Several more seconds of silence hover between us. She yawns, stretches to the left and right, wipes her eyes, and resituates in her chair in a way that suggests she has mentally evacuated and re-entered her own body, and, therefore, my office. She seems to see with different eyes. Her gaze floats around the room and rests on my multi-colored tapestry of an elephant on the wall.

Figure 3

"It's how... black carves... the elephant face...he is stuck inside the fabric because of the black..." Between phrases, her wand-like fingers gesture again, as if speaking in a sign language she's simultaneously inventing and learning.

"What does that mean to you?" I ask.

"It means..." She drums her sternum. Then her palms push the air as if shoving something out of the way. "In or out."

"Tell me about 'in or out'." I try not to move in my own chair. I can sense she's about to encounter resolution. I see it in the way her eyes and fingers seem to draw the same pattern in the air. I wish I could see what she's seeing.

"I don't know." Her eyes close and grimace.

"Okay, describe the feeling," I offer. "How does 'in and out' make you feel? What does 'in and out' remind you of?"

A full minute goes by in silence: a salient reprieve. If clarity that strikes before invention had scent, I could smell it. She shifts and twirls her hair, then her eyes rest again on the elephant tapestry. Her chin bobs up and down; I find myself holding my breath. Suddenly, she pulls her chair forward and sharply inhales. Her eyes focus on something I cannot see on the desk between us.

"I am lonely," she nearly whispers, staring into her blank computer screen. Her finger calmly traces that black rim again. I realize I've finally exhaled.

"What about black?" I softly ask. I read the subtle shift in her posture and muscles around her eyes. A little more energy trickles back into her limbs, which begin to twitch as if thawing.

"Black is safe."

She finally looks up at me a little bleary-eyed. Her spine stiffened and her voice dropped an octave, indicating a nexus had just congealed in her mind's eye. I continued to offer brief, vague guiding questions, inviting her proprioception to guide this quest for meaning. As her body worked for words, her understanding of black unfolded in snowball effect. She told me how, at various ages, black allowed her to hide her evolving forms of shame: dirt stains on new clothes from her angry father; thickening thighs from judgmental school girls. Her gestures quickly began to lose rhythm and gain frenzy. I could tell we simultaneously hit the jackpot and a raw nerve. But this was not the time for me to intrude, so I settled in as the audience. That day she left my office with a writing plan.

As Anne reminds us, we can choose whether to respond or react to psychological discomfort. We choose whether to crash into and wrestle waves of anxiety or difficult emotions or shiftily roll away from dis-ease like a martial artist, letting its counter energy propel us in brand new exploratory directions. A recent personal example:

> *I've been writing for a solid nine minutes, no pause. My mind stutters. I eat a mint. Sip coffee. Spit out mint. Stand and stretch. Sit back down. Rearrange paragraphs. Jot down erratic jumble of inspired sentences. Bite inside of cheek ten times. Read. Copy/paste elsewhere. Do five pushups. Walk outside. Return to office. Lie on floor. Watch my belly rise with breath. Deflate it by rolling over. Imagine writer's block sucked into wall, like into a vacuum. Wonder why vacuum is spelled so funny. Wonder why words flit around in my mind like illusive fireflies. Remember a lost word. Return to computer before I forget. Print out draft. Spread pages on floor. Remove shoes. Scratch itch. Explain my point out loud to myself. Walk in three circles. Feel my focus go fuzzy. Thank my body for writing revelations to come and immediately go to lunch.*

I honor the surge of mental fuzziness because I trust my rhythm will come back once I've eaten. When we move, and pause between, we notice subtle shifts and potential salience in our language's musicality—whether a sentence sounds like a song or a series of sour notes. In the pause, a sentence can *feel* too long or too vague before we *know* why, like the performer, who, as a child, intuitively improvises the transformation of one leap into its landing. As a dancer on stage or yogi on her mat, I try to listen to micro discomforts as well as Anne. I am fascinated by how an itch to move or an external distraction, when attended to, often reveals the word for which I was searching. When resting on my belly on my office floor, I allowed my mind to compare words to illusive fireflies. This fanciful respite cleared room for invention to take root.

Nudges of physical discomfort, exhaustion, hunger, or anxiety are simply my mind's wiser layers poking at my subconscious, reminding me not to waste time staring at my keyboard when words evade me. Instead, I get up, move, gesture, dance, spin in circles and wait for meaning to show itself. It sounds cheesy, but it feels Newtonian.

Kinesthetic scripting encourages thought to evolve, but our bodies' promptings speak in enigma and emotion, neither of which are our primary languages in adulthood. I like to ask students to "show me" rather than tell me their writing concerns. When they quickly point to the troublesome passage, their fingers, eyes and body language begin to illustrate lack of clarity or a muddled thesis before they speak. I regularly work with language learners like Anne who struggle with run-on sentences and misused commas. We realize while they may not *know* when to end a sentence and when a conjunction is needed, they can often literally *feel* it. I ask these students to point out the commas that make them feel uneasy. They often immediately highlight misused commas scattered throughout their writing when invited to this primal act of pointing at something that threatens them. For many language learners I see, those tiny squiggles can be terrifying.

I watch a group of composition students read each other's drafts during a writing center peer review workshop. Their legs violently quiver; pencils tap tap tap; hands doodle, flip pencils, drum tables; bubblegum is popped and smacked. But I don't hear distraction. I hear bodies working for words, and I wonder if the pencil tapper is actually inspiring the bubble gum popper. Is the subtle cacophony actually a form of collaboration? Where in their bodies do they hold and process this information? How do they know to listen to others' rhythms? I also wonder how various types of bodies physically script in different ways. Do the athlete's feet run practice drills under the desk while brainstorming or does the singer hum vocal warm-ups when remembering APA format? Witnessing this improvised ensemble, I am grateful for daily conversations about moves we can make toward more lucid, juicier writing. My favorite writing conversations end with definite questions and loose plans of action: one step, stretch, gesture and stroke in front of another. After all, we are guaranteed nothing else, except, perhaps, our next move.

Work Cited

Elbow, Peter. "The Process of Writing–Cooking." *Writing Without Teachers*. Oxford University Press, 1973, pp. 48-75.

IUPUI

JOURNAL OF TEACHING WRITING

SCHOOL OF LIBERAL ARTS

Indiana University
Indianapolis

The *Journal of Teaching Writing* (*JTW*), now in its 36th year, is a journal devoted to the teaching of writing at all academic levels and in any subject area. Our mission is to publish refereed articles and reviews that address the practices and theories that bear on our knowledge of how people learn and communicate through writing. Topics include writing and literacy, composition theory, revision, responding to writing, assessment, diversity in writing, information literacy, and others. An important part of our mission is demystifying the editorial review process for our contributors and modeling the teaching of writing as a process of reflection and revision. Submissions and subscription requests may be sent to our editorial assistant via email at jtw@iupui.edu.

Contributors to *JAEPL*, Vol. 24

Lindsey Allgood is a Writing Specialist at the University of California, Irvine's Center for Excellence in Writing and Communication (the Writing Center) where she focuses on outreach to the fine arts. Formerly, she taught English Composition at the University of Oklahoma and held a graduate assistantship as Lead Consultant and Fine Arts Liaison at the University of Oklahoma Writing Center. She is also an artist and yoga practitioner. (lallgood@uci.edu)

Anastassiya Andrianova is an Assistant Professor of English at North Dakota State University in Fargo, ND, where she teaches courses in British, postcolonial, multicultural, and world literatures. She holds a Ph.D. in Comparative Literature from the City University of New York and has published on animal studies, drama, nineteenth-century pedagogy and culture, and postcolonial literature. Her current projects are on animal consent and the representation of animals in children's books. (anastassiya.andriano@ndsu.edu)

Kristina Fennelly is an Assistant Professor of English at Kutztown University. Her teaching and research interests center on non-adversarial approaches to argument via the exploration of Rogerian and listening rhetoric. She has recently presented at the Conference on College Composition & Communication, Computers & Writing, and MAWCA. She is also an active member of the Women's, Gender, & Sexuality Studies program at Kutztown where she teaches WGSS courses for students working towards the minor. (fennelly@kutztown.edu)

Michael S. Geary, MA, is Associate Professor of English and Writing Center Coordinator at Bristol Community College in Fall River, MA. A 19-year veteran of the community college system, he is noted for his theme-based writing classes and as the creator of Bristol's Science Fiction Literature class. He currently oversees Writing Center tutoring on all four campuses and is a former Chair of the English Department's Portfolio Assessment Project. (Michael.Geary@bristolcc.edu)

Brian Glaser is an assistant professor of English at Chapman University in Orange, California. (bglaser@chapman.edu)

Mara Lee Grayson is an assistant professor of English at California State University, Dominguez Hills. She is the author of the book *Teaching Racial Literacy: Reflective Practices for Critical Writing*. Her work has also appeared or is forthcoming in *English Education*, *Teaching English in the Two-Year College*, *English Journal*, *St. John's University Humanities Review*, and numerous edited collections. Grayson holds a Ph.D. from Columbia University and an MFA from the City College of New York. (maragrayson@gmail.com)

Jacquelyne Kibler is an instructor for Arizona State University's online writing program. She is also a Ph.D. student in the University of Arizona's Rhetoric, Composition, and the Teaching of English program. Her research circulates around mindfulness practice in first-year composition, Buddhism, new materialism, and Indigenous pedagogy. (jkibler@asu.edu)

Faith Kurtyka is an associate professor of English at Creighton University in Omaha, Nebraska. She has published articles on feminist rhetorics, extracurricular literacies, and the relationship between genre and emotion. She is currently at work on a book project about conservative young women. (fmkurtyka@gmail.com)

Mare Leonard lives in an old school house overlooking the Rondout Creek in Kingston NY. Away from her own personal blackboard, she teaches through The Institute for Writing and Thinking and the MAT program at Bard College. Finishing Line Press just released her sixth chapbook, *The Dark Inside My Hooded Coat*, and *The Pickled Body* recently nominated a poem for a Pushcart. Her latest publication will be forthcoming in *Oyster River*. (aggiemaggie66@gmail.com)

Sharon Marshall coordinates and teaches in the First-Year Writing Program at St. John's University in Queens, N.Y. She writes about composition pedagogy and applying principles derived from Nichiren Buddhism and Critical Race Theory to teaching writing. She is the author of *Water Child*, a novel. Currently, she is working on another novel *Deep Rivers* and *Pedagogy as Poetry or How Teaching First-Year Writing Became My Life's Poem*, an autoethnography. (Marshalls@stjohns.edu)

Monica Mische is a Professor at Montgomery College where she coordinates the Integrated English and Reading Program, teaches writing and literature, and trains tutors to work with students with disabilities. Her work has appeared in *Journal of Basic Writing* and is forthcoming in *Pedagogy* and in the anthology *Deep Beauty*. (monica.mische@montgomerycollege.edu)

Dan Mrozowski is the director of Graduate Studies in English at Trinity College in Hartford, CT. His most recent work, "The Spirit of Revolt: Hamlin Garland's Paranormal Writing," appeared in *Haunting Realities: Naturalist Gothic and American Realism*. He also co-edited a collection, *The Great Recession in Fiction, Film, and Television: A Busted Culture*, published by Lexington Books. (Daniel.Mrozowski@trincoll.edu)

Laurence Musgrove is Professor of English at Angelo State University in San Angelo, Texas, where he teaches undergraduate and graduate courses in creative writing, literature, visual thinking, and mindfulness. Laurence has served as a past executive committee treasurer, chair, and conference chair of AEPL. He is also the author of three books: *Local Bird* – a collection of poetry, *One Kind of Recording* – a collection of aphorisms, and *Start Again, Dignity* – a collection of contemporary Buddhist sutras forthcoming from Lamar University Literary Press. (LMusgrove@angelo.edu)

Amy Nolan lives in Iowa, where she teaches creative writing and film history at Wartburg College. Her platform for teaching, research, and writing is to express and examine the connections between our treatment of our bodies and our treatment of the planet. Her essay on anorexia, "Close to the Bones," was published in *The Bellevue Literary Review*, which awarded the essay with an Honorable Mention for the Carter V. Cooper

Prize contest. Most recently, her essay, "My Mother's Hips," was nominated for a Pushcart Prize by *Ruminate Literary Magazine*. (amy.nolan@wartburg.edu)

W. Kurt Stavenhagen is an Instructor in the Writing, Rhetoric & Communications Program at SUNY College of Environmental Science and Forestry. He researches the intersections between ecological literacy and contemplative practices, and recently co-authored "Contemplation as Kairotic Composure" with Tim Dougherty. (wkstaven@esf.edu)

Christy I. Wenger is an Associate Professor of English, Writing and Rhetoric at Shepherd University in Shepherdstown, WV, where she serves as the Director of Writing and Rhetoric. She is the author of *Yoga Minds, Writing Bodies: Contemplative Writing Pedagogy* and her articles have appeared in *Pedagogy*, *JAEPL*, and *WPA: Writing Program Administration*. She has also published chapters in collections such as *Women's Ethos: Intersections of Rhetorics and Feminisms*, and *Next Steps: New Directions for/in Writing about Writing*. She serves on the board of the Assembly for Expanded Perspectives on Learning and is "Connecting" editor for the *Journal for the Assembly for Expanded Perspectives on Learning*. (CWENGER@shepherd.edu)

PARLOR PRESS
EQUIPMENT FOR LIVING

New, in Living Color!

Exquisite Corpse: Studio Art-Based Writing Practices in the Academy ed. by Kate Hanzalik and Nathalie Virgintino

The Afterlife of Discarded Objects: Memory and Forgetting in a Culture of Waste by Andrei Guruianu and Natalia Andrievskikh

Type Matters: The Rhetoricity of Letterforms ed. Christopher Scott Wyatt and Dànielle Nicole DeVoss (**BEST DESIGN AWARD-Ingram**)

New Releases

Tracing Invisible Lines: An Experiment in Mystoriography by David Prescott-Steed

KONSULT: Theopraxesis by Gregory L. Ulmer

Best of the Journals in Rhetoric and Composition 2018

Other People's English: Code-Meshing, Code-Switching, and African American Literacy by Vershawn Ashanti Young, et al.

Networked Humanities: Within and Without the University edited by Brian McNely and Jeff Rice

The Internet as a Game by Jill Anne Morris

Congratulations, Award Winners!

Strategies for Writing Center Research by Jackie Grutsch McKinnie. **Best Book Award, International Writing Centers Association (2017)**

Antiracist Writing Assessment Ecologies: Teaching and Assessing Writing for a Socially Just Future by Asao Inoue, **Best Book Award, CCCC, Best Book, Council of Writing Program Administrators (2017)**

The WPA Outcomes Statement—A Decade Later edited by Nicholas N. Behm, Gregory R. Glau, Deborah H. Holdstein, Duane Roen, & Edward M. White, **Best Book Award, Council of Writing Program Adminstrators (2015)**

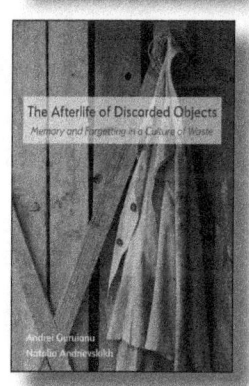

www.parlorpress.com

Every One Has a Voice!

Listening, Empowerment, Compassionate Confrontation, and Healing
The 25th Annual Conference of the Assembly for Expanded Perspectives on Learning

June 20-23, 2019
YMCA of the Rockies, Estes Park, Colorado

If we really want to change things…It's going to start at the grassroots level, and with our [youth].
— Barack Obama, 1995

Democracy will come into its own [--] for a life of free and enriching communion [--]...when free social inquiry is indissolubly wedded to the art of full and moving communication.
— John Dewey, 1927

Perhaps the times we are now living through will at some point come to be known as The Age of Donald Trump and #MeToo! With the former comfortably in the past. And the latter the permanent democratic norm. Historically exemplified by the multitude of voices - prominent among students and teachers - now speaking out, in these very times, for healing. The healing of the multitude of abuses brought about by people's long submission to unjust, dehumanizing, and unnatural hierarchies of many kinds. Through these voices the motto "We are the ones we've been waiting for" will have become not just a one-time inducement to vote, but an everlasting call for all to live in truth.

This is the vision inspiring the 25th Annual Summer Conference of the NCTE Assembly for Expanded Perspectives on Learning - a vision that will be greatly, and directly, amplified by the presence of the voices of you and your students!

Principal Keynote Speaker (other keynotes on back)
(We are also seeking to bring students and teachers from Parkland, Florida)

CAROL GILLIGAN, of Harvard & NYU - named by TIME Magazine as one of the 25 most influential people in the US - has been a powerful public voice for the power of democratic voice since the 1980s, with the publication of her landmark *In a Different Voice: Psychological Theory and Women's Development*. And it was her comment that "a democracy is not just a place where everyone has a vote, but where everyone has a voice" - at our 2003 conference "Building a Culture of Listening in Our Institutions of Learning" - that inspired this year's theme. Her brand new book (with David A.J. Richards) *Darkness Now Visible: Patriarchy's Resurgence and Feminist Resistance* is of breathtaking timeliness and importance, its message summed up by Gloria Steinem: "it is the sleight-of-hand of every unjust system to become the rule, and to make everyone else the exception. [This book] end[s] the idea that patriarchy represents everybody, and show[s] that feminism turns patriarchy into democracy. [It is] a prescription for tearing down Trumpian walls…[by] seeing each other as unique and equal."

Questions and Topic Areas for Proposals
(though let your own voice be your main guide)

What are the ideas and practices in your classroom that, in the words of Mary Rose O'Reilley "listen [people] into existence"? That help them know that their voices and stories are meaningful and resonantly empowering to others, and need to be heard in both intimate and public spaces?

How have they learned to use those voices to speak personally storied truth to power in both small and large ways? And how have new possibilities for healing and transformative change in our collective stories, writ large or small, been brought about through their—and your—speaking out? (We use the word "possibilities" here because we know that the many of the stories you will share will likely involve the witnessing of the many tragedies and martyrdoms that are so often required to impel us to compassionate change.)

What are the various ways that prevailing educational practices make the hidden claim "I am your voice" that has been blatantly asserted by our current president? And how can we broadly institute educational practices that will educe the great chorus of voices that constitutes authentic democracy?

Please find topic suggestions on back.

To Propose:

Send an abstract of up to 250 words for a 75-minute interactive workshop (preferred format), making sure to include descriptions of the activities in which you will involve participants; or a 20-30 minute talk or short teaching demo, to AeplVoice19@gmail.com by December 15 for early consideration, January 15 for regular consideration. Proposals submitted after January 15 will also be considered.

Registration:

$270 February 2 — April 15, 2019; $350 after April 15; discounts for students, adjuncts, and retirees and for multiple attendees from the same organization. Discount policy, lodging and membership info, and preconference workshop description on website.

Registration available at **www.aepl.org**.

Every One Has a Voice!

Listening, Empowerment, Compassionate Confrontation, and Healing

The 25th Annual Conference of the Assembly for Expanded Perspectives on Learning
Preconference workshops on Alexander bodily poise and Linklater vocal focus

June 20-23, 2019
YMCA of the Rockies, Estes Park, Colorado

REGISTER NOW www.aepl.org

Hephzibah Roskelly retired in 2016 from the University of North Carolina Greensboro, where she taught rhetoric and writing and directed the Women's and Gender Studies program. She has collaborated with Kate Ronald in lots of enterprises, including their book *Reason to Believe: Romanticism, Pragmatism and Teaching of Writing* (1998). The second edition of her textbook with David Jolliffe, *Writing America* (Spring 2020) is designed to engage high school and early college students in confronting current civic issues using American history and literature. She lives in Louisville, Ky, teaches distance courses, and mentors area high school English teachers.

Kate Ronald retired from Miami University in 2016, where she served as the Roger and Joyce L. Howe Professor of English and Director of the Howe Center for Writing excellence and taught graduate and undergraduate courses in composition and rhetoric. She directed more dissertations than she remembers. Her two favorite publications remain *Reason to Believe: Romanticism, Pragmatism, and the Teaching of Writing*, co-authored with Hephzibah Roskelly (SUNY, 1998), and *Available Means: An Anthology of Women's Rhetoric(s)*, co-edited with Joy Ritchie (Pittsburgh, 2001)

Proposal topic suggestions:
- Making marginalized lives and voices matter
- Making humanity and the humanities matter
- Making nature and biodiversity matter
- Feminisms and new understandings of manhood
- Diverse community building
- Empathy and compassion, including "speaking truth to power with love" (Cornel West), with compassion for the concealed inner pain of oppressors
- Speaking and public speechmaking through embodied voice
- Public discourse in the writing classroom and elsewhere
- Truth and reconciliation: Confession and forgiveness
- Practices of nonviolence
- Understandings of the psychology of violence and its prevention
- Courage
- Embodiment
- Mindfulness
- The Arts
- Rhetorical practices
- Reading practices
- Specific readings: works of literature and theory
- Important thinkers and role models
- Activism—online and in person
- Personally encountering meaningful history
- Listening
- Healing

Dr. Veronica House is the founding Executive Director of the Coalition for Community Writing and founding chair of the Conference on Community Writing. She is a faculty member in the Program for Writing and Rhetoric at the University of Colorado Boulder, where she has served as Associate Faculty Director for Service-Learning and Outreach for eight years. As founder of the University's award-winning Writing Initiative for Service and Engagement, she coordinated the Program for Writing and Rhetoric's transformation into one of the first writing programs in the country to have integrated community-engaged pedagogies throughout its lower- and upper-division courses. She enjoys working with faculty at colleges and universities across the country to design community-engaged courses and programs.

Ruth Rootberg, M.Ed, M.M, M.A., trained with Kristin Linklater and was Associate Professor in voice at the Yale School of Drama from 1995-2000. Other faculty positions included Northern Illinois University, the Theatre School DePaul, and Mt. Holyoke College. She is certified Laban Movement Analyst (2000) and an AmSAT-certified Alexander Technique teacher (2003). Ruth has presented integrated voice and movement workshops at the Voice Foundation, Alexander Technique conferences, the Association for Theatre in Higher Education (ATHE), SAPVAME (South Africa), and has given workshops at music, theatre, and dance programs around the country. Ruth resides in Amherst, Massachusetts.

About AEPL: The Assembly for Expanded Perspectives on Learning (AEPL) is an official assembly of the National Council of Teachers of English. AEPL is open to all those interested in exploring the boundaries of teaching and learning beyond traditional disciplines and methodologies. Areas of interest include but are not limited to aesthetic, emotional, and moral intelligence, archetypes, body wisdom, care in education, creativity, felt sense theory, healing, holistic learning, humanistic and transpersonal psychology, imaging, intuition, kinesthetic knowledge, meditation, narration as knowledge, reflective teaching, silence, spirituality, and visualization. More information at www.aepl.org.

About the YMCA of the Rockies: Stunningly situated, the YMCA of the Rockies is a premiere conference venue. The YMCA provides comfortable, modern lodging and access to a range of activities including hiking, biking and horseback rides through Rocky Mountain National Park. Attendees are responsible for reserving lodging separately from conference registration. Rooms must be reserved by April 15, 2019. Visit the YMCA website at https://ymcarockies.org/lodging/.

www.ingramcontent.com/pod-product-compliance
Lightning Source LLC
Chambersburg PA
CBHW031321160426
43196CB00007B/610